# Music Composition FOR DUMMIES®

**by Scott Jarrett and Holly Day**

WILEY

Wiley Publishing, Inc.

**Music Composition For Dummies®**

Published by
**Wiley Publishing, Inc.**
111 River St.
Hoboken, NJ 07030-5774
www.wiley.com

For general information on our other products and services, please contact our Customer Care Department within the U.S. at 800-762-2974, outside the U.S. at 317-572-3993, or fax 317-572-4002.

For technical support, please visit www.wiley.com/techsupport.

Wiley also publishes its books in a variety of electronic formats. Some content that appears in print may not be available in electronic books.

Library of Congress Control Number: 2007943296

ISBN: 978-0-470-22421-2

Manufactured in the United States of America

10 9 8 7 6 5 4 3 2 1

WILEY

# *About the Authors*

**Scott Jarrett** is a musician and producer who has worked with numerous artists, including Willie Nelson, Fiona Flanagan, Mary Klueh, and Keith Jarrett. He has served as music director for many live theatrical productions including the Broadway production of *The Best Little Whorehouse in Texas*. He currently runs Monkey House recording studio in Hudson, Wisconsin. He has released two original albums, *Without Rhyme or Reason* and *The Gift of Thirst*. He has taught music theory, composition, production, and/or recording at the Full Sail Center for the Recording Arts in Orlando, The Acting Conservatory in Nashville, and McNally-Smith School of Music in St. Paul, Minnesota.

**Holly Day** is a music journalist whose articles have appeared in publications all over the world, including *Computer Music Journal*, *ROCKRGRL*, *Music Alive!*, *Guitar One*, and *Mixdown* magazines. Her writing has received an Isaac Asimov Award, a National Magazine Award, and two Midwest Writer's Grants. She is co-author of *Music Theory For Dummies* (Wiley).

# Dedication

To Irma Jarrett, who along with being a nurturing teacher would have also been an excellent Jedi knight, but for the fact that for her the Dark Side doesn't exist. — Scott

To Sherman, Wolfegang, and Astrid, without whose love and support I am nothing. — Holly

# Authors' Acknowledgments

I would like to express my deeply felt thanks to my 10th-grade English teacher, Mr. Sims, wherever he may be, for his encouragement. I would also like to thank Ruth Sweet for introducing me to the effort shapes and their many uses. Stu Kuby and Louise Messina deserve credit for giving me some of my first professional music-composition opportunities. My heartfelt gratitude goes out to Tom Day, Mike Bogle, and Steve Horlick for their generous help, support, and resources. And lest I forget from whose well of patience I drink and whence springs my motivation, I acknowledge my wife, Meg, and my two sons, Garner and Colin. — Scott

I'd like to thank the amazing musicians whose invaluable advice was essential to the writing of this book: Jonathan Segel, Genesis P-Orridge, Steve Reich, Philip Glass, and Mark Mothersbaugh. I'd also like to thank Corbin Collins, Matt Wagner, and especially my father, Tom Day, for helping make music such an important part of my life. A special thank you goes to Katherine Tondra, whose help during the deadline crunches is immensely appreciated. — Holly

## Publisher's Acknowledgments

We're proud of this book; please send us your comments through our Dummies online registration form located at www.dummies.com/register/.

Some of the people who helped bring this book to market include the following:

*Acquisitions, Editorial, and Media Development*

**Project Editor:** Corbin Collins

**Acquisitions Editor:** Stacy Kennedy

**Copy Editor:** Corbin Collins

**Technical Editor:** Delbert Bowers

**Project Manager I:** Laura Moss-Hollister

**Media Development Specialist:** Kit Malone

**Editorial Manager:** Michelle Hacker

**Editorial Supervisor and Reprint Editor:** Carmen Krikorian

**Art Coordinator:** Alicia B. South

**Editorial Assistants:** David Lutton and Leeann Harney

**Cartoons:** Rich Tennant (www.the5thwave.com)

*Composition Services*

**Project Coordinator:** Lynsey Osborn

**Layout and Graphics:** Claudia Bell, Carl Byers, Alissa D. Ellet, Laura Pence, Ronald Terry, Christine Williams

**Music and Graphic Design:** W. R. Music Service, Woytek and Krystyna Rynczak

**Proofreaders:** Jessica Kramer, Shannon Ramsey

**Indexer:** Valerie Haynes Perry

**Special Help:** Alissa D. Ellet

---

### Publishing and Editorial for Consumer Dummies

**Diane Graves Steele,** Vice President and Publisher, Consumer Dummies

**Joyce Pepple,** Acquisitions Director, Consumer Dummies

**Kristin A. Cocks,** Product Development Director, Consumer Dummies

**Kathleen Nebenhaus,** Vice President and Executive Publisher, Consumer Dummies, Lifestyles, Pets, Education Publishing for Technology Dummies

### Composition Services

**Gerry Fahey,** Vice President of Production Services

**Debbie Stailey,** Director of Composition Services

# Contents at a Glance

# Table of Contents

# Introduction

*W*elcome to *Music Composition For Dummies*!

Are you the type of person who walks around all day with a maddening melody in your head that makes you stop whatever you're doing so you can pay it full attention?

Do you often find yourself tapping out rhythmic passages from these melodies on your desk at work or scribbling down song lyrics on scraps of paper?

Is music sometimes more of a slave driver to you than a muse?

If you said yes to any of those questions, all we can say is this: We are here to help.

## About This Book

*Music Composition For Dummies* contains everything you need to know to get started

- ✔ Picking out the perfect rhythm and tempo for your composition.
- ✔ Matching keys and chord progressions to the moods you want to convey.
- ✔ Working within the confines of musical form without confining your creativity.
- ✔ Forcing yourself to sit down and come up with musical ideas, even when your mind is drawing a complete blank.

In this book, we discuss the basics of composition, from writing natural-sounding chord progressions and cadences, to composing atonal music, to making yourself a demo recording and getting it in the hands of the right people. If there's any one thing we've tried to do here, it's to demystify the process of composing music and writing songs.

There are few things more satisfying than plucking a melody from inside your head and nurturing it into a full-fledged song or even an orchestral piece. This book will make that process a whole lot easier for you.

Because each chapter is as self-contained as possible, you don't have to read every single chapter to understand what the next one is talking about — unless you want to, of course.

To find the information you need, you can use the Table of Contents as a reference point, or you can just flip through the Index at the back of the book.

# Foolish Assumptions

This book is written for many types of budding composers: the classical music student who never learned how to improvise, the backup musician who wants to start taking the lead and writing material, and the seasoned musician who wants to start writing music in genres outside his or her comfort zone.

You are probably at least a familiar with playing a musical instrument. Perhaps you were trained on piano and now want to strike out on your own and start composing your own music. Maybe you're a self-taught rock guitarist who wants to learn about composing in other genres. Or perhaps you're just a person who has had this maddening tune dancing around in your head, and you want to figure out how to turn it into a real song.

We do assume that you have at least the rudiments of music theory knowledge. We expect you to know how to read music at least at a basic level, what chords are, how many beats a whole rest gets in 3/4 time — stuff like that. Unfortunately, there is not enough room in this book to teach you music theory, too.

If you're an absolute newcomer to music, we recommend you first go out and get yourself a copy of *Music Theory For Dummies* (Wiley) by Michael Pilhofer and Holly Day to give yourself a good grounding in the language of music. Then come back here.

# How This Book Is Organized

*Music Composition For Dummies* is organized into five parts. The first four are each focused on a particular aspect of music, with the fifth part, the Part of Tens, containing information about some of the fun aspects of composition that may have little or nothing to do with actually playing music.

This system makes it easy for you to find what you need to know quickly — because, after all, this is a reference book, and nobody wants to spend all day thumbing through pages to find one simple technique.

# Part I: Basics and Rhythm

Without rhythm, "music" would be one long, unbroken, unwavering note, and that would be awfully tricky to dance to. Rhythm is the most basic component of any type of music, and being able to use rhythm properly can make or break a composition. In this section, we discuss the moods you can create by using different types of rhythm, as well as all the tools you should bring to the table with you when you first set out to be a composer.

# Part II: Melody and Development

Melody is the lead line of the song that stays stuck in your head long after the song is over. It's the basic theme running through a piece of music that ties the whole thing together. In this section, we show you how to build melodic lines around spoken or written phrases, how to build melodic motives, and how to use the moods associated with different scales and modes.

# Part III: Harmony and Structure

Harmony is the part of a song that fleshes everything out. The proper use of harmony could turn the melody of "Twinkle, Twinkle, Little Star" into a full orchestral number. In this section, we go over writing harmonic accompaniment with existing melodies, composing music with chord progressions, using effort shapes as compositional tools, understanding basic musical forms, and getting going in songwriting.

# Part IV: Orchestration and Arrangement

At the end of the day, your music can't just sit there looking lonely on paper. It has to be either played by instruments, or sung, or both. In this chapter, we discuss the playable ranges of the major instruments of pop ensembles and the traditional orchestra. We also show you how to write music for pieces with multiple voices, write music for profit, compose electronic and experimental music, and put together a demo recording of your work.

## Part V: The Part of Tens

Here we introduce you to a few things to do with composition outside of playing music. We profile some fascinating composers without whom this book, or any other book like it, would not be possible, as well as some additional music theory and music history books you can pick up to further your education on the subject. We also go over some of the most revolutionary periods of music history that every musician should know about, and discuss why those periods of music were so important.

# Icons Used in This Book

*Icons* are handy little graphic images that are meant to point out particularly important information. You'll find the following icons in this book, conveniently located along the left margins.

This icon indicates good advice and information that will help you understand key concepts.

When we discuss something that might be problematic or confusing, we use this icon.

This icon flags information that's, well, technical, and you can go ahead and skip it if you want to.

When we make a point or offer some information that we feel you should keep with you forever, we toss in this icon.

# Where to Go from Here

If you're just starting out as a composer, then go ahead and plow into Part I.

If you're already familiar with the basics of rhythm and want to start writing melodies, then head for Part II.

If you've already got a hot melody, but want to know how to turn it into a more full-fledged composition, Part III covers the basics of matching melodies to harmonies.

Part IV can help you decide what instruments you want to use in your composition, or to whom you might want to sell that composition.

It's important to relax and have fun with this — listening to, playing, and writing music are some of the most enjoyable experiences you'll ever have. *Music Composition For Dummies* may have been written by teachers, but we promise that no clock-watching music instructors will show up at your door to check on how fast you're plowing through this book. Composing music is a magical, mysterious, wonderful thing. Yet it's also based on surprisingly simple principles. In Western music, there are only twelve pitches in each of eight octaves on the piano, but think of just how different one piece of music can be from another.

Limits can actually be freeing: Just as with poetry or prose, the more comfortable you are working inside a specific form, the greater your ability to successfully express yourself within that form becomes.

# Part I
# Basics and Rhythm

The 5th Wave                    By Rich Tennant

D. BOYD
JAZZ
STUDIES
2ND Floor

"Okay, did you feel that rhythm on the way down?
That's the syncopation I'm looking for."

## In this part . . .

We tell you what you need to know before you start seriously composing music — and it's not just knowing how to read sheet music, either (you should already be familiar with that). Everything from a breakdown of music-composing software programs to developing file-management systems for your compositions is discussed in this section. We also talk about how important rhythm is to creating specific moods in your compositions and discuss how to use rhythmic variations to make your music more interesting.

# Chapter 1

# Thinking Like a Composer

Music is the one art form that is entirely defined by time. Once a piece of music is finished being performed, technically, when the last of its echoes fades, it's gone. Each piece of music is literally sandwiched in silence, or external noise, and if your listeners aren't paying attention, they're going to miss it.

Your job, of course, is to make them pay attention.

## Limitations as Freedom

Going further, music can be considered to be *the sculpting of time*. You can think of your three minutes — or half hour, or 36 hours — as a block waiting to be chiseled into a specific shape that's meant to tell a story or convey an emotion. You just have to figure out which carving technique(s) will work best to get your particular idea across to your audience.

This is where *form* comes in. Forms are the specific ways of composing pop music, classical music, blues music, jazz, country, and even atonal and serial music. If you know what form you want to compose your song in, part of the groundwork for your composition is already done for you.

And don't fret about this "constraining" or "limiting" you. Does the net limit you in tennis? No, it gives both players something in common to go by. In music, a form does the same thing: Your listener knows more or less what to expect, and you know more or less what to give them. The rest — the uniqueness of your contribution — is up to you. Plus there's nothing wrong with combining forms to make new ones. You've heard of jazz/rock fusion, porch punk, country blues, and so on? In fact, you may even find yourself combining forms without thinking about it.

After choosing a main form, you may want to pick the key you want to write your piece in. Knowing how the different keys and modes lend themselves to specific moods is a great help in trying to get a specific emotion across in your music. And how do you know about keys and moods? By listening to music written by other people, of course. You have already internalized a lot of musical mood information, probably without even realizing it.

You may have a melody already bumping around in your head that needs harmonic accompaniment. You can either plug that melodic line into your chosen form or start adding some chordal accompaniment and see where it goes on its own.

There's no real pre-ordained order in which you should begin composing music. The end result is all that matters, and if you end up with a piece of music that you're even partially satisfied with, then you are on the right track.

You don't have to re-invent the wheel. Much of the work in composing music has already been done for you by others. Instead of re-inventing the wheel, make your wheel different, more interesting, more unique and truer to what's inside you than any other wheels.

# Composing as an Extension of Listening

As a music teacher, Johann Sebastian Bach, like other great composers of his day, trained his students to be not just impressive little robotic pianists, but to be improvisers and composers. This is something that's not often taught by music professors today. Back then, learning how to read scores and perform other people's music was not a separate or independent skill from learning about the creation of music itself. The music of the masters was presented to students as something to improvise on — and possibly even to improve on.

This practical musicality was a comprehensive craft that involved thinking creatively and realizing it in sound. Music meant more than merely following instructions. The rote repetition of other people's music, including Bach's own, was used as example *and was not the end itself.* Students were encouraged to alter scores by adding notes, reducing the time value of notes, dropping notes, and changing or adding ornamentation, dynamics, and so on. One couldn't even get into Bach's teaching studio without first showing some rudimentary composing ability.

If you're a classically trained music student who has just not had a lot of opportunities to spread your wings and write your own pieces of music, this book is especially designed to help you find your own voice, both by drawing from what you've learned in all those years of rote memorization and mining your own feelings about how music should sound.

# Rules as Inspiration

If you didn't know better, you might think that music was something that could start on any note, go wherever it wanted to, and just stop whenever the performer felt like getting up to get a glass of iced tea. Although it's true that many of us have been to musical performances that actually do follow that, ahem, style of "composition" — for the most part, those performances are confusing, annoyingly self-indulgent, and feel a little pointless. The only people that can pull off a spontaneous jam well are those who know music enough to stack chords and notes next to one another *so that they make sense* to listeners. And because music is inherently a form of communication, connecting with your listeners is an important thing to try to do.

You really need to know the rules before you can break them.

Knowing about song forms, how to meld harmonic lines into a real melody, and how to end a song on a perfect cadence can be incredibly inspiring. There's just no describing the power of the light bulb that goes off in your head when you suddenly *know* how to put a 12-bar blues progression together and build a really good song out of it. The first time you make music with your friends and find you have the confidence to present your own ideas is thrilling.

It's our intention that the reader of this book will end up putting his or her copy down on a regular basis because the urge to try out a new musical technique is just too hard to resist!

# You as Your Own Teacher

As with any creative activity, composing music requires that you trust yourself. An understanding of music theory and a lot of playing skill can be a good starting point, but what an idea means to you — how it makes you feel and what you ultimately say with it — can be the only real criterion of its validity.

As you read the following chapters, keep the ideas in this section in mind.

## Know what your options are

Once you have an idea, learn how to work it, with methods for (re)harmonization, melodic and rhythmic development, counterparts, variations, and other compositional techniques. A good composer never stops learning and can never have too many "tools" in his or her musical toolbox. Learn as many compositional styles and techniques as possible and try to get an intuitive grasp on how and when to apply them.

With practice, this information will become second nature — as easy to summon and use in your compositions as it is for an electrician to pull a screwdriver or wrench out of his toolbox. A firm, intuitive grasp on music theory and basic composition and arranging techniques will take your farther than you can imagine.

## Know the rules

Every form has a set of rules, and as a composer, you should be familiar with all of them. Rock, folk, classical, and even experimental genres have specific rules that define them, and knowing those rules is sometimes half the work. Are rules made to be broken? Sure, sometimes. But they are also made to be hard-earned guidelines that many, many people before you had to figure out by trial and error. Use their wisdom for all it's worth — don't unthinkingly discard it.

## Pick up more instruments

Each instrument has its own beautiful, specific sound. Sometimes, becoming halfway fluent on a new instrument can completely change the way you want to put music together. It can also expand your appreciation for those other musicians who will be (we hope) putting your music into action.

## Understand when to put something aside

The compositions that cause you persistent, frustrating problems are probably the ones you need to put away for a later date. Often (but not always), the best ideas for compositions are the ones that come together naturally, easily, and quickly. If you're struggling with a piece of music, sometimes the best thing you can do is put it away for the day, or even longer, and come back to it later with a fresh perspective.

## Get something from nothing

A great idea is a gift and cannot be produced at will. However, lots of great composers can do just fine without divine intervention. If you look at many of J. S. Bach's compositions, for example, you can see that many sections are directly technique-inspired, built around very basic melodic lines and musical ideas.

If you can't come up with a brilliant start from thin air, then just try to start with a random one by taking a pen and writing down a series of random notes. Fill a whole music sheet with random dots and see if there's anything interesting. Yes, we're serious. Or pick up a guitar and play random chords until something sounds interesting. Or fiddle around on a keyboard until something makes your ears perk up. Countless classic pieces of music have begun with little more than these simple techniques.

Once you have a bit of something you want to explore, you can use rules to help you. It may sound corny, but it's true: The biggest oak began as a tiny acorn. The chapters in this book can show you how to fill out the melodic line you've just created as well as build a harmonic accompaniment.

## Trust your own taste

If you like it, someone else will too. Composing music is about self-expression, and if you've written a piece of music that sounds wonderful to you, then by all means, go with your gut. As beautiful and unique as all members of the human race are, there are more similarities between us than differences.

On the other hand, even if what you've written doesn't follow any set of rules, and even if most people who hear it hate it, *if you love it, it's worth keeping*. Eventually you'll bump into other people who will truly *get* it, and you'll be happy you saved that one odd bit of music that everyone else thought was unlistenable.

We mentioned a composer's toolkit. In the next chapter, you start building yours.

# Chapter 2

# Tools of the Trade

• • • • • • • • • • • • • • • • • • • • • • • • • • • • • • • • • • • • • • • • • • • •

*In This Chapter*

▶ Writing music by hand

▶ Composing on an instrument

▶ Using software to help you write music

▶ Training your ears

▶ Understanding the importance of music theory

▶ Finding the space, time, and ideas to compose

• • • • • • • • • • • • • • • • • • • • • • • • • • • • • • • • • • • • • • • • • • • •

*J*ust as electricians, plumbers, and mechanics use toolboxes to organize their tools, composers also bring toolboxes with them to work. The difference is, of course, that the aforementioned tradespeople's toolboxes can be seen, felt, and tripped over in the dark, whereas the composer's toolbox is contained mostly within his or her mind.

But they are still tools, and you need to use and develop them if you are going to get very far composing music. If you could open up a typical composer's toolbox and take a peek inside, you would find the tools covered in this chapter within.

# The Ability to Compose with Pencil and Paper

Believe it or not, even in this computerized world there are still many situations where a sheet of paper and a pencil are the best tools for the music composer. Many important modern composers, especially those born before 1940, won't work with anything *but* paper and pencil. So, never think you are too advanced for these humble tools.

Writing music with only paper and pencil has some amazing advantages to composing at a piano or other instrument. For one thing, many composers find the actual sound of the instrument itself interruptive to the composition process. Just imagine yourself deep in thought, hearing the perfect sequence of notes in your head, when suddenly, your finger touches the actual piano key, and it doesn't sound exactly like you imagined. Real sound is jarring, and hearing even the first note of your imagined phrase before you've written it down can cause you to lose an entire piece of music.

Conversely, many musicians work directly on their instrument of choice, usually a piano or guitar, and simply jot down their musical ideas on paper while composing. The ability to work with pencil and paper comes in especially handy in this context — you don't have to wait for a computer to boot up, and you don't have to compose solely in the same room as your computer. Computers can't be beaten for neatness when you need a printed *score* (written music for all the instruments that play a piece of music), a *part* (written music for just one instrument, extracted from a score), or *lead sheet* (written music using chord charts and a melodic line) — but you can take a pencil and paper anywhere.

In order for the pencil and paper to be useful, though, you have to be able to translate what you hear in your head into music notation. A good knowledge of *solfege* (the basic system of *do*, *re*, *mi*, *fa*, *so*, *la*, *ti*, in which each syllable represents a note on the major scale), or the numeric system of melodic representation (*Do* is 1, *Re* is 2, and so on) is essential.

If you aren't fluent enough in your head with different keys, you can write everything out in the key of C and *transpose* it to a different key later, probably on the computer.

Pencil and paper are often useful to just jot a rhythmic idea down quickly. This can be done on any type of paper; notation paper is not necessary — you can even just write X's for note heads and draw in the measure lines.

When using a pencil and paper, be sure to have a good eraser on hand, too.

## Performance Skills

Most composers use a keyboard or guitar to compose on, but you can use any instrument you're comfortable with. Although most composers are proficient instrumentalists, some composers actually do it all in their heads.

At any rate, being able to play melodies and chords on an instrument is a definite plus. The piano with its 88 keys encompasses the ranges of all other orchestral instruments, so it is traditionally the best choice. An electronic keyboard hooked into the right computer program (see next section) can provide a broad sound palette that can give the composer a rough idea of what a composition might sound like later played on real instruments. Keep in mind that a violin, for instance, played with a bow, can never really be accurately portrayed by a violin sample coming out of a keyboard.

*Some* skill at playing, plus the easy availability of an instrument, is almost essential for a music composer. The first time Scott wrote music for orchestral instruments, he had only enough skill on the piano to play two or three parts together at the same time, so he had to play the oboe part with the French horn part, and then the French horn with the trumpet, and so on. He never actually heard all the notes played together until he was in the recording studio in front of the orchestra. Exhilarating? Yes. Scary? You bet!

# Composition Software

It is impossible to overstate the important role of computers in music composition today. The following are some ways computers are involved in composing music today. Computers

- ✔ Provide various sounds to work with.

- ✔ Print out your parts quickly and neatly.

- ✔ Help you organize your ideas.

- ✔ Fit music to film easily.

- ✔ Provide tools for piecing together entire compositions while enabling you to test out ideas before committing to them.

- ✔ Can even produce and deliver a final recording of your work, if you use a good composition program.

As we mentioned, many great music composers out there do not use computers at all in their work, whereas others would be completely lost without computers.

So where do computers fit into *your* musical world? Ask yourself a few questions:

- ✔ Are you computer savvy?

- ✔ Do you have access to a fairly late-model computer?

- ✔ Can you get around the operating system?

✔ Do you understand the basics of file management?

✔ Have you had success learning other computer programs before?

If you answered yes to most of these, then you will probably do all right, as long as you don't pick the wrong software for the job.

In this section we briefly discuss a few major industry software packages, focusing on what each is good for and not good for.

# Finale

`www.finalemusic.com`

Finale is a music notation, scoring, layout, and publishing program. It is probably the most popular choice for bringing musical ideas into print. The program does enable you to audition your ideas with traditional orchestral sounds, but it is mostly used to print scores and parts. It does this very well, and many music programs in colleges and universities are now requiring the study of this program. Finale 2007 runs approximately $350.

# Sibelius

`www.sibelius.com`

Sibelius is a competitive program to Finale. It has better playback features for hearing scores that you've just input than Finale, but is less straightforward to navigate through. It is largely a matter of personal taste which of these two programs suits your writing style better. Sibelius 5 Pro Edition runs approximately $600.

# Pro Tools

`www.digidesign.com`

Pro Tools is found in almost every recording studio in the U.S. It is primarily designed for recording and editing audio tracks, though the last few versions of Pro Tools have included access to sample players and synthesizers through its MIDI capabilities. Pro Tools includes some integration with Sibelius, and the compositional side of Pro Tools is likely to expand more in the future. At present, it doesn't offer a lot in the way of compositional tools. Pro Tools is said to be unparalleled for cutting, pasting, and otherwise processing audio recordings. Pro Tools LE runs approximately $500.

## Logic Pro

www.apple.com/logicpro

Apple's Logic Pro is a complex and very deep program that aspires to be everything in one package. It offers sophisticated notation, scoring, layout, and printing tools, audio recording and editing capabilities, MIDI production with sample and synthesizer plug-ins, excellent cut-and-paste arranging and compositional tools, and more. You can even burn CDs and create MP3 and AAC audio files right in the program.

Logic Pro has a fairly steep learning curve, but most people who have tackled it find it is worth it. It is a popular program for electronic composition, sound design, and music composition for film and video — and is as popular in the studios of Europe as Pro Tools is in the U.S. Many of the notated figures in this book were created in Logic Pro. At the time of this writing, Logic Pro is only available for Macintosh computers. And it's not cheap: Apple Logic Pro 7.2 runs around $1000.

## Cubase

www.steinberg.net

Cubase is similar to Logic Pro, though with less power in the scoring printout area and fewer compositional features. Cubase is easier to learn than Logic Pro, though, and it's available for Mac and Windows machines. Cubase 4 runs approximately $1000.

If you are already using a music-composition program and feel comfortable with it, there's no real reason to change your routine. However, if you're planning on moving your work around a lot from place to place or studio to studio, you might start learning how to use Pro Tools, especially if you're doing a lot of audio recording of performances. If you're also doing sound design or electronic composition, need music printed out, or if you work with *loops* (repeated samples or recorded sounds that run through part or all of a composition) in addition to working with audio recordings of performances, Logic Pro may be your best bet.

# A Pair of Moderately Well-Trained Ears

When you think about it, we don't really "train" our ears at all. We develop *listening skills* and, therefore, develop our communication skills. We do this by training our *brains* to exercise a more focused type of attention on the stimuli arriving at our ears. It's just like when you're learning to speak a foreign language — you learn to pick out familiar words and phrases spoken in that new language and build your vocabulary from there. Music is as much a language as Mandarin or English or Swahili, and it just takes time, patience, and good listening skills to understand its "words." You probably won't pick it up instantly, but with perseverance, you will pick it up.

There are a lot of good courses available for developing good musical listening skills. If you're the self-teaching type, sitting in front of a piano and hitting notes over and over until you can identify pitches by ear is a good way to start.

Very few of us are born with perfect pitch, but most people can become able to identify *intervals* (the difference in pitch) between two or three notes and can pick those notes out on the piano without much trouble. With practice, the same person can learn to pick out simple phrases and chords on the piano and therefore learn how other composers put their songs together.

What we're saying here is that being one of the gifted few with perfect pitch isn't critical to being a good composer. With a set of moderately well-trained ears, you can learn to play and compose just about anything.

# Knowledge of Music Theory

It is important to be able to communicate your musical ideas to others. That's why you want to compose music in the first place, right? Part of this communication is being able to define the music you hear in terms that others can understand. *Music theory* is the study of music and the way it works and it encompasses the language through which musicians communicate their musical ideas to one another.

We assume that if you're ready to compose, you can already at least read music. With practice, you should be comfortable enough reading music that you can hear the notes in your head as you read them on the page. Have you ever seen someone reading a piece of music aloud to themselves, often humming loudly as they work their way through a piece? That's the level of comfort you should aim for — being able to "hear" a song just by looking at a lead sheet or a section of sheet music.

If you are weak in the music theory department, we recommend that you read *Music Theory For Dummies* by Holly Day and Michael Pilhofer (Wiley).

# Space, Time, and Ideas

The rhythmic beatings and messages that we get from the sounds around us in everyday life strongly influence the music that we compose. To a city dweller, a bird song is a signal from a world beyond the din of street noise. To a more rural ear, the sound of a jet flying by is also a signal from another world. Such influences affect the making of our inner music. The background of a song, either supporting or contrasting a theme, is what commands our attention. The best music is about a place, time, mood, setting, or vibe that offers a silver string of melody and throbs with the rhythmic urgency of our lives.

Engaging in musical composition often requires silence. Silence is the container of musical imagination. Your best melodic and rhythmic ideas may come to you amidst the hustle and bustle of life, but if you can't find a quiet place and time to spend nurturing these ideas, they will bear little fruit.

# A Pack Rat Mentality

Keep everything. Tape everything. Whether you compose with pencil and paper or on a computer, or just hum lines into a portable tape recorder while you're out for a walk, it is essential that you try to keep all the little beginnings, endings, chord progressions, melodies, grooves, and musical ideas of all shapes and sizes on file somewhere. A melody that leads to a dead end today may inspire you next year. A dumb little ditty that you have rolling around in your brain may not be your next masterpiece, but it might work great for a TV or radio jingle.

Many great composers disliked the very works that earned them notoriety. Bizet hated *Carmen*, for example. And maybe fame and fortune aren't all they're cracked up to be, but along with them comes the freedom to continue to pursue the craft of music composition. To a musician, money equals time, meaning that the more money you've got coming in, the more time you can spend working on the music you truly love to write. So don't be so quick to condemn your "unfinished" works. Just know how to recognize when a particular musical idea isn't working and don't try to force pieces of a puzzle to fit together. If something doesn't work, put it away and save it for a rainy day.

# Chapter 3

# Musical Scrapbooks: Writing on Paper and Screen

*T*here are not a whole lot of things worse than coming up with a great melody line, or even the beginnings of a great song, only to forget what you came up with simply because you didn't write it down.

You may think you've got a great memory for music, especially your own, but if you don't find some way to write down those notes or record that riff, there's a very good chance that the last time you hear that brand new music might be the first and only time you play it.

To avoid this kind of heartbreak and potential tragic loss for humanity, get in the habit of getting every idea you ever have down somehow — recorded, written, typed, whatever. This is so important we are dedicating this chapter to it.

## Writing It Down

There's an easy way to keep from losing those beautiful moments of inspiration, and that is to keep a pad of paper and a pencil or pen with you at all times. It only takes a few seconds to write down that engaging little melody or riff that's been banging around in your head.

Keep a pad and pencil by your bed, too, in case you wake up inspired and need to write down something quick.

When composing by hand the old-fashioned way, a good mechanical pencil with a good eraser is a must. A mechanical pencil — one of those with the clicky thing at the end that pushes the lead through the tip — is perfect because it ensures that your note stems, heads, and so forth will all be a consistent size. Use a pencil with larger diameter leads, at least 0.5 mm and up to 0.7 mm. You will find it easier to fill in note heads, and the tip won't break off quite as often. Have a standalone eraser nearby as well. Usually the areas to be erased are larger than the areas to be rewritten.

You can probably buy staff paper at your local music store by the sheet, notebook, or even by 500-page ream. If not, order through online bookstores like Amazon or download printable PDFs from many free music Web sites, including www.incompetech.com and www.blanksheetmusic.net.

# Using Software

Printed music these days is made, as mentioned in Chapter 2, with the aid of computer music scoring/notation/composition programs such as Sibelius, Finale, and Logic. Even a simple chord chart can quickly and neatly be printed out with these programs. After years of working with nearly illegible handwritten charts, almost everyone is happy about this development. Most of the figures in this book were created in Logic and Finale.

In college music courses, learning your way around these computer programs is often part of the required curriculum. Understanding one of these programs can aid tremendously in the generation of scores and parts.

Within these computer programs, you have the option of playing your music into the computer with a MIDI controller (and a metronome to keep you in time) or entering the notes with a mouse or keyboard. The MIDI controller is usually a keyboard, but you can use guitar, drums, woodwind, and even vibes MIDI controllers if you are more at home with one of these.

The important thing is to get your tune into the machine. You can edit your music within the program later, if need be. Notes can be moved around, deleted, copied, pasted, lengthened, shortened, and otherwise ornamented. You can add or enharmonically change accidentals. Your work can be auditioned within the program using the sound libraries that are included in most packages, and you can easily transpose into any key. The printout can be formatted in various ways and with various styles, including guitar tablature.

Making your lyrics conform to note positions is simple. You can even extract chord symbols and put them on the printout. Speaking of printing, you can print out an entire score, individual parts, or even just a small bit of something from your screen (as we have done frequently for the figures in this book).

In short, these computer applications are very sophisticated music notation processors, much as Microsoft Word is a sophisticated word processor. An expert with Finale can pretty much type his or her music into the computer.

Using these programs means you don't have to carry around a ream of sheet music, or even a notebook, for making notes about ongoing compositions. (Instead, you may be carrying a laptop computer.) With music notation software, the music you play on your instrument has already been automatically notated, from the barest melody line to the rhythm track you beat out during warmup.

You can erase the things you don't want to use, of course, but the little unfinished gems that come to you while fooling around can now be saved, instantly, for use in the future. A good rule of thumb is if you're in doubt, save it.

Having a large cache of little musical bits to listen to and draw on for inspiration is so much better than having no unfinished music at all. Besides, you never know when someone will want ten seconds of music from you for television filler music, a videogame sound effect, or even a ringtone.

# Computer versus Paper and Pencil

Of course, even in the computer age there is still no replacement for an actual printed copy of your work. Print everything and keep a file folder of the printed paper copies of any of your work that actually gets recorded or performed. With the speed at which technology advances there is no telling what sort of computer applications and storage media we will be using in five or ten years. Retrieving data from the sorts of media we use today could become difficult in the future. It has already become difficult in many cases to retrieve work that was saved on floppy disk, ADAT, and DAT tapes. And have you noticed that good quality audio cassette players are becoming scarce?

Despite the overwhelming advance of computer technology into the world of music composition, there are still advantages to working with pencil and paper. Pencil and paper are cheap and can be taken anywhere. At the beach or in a kayak are not great places for computers. And they don't need to be plugged in or charged up. If you are skilled at transcribing the music in your head into music notation, you may not need all of the automatic help that you get from a computer during the early, creative phases of your composition. You might still want the power of making your work legible enough for anyone to read, and you may want to publish your work, so the computer will come in handy later — but there is something freeing about working with simple, primitive tools. The process of writing becomes more direct without the distractions of a computer environment to confront you.

Some composers feel more comfortable with the light reflecting off of a piece of paper than by the light transmitted through a computer monitor. You may also find it easier to navigate through a pile of papers than click through the pages onscreen.

Few things in life are more rewarding than sitting out on your porch on a sunny spring day with a book of staff paper and a pencil, writing down whatever comes to your imagination. Try it.

# File Management

One of the dangers of working solely in the computer realm is that important pieces of music might get lost if you aren't careful with file management. Sometimes it is hard to say which pieces of music are going to end up being important ones, so we offer some tips here about file management.

To start with, let's define *file management* as the organization and logical arrangement of hierarchical structure in various data storage media, such as hard drives, CDs and DVDs, file folders, and files used for your work. More simply: It's where you keep stuff in your computer.

It is a good idea to keep all your computer applications on your boot drive, but storing your music on the same drive can end up being a very bad idea. Fragmentation can occur or you could just run out of space. Moreover, if the drive crashes (which it will, sooner or later) you could easily reinstall your applications, but your work could be lost forever. To prevent this from happening, you should probably get an extra, external hard drive and dedicate it to your saved music files. They are not so expensive anymore; you can probably find a perfectly good one for $75 or so.

Start by creating a folder on your drive called My Compositions, or something like that, and create organizational folders within that folder. They could be named for the different styles of music you are working with: Rock, Jazz, and so on. Or you could organize your work using folder names like Jingles, Film Scores, and Songs.

# Electronic versus "real" Instruments

Some composers feel that auditioning compositional ideas using the synthesized or sampled sounds inside a computer is a bad idea. It can steer a composer's editing choices away from the capabilities of musicians and toward what seems to work with the particular sound you are listening to at the moment. These composers feel that many good ideas get tossed out this way. For them, a better choice is to present the parts to musicians and meet the challenges then, with the input of the musicians who have to play the parts.

Hearing your music played by real musicians first *is* a decidedly different experience than testing and editing your music with computer sounds and then giving it to real musicians. You still have a lot of work to do when the musicians finally get ahold of your music.

Nothing ever quite plays exactly the way you think it will, so always be ready for compromises, rewrites, and other surprises. When the musicians are trying to play your piece for the first time, you are obliged to radiate a sense of confidence about what you are going for, and an ability to be fast and flexible with your edits and changes.

Inside these folders you should create a folder for each group of compositions that belong to a particular project or client. For example, in a folder named Productions, there could be a folder named Albums, in which there is a folder named The Gift of Thirst, inside which there is a folder for each song from that album.

If this seems like a lot of work, you have probably never lost anything on your computer — *yet!* It just takes one time to lose years of work. And then you'll be kicking yourself for not having taken advice like we're giving here. And you won't be just gently kicking yourself, either.

Frequently making a backup of your work is a must. You can do this by having yet another hard drive, and copying your work across to it from time to time. Or you can burn your work onto a DVD-R or CD-R disc from time to time. These hard media copies are not subject to mechanical breakdowns, though they can get scratched into uselessness if you don't treat them with care. To be really safe, make an extra copy every once in a while and take it to work or give it to a neighbor.

# Chapter 4

# Rhythm and Mood

● ● ● ● ● ● ● ● ● ● ● ● ● ● ● ● ● ● ● ● ● ● ● ● ● ● ● ● ● ● ● ● ● ● ● ● ● ● ● ● ● ● ● ● ● ● ●

## In This Chapter

▶ Making music out of time

▶ Deciding on rhythm and tempo

▶ Feeling different rhythms

▶ Varying rhythms

▶ Understanding back phrasing, front phrasing, and syncopation

▶ Finding your own rhythmic phrasing

▶ Exercising your rhythms

● ● ● ● ● ● ● ● ● ● ● ● ● ● ● ● ● ● ● ● ● ● ● ● ● ● ● ● ● ● ● ● ● ● ● ● ● ● ● ● ● ● ● ● ● ● ●

*T*ake a few minutes to listen to the rhythms around you. Is a bird singing? A train rattling by? Is someone hammering something down the block?

You may notice the repetitive sounds of your tires as you drive over a bridge, your footsteps as you walk or run, the cash register tapping out its tune. There are even rhythms from within: the sound of your breathing, your heartbeat. Life is full of rhythm if you're paying attention.

The rhythms of life have always influenced composers, both consciously and subconsciously. During the era when people regularly made long trips in horse-drawn carriages, quite a lot of music was written with a trotting or cantering rhythm. It's easy to imagine being a bored composer on a long trip through England when suddenly, your next composition pops into your head, spurred on by the relentless, rhythmic hoof-falls of the horses pulling your buggy.

The same types of influences are around us today. It's not such a big stretch to hear the clanging of assembly-line machinery when listening to industrial music. Obviously, rap music wasn't invented by cattle ranchers languidly following a herd along the trail, and there's no way you can listen to rap and think that there was any such connection. You can, however, hear the colorful banter of urban neighborhood streets in rap music, and you can easily feel the sway of a horse's walk in traditional country and western ballads.

In short, different rhythms convey different moods, and learning how to corner and manipulate those rhythms is the first step to getting your musical ideas across to another person.

# Sculpting Time into Music

A composition can be thought of as the *sculpting of time*.

Time is relative. Einstein once explained his concept of relativity by saying, "When you are courting a nice girl an hour seems like a second. When you sit on a red-hot cinder a second seems like an hour."

Rhythm is a large part of music's ability to sculpt time and produce different moods. The right rhythm can sculpt a five-minute piece of time to convey a sense of urgency and hurriedness — or to make the listener feel laid back and relaxed. These are examples of the mood messages that can result from rhythmic choices in music composition.

Let's say you're scoring a film. You wouldn't use a slow, pensive, loping rhythm to score a crowded party or a parade scene, and you wouldn't even think about an exciting 2/4 march for a funeral scene — unless, of course, your intention was to create an unnatural mood or feeling. Just like how your heart beats faster when you're happy or excited, lively rhythms to lively scenes just make sense. In music, lively rhythms convey a happy, excited, or just plain agitated sense, whereas slower rhythms can't help but invoke feelings of somberness, sadness, or even drowsiness.

Rhythm in music is more than just a regular, clocklike pulse chosen at random. When used wisely, it can set the tone of your composition and convey moods and mood changes throughout a composition.

# The Feel of Different Rhythms

Look at the following list of moods or emotions and try to decide the general *tempo* (the speed or pace of the underlying pulse) that might best convey these moods. There are no wrong answers, and you can just say "fast" or "slow" for now, although there is a fairly sophisticated musical language for different tempos.

- Fear
- Anticipation

- ✔ Sorrow
- ✔ Joy
- ✔ Anger
- ✔ Love
- ✔ Hate
- ✔ Compassion
- ✔ Surprise
- ✔ Tenderness
- ✔ Anxiety

As we said, there are no right and wrong answers. One reason for this is that emotions and moods can have variations within themselves. For example, fear can have a fast rhythm or a slow rhythm, with the "fast" fear being more flight-oriented, and the "slow" fear being more dread-oriented or suspense-oriented.

However, in general, the way these moods broadly affect your bodily functions is pretty universal. Surprise gets your heart rate up, whereas sorrow slows it down. It's a known fact that the rhythms of music can affect your heart rate and other bodily functions. Have you ever been to a rave or dance club? The DJ uses the rhythms of each song to adjust the heart rates of the dancers like so many metronomes and thereby manipulates the emotions of a whole crowd up and down over the course of the evening.

But there is more to rhythm than tempo alone. Have you ever noticed that there is a difference in the feel of walking and skipping? Walking is quite regular and even: Clop, clop, clop, clop, clop. Figure 4-1 shows how the rhythm of walking looks on a musical staff.

**Figure 4-1:**
A walking
rhythm is
steady and
regular,
loping
along.

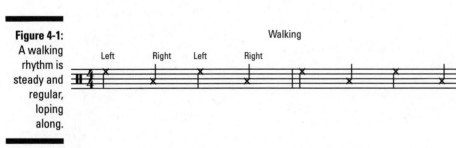

Skipping, on the other hand, has an uneven groove (Figure 4-2), with two steps close together and then a pause. Da, da-da, da-da, da-da.

**Figure 4-2:**
A skipping
rhythm
proceeds
irregularly,
in jerks and
delays.

If your friend walks at a rate of one step per second and you skip at the same rate, you could call these two rhythms *variations*. You are both moving at the same tempo, but the feel of the rhythm is different. Sometimes we use the term *mood message* to describe the feel of a rhythm. What is the difference in the mood messages of walking and skipping?

# Using a metronome

For many composers, exact metronome settings are critical for setting the groove and the mood of the piece. Today's computer music workstations provide a great deal of precision in this area, with many of them offering *click-track* (a virtual metronome you hear through headphones) settings down to the ten-thousandth of a beat per minute (abbreviated bpm, also sometimes called MM).

Such precision comes in particularly handy when you're trying to fit a particular musical mood to a set length of film or video. That piece of music you composed at 92 bpm (or MM-92) may need to be changed to 90.785 bpm in order to fit the length of the scene exactly. Another thing to consider is that, if you are working with a singer, the lyrics have to be allowed to flow naturally —— even if the musicians might enjoy playing the music at a faster or slower tempo.

Terms for ranges of metronomic tempo were established long ago and are still used today. You will undoubtedly encounter them in sheet music. They are Italian words, and the following are a few of the more common ones:

Largo: 40 to 60 beats per minute

Larghetto: 60 to 66 beats per minute

Adagio: 66 to 76 beats per minute

Andante: 76 to 108 beats per minute

Allegro: 108 to 168 beats per minute

Presto: 168 to 200 beats per minute

And once you have decided on a tempo, you have to determine the meter of your piece. In other words, how many beats will be contained in each measure, and what type of note — quarter, eighth, and so on — will be counted as a single beat. This choice is represented as a time signature (4/4, 3/4, 6/8, and so on). It is a lot easier for musicians to count up to three over and over again than it is for them to count each beat in a piece of music separately. Besides this, it seems that rhythms in life tend to work in simple repeated patterns like the beating of your heart or the rhythm of walking.

The point here is that it can be useful to start a composition by choosing the mood you want the piece of music to convey and matching it up with a rhythm that is appropriate. When you're starting from the rhythm up — a very common way to compose music — choosing the best tempo for the job is half the work.

You want your composition to tell a story. And, just as a story contains passages of contentment, change, tension, crisis, and resolution, for example, so the mood needs to change at some point within the music. You can change and vary the tempo (mood) to fit that mood change. You can use rhythm to create contrast, conflict, development, resolution, and other story-building components.

# Speed Bumps and Rhythmic Phrases

A composition traveling along at a set meter and tempo can get boring or even exhausting after awhile. That's another reason why it's a good idea to break up the rhythmic landscape with a few bumps along the way — to keep things interesting or keep your listener awake.

Beethoven's "Ode to Joy" offers a familiar example of varying the rhythmic landscape in order to throw things off a little bit (Figure 4-3).

Ode to Joy

**Figure 4-3:** Beethoven's "Ode to Joy" clips along regularly until you get to the end of the twelfth measure.

At the end of the twelfth measure, after a section of mostly straight quarter notes, he surprises the listener by putting a strong accent — unexpectedly — on beat *four*. Beat four is usually a weak pulse, but the German genius makes it strong by starting a phrase there, and then makes it even stronger by tying the note over into beat *one* of the following measure. Beat one is usually expected to be a strong beat. The result almost feels like you were walking along and then slipped on a patch of ice, yet managed somehow able to hold on and continue with an unbroken stride.

This technique of putting a strong accent on a beat that is usually weak (an up-beat, for example) is called *syncopation,* and can be applied to a single note, a group of notes, or an entire melody.

Breaking up the rhythm is an excellent way to hold the listener's attention, and it may provide opportunities later on for different instrumentation choices and arrangement ideas when you start to flesh out your composition.

Figure 4-4 shows another section of "Ode to Joy" in which Beethoven "skips" with the same melody he "walked" with earlier in Figure 4-3.

**Figure 4-4:**
Taking another look at Beethoven's "Ode to Joy" — same notes, different rhythm.

Ode to Joy

Beyond the steady persistence of the underlying tempo of your composition, there are brief sections of music called *rhythmic phrases*. Think of the old "Shave and a Haircut" ditty (it's actually a *couplet*), the rhythm of which is shown in Figure 4-5.

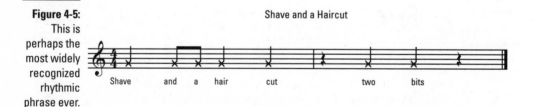

**Figure 4-5:**
This is perhaps the most widely recognized rhythmic phrase ever.

Shave and a Haircut

Shave    and    a    hair    cut    two    bits

You don't even need the melody for the rhythmic phrase in Figure 4-5 to be immediately recognized. In fact, if you knock the first five notes out on your desktop at school or work, someone is bound to finish it for you. The rhythm suggests the melody, shown in Figure 4-6.

**Figure 4-6:**
Adding the familiar notes to the familiar rhythm.

This is an important idea: A simple rhythmic phrase can suggest melodies. It can also, therefore, render some melodies unsuitable.

# Mixing It Up: Back Phrasing, Front Phrasing, and Syncopation

There are a few ways to change up the rhythm of your composition.

## Back phrasing

Let's have some fun by pushing the phrasing of "Shave and a Haircut" out by one beat. Our result looks like Figure 4-7.

**Figure 4-7:**
"Shave and a Haircut" — back phrased.

When you move your music phrase later in the measure, so that the melody starts after the beat, it's called *back phrasing*. As you can tell from Figure 4-7, our song now starts on beat *two*, with a rest on beat one. Try it out! Make sure you are playing or singing this with the strong accent, as usual, on the first beat of the measure. ONE two ONE two. Back phrasing can be a tricky thing to get a handle on, so if a natural-sounding rhythm eludes you the first couple of times, that's okay. You see how it changes the song?

## Front phrasing

If we go the other way and *front phrase* it — or move the melody forward by one beat — the result looks like Figure 4-8.

**Figure 4-8:**
"Shave and a Haircut" — front phrased.

Now, going back to tempo for a second, try playing or singing these variations at a very fast or ridiculously slow tempo, just to see what those changes do to the overall feel of the song. Bet you never thought that "Shave and a Haircut" could sound so spooky! It's funny how even slight changes in tempo can change the mood of a song so much.

Let's try to do a skipping variation of the back-phrased version of "Shave and a Haircut" (Figure 4-9).

**Figure 4-9:**
Making "Shave and a Haircut" skip along.

Bear with us for one more example as we now syncopate the original melody (Figure 4-10).

# *Syncopation*

Notice in Figure 4-10 how the "syllabic emphasis" is not where the strong nat-ural beats are. Syncopation is basically about putting the em*pha*sis on the wrong syl*lab*le. That doesn't mean it's "wrong," though. Syncopation just makes things a bit different, surprising, and spicy. In short, it's a good way to break up the rhythmic landscape and thereby change the mood of your composition.

If you were counting out just the rhythm from Figure 4-10, you would get something like the following:

> one-AND two-and THREE-and four-AND one-and two-AND three-AND four-and

As you can guess from all the examples, a composer could nearly build an entire composition around "Shave and a Haircut" — with just a few minor variations, we might not even know it. Depending on the accompaniment, tempo, musical context, and any number of other variables, "Shave and a Haircut" could completely escape our notice in a composition.

Using familiar themes in new ways is incredibly common in composition. There's nothing new under the sun — only a lot of old stuff, being used in new ways. A composer could, if he or she wanted to, throw a lot of old, stale, familiar little chestnuts at his or her listeners without their even realizing it.

Don't be afraid of trying out some variations of a strong rhythmic phrase or theme by offsetting the starting point of the phrase in time or using syncopa-tion to spice it up.

By the way, such rhythmic tinkering is easily done in music software (such as Logic Pro) by just creating or even copying someone else's phrase or theme and dragging it around a little. (See Chapter 2 for more on music software.) On paper, it's a matter of visualizing and auralizing the newly displaced nugget of your rhythmic ingenuity.

# Finding Your Own Rhythmic Phrases

Although it's possible to build your entire arsenal of musical compositions on variations of the "Shave and a Haircut" riff, it's so much more fun and satisfying to come up with your own rhythmic phrases to build songs around. So where can we get these rhythmic phrases? Everywhere — there's one right there, in the last sentence (Figure 4-11).

**Figure 4-11:**
You can often find interesting rhythmic phrases embedded in everyday language.

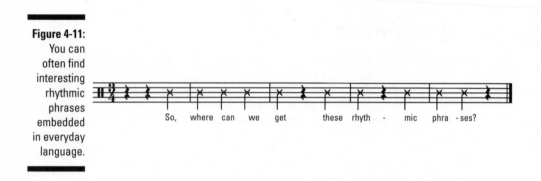

So, where can we get these rhyth - mic phra - ses?

What kind of melody would the rhythm in Figure 4-11 suggest or reject?

It has been said that music is a universal language, but even rhythms on their own, without a melody, are capable of universal communication. Think of the talking drums in West African culture, which seem to mimic the human voice — or the tablas of India with their huge vocabulary of variable sounds. Though we all speak different languages, all languages have rhythms and melodies in them. So perhaps we should say instead that language universally uses the elements of music to communicate.

For now, start paying attention to the tempos and rhythmic phrases present all around you. They will contribute much to your musical compositions, whether you want them to or not.

# Exercises

1. **Find and notate a rhythmic phrase from your own personal environment.**

   It could be anything from the rhythm of a washing machine to the sound of your breathing or heartbeat. Maybe your engine makes an interesting rhythm when it starts in the morning. Maybe your dog barks in a rhythmic pattern. Maybe someone is hammering down the street or your door or mailbox makes a rhythmic creaking noise. Whatever it is, if it has rhythm, you can use it in your composition.

2. **Notice the tempo of your walking.**

   Most people settle into a habitual pace when they walk. Try to change it up today. Go a little faster or slower and see how that feels. Try to feel the upbeats between your footsteps as you walk. What kind of melody suggests itself when you listen to the rhythm of your walk?

3. **Notice the unconscious rhythms of human interactions.**

   Notice the rhythm of conversation while you are chatting with friends, for example. Most activities have a generally accepted "normal" pace that we almost always adhere to. How do you feel when someone moves too slow or too fast for the circumstances? What makes you slow your pace or speed it up? And most importantly, how can these things be incorporated into your music?

4. **Write or copy three short sentences and notate their rhythms.**

   Is the meter of the sentence four beats to a measure or three? Where are the accents? Which syllables move the melody up and which move it down?

5. **Analyze several of your favorite songs or compositions.**

   Can you find rhythmic phrases that recur? How many variations can you find of the same phrase? How many different phrases were used? How do the rhythmic phrases interact with the melody choices?

6. **Pick a rhythmic phrase from these exercises that you would like to develop for future use.**

# Part II
# Melody and Development

The 5th Wave                    By Rich Tennant

"Okay, we're approaching some swimmers. Start
playing the notes, E and F in the lower register.
Slow at first, gradually picking up tempo."

## In this part . . .

We discuss how to find inspiration for musical pieces in spoken and written phrases, as well as how using specific keys and modes can instantly create specific moods in your music. We also discuss how you can begin writing your own melodic motifs to build music around, as well as how to develop your melodies.

# Chapter 5

# Finding Melodies Where You Least Expect Them

. . . . . . . . . . . . . . . . . . . . . . . . . . . . . . . . . . . . . . . . . . .

. . . . . . . . . . . . . . . . . . . . . . . . . . . . . . . . . . . . . . . . . . .

*W*hat exactly is a melody? Or, from a composer's standpoint, perhaps a more important question is: Why do you need one (or several)? Where can you find them?

To answer the first question, putting it very, very simply: A melody is a succession of notes built on a musical framework.

A melody is probably the most important part of a composition. It's the lead line you find yourself humming after hearing a song, and it's the part of a song that seems to be the hardest to get out of your head.

Sounds simple enough. Maybe too simple, but it's a good start.

## What Is a Musical Framework?

Obviously, throwing a random succession of notes together will almost certainly not produce a good melody. Yet many successful compositions might sound to many listeners as though that's just what the composer did. And believe it or not, there are tools available in several computer programs that will do just that — randomize notes into musical phrases (see Chapter 2 for a brief survey of music software).

Anyone, with or without the help of technology, can come up with a succession of notes. But what makes a *good* melody? And just what do we mean by a musical framework?

For one thing, a *musical framework* is the duration of a particular section of your composition. Or to be more abstract: A musical framework is the amount of time during which you are hoping to secure the attention of your listeners.

Because music is the sculpting of time, without a framework of some kind, you don't have music. Many times when you are composing, the melody itself creates or even demands a framework to grow around it. Even a lonely, solitary melody has a little rhythm built into it. (The other elements of the musical framework are the chords and instrumentation that you have chosen, which we talk about in Part III.)

Now, where do you find melodies to go into this framework?

# Finding Melody in Language

If you are ever in need of inspiration, try slipping a tape recorder in your pocket and heading out into the street. Go into a cafe or get on the bus, turn on your tape recorder, and just let the din of the other passengers' voices wash over you. You don't even have to listen to the tape afterwards — oftentimes, just being an active listener can be enough to get you started in learning to pay attention to the music of language.

There is so much to get from the way a person talks. Consider the rhythm of a speaker's voice — is it clumsy, staccato, languid? What about the quality of a voice — high-pitched, low-pitched, childish, aggressive? Each person is a self-playing instrument. Put two or more people together, and you've got the most basic orchestra.

Take another look at the example of finding the rhythmic phrase in speech from Chapter 4 (Figure 5-1).

**Figure 5-1:**
Rhythmic patterns are found everywhere in speech.

So, where can we get these rhyth - mic phra -ses?

Looking at Figure 5-1, let's see what kind of melody is suggested by this phrase. When you speak the phrase out loud, notice that some of the words rise upward in pitch, while others go down in pitch. There might be some variation in emphasis or intention when different people say the phrase, but by and large these words almost demand a natural melodic movement, something like that shown in Figure 5-2.

**Figure 5-2:**
Adding natural melodic movement to the phrase, based on the way the words rise and fall in speech.

All well and good. Now try speaking the phrase with an *unnatural* melodic movement, something like the one shown in Figure 5-3.

**Figure 5-3:**
Making the phrase sound wrong by adding unnatural melodic movement to it.

Now the phrase doesn't work musically. The melody of it is off somehow. Or is it the rhythmic emphasis? See how important the elements of music are to basic spoken communications? It's fairly easy to determine the direction that the melody wants to move in this example — and a direction where it doesn't. We can see the basic landscape, given this phrase.

But where will we find the exact notes to give to our melody? One way would be to limit ourselves to the notes within a particular scale. In our examples, we've stuck to the key of C major and used notes that we know make musical sense together — that is, notes from the C major scale. So, using notes from the major scale is one very common method of finding notes.

# Let's Eat (,) Grandma!

It's fun and instructive to see how meanings can totally change depending solely on your melodic choices. Figure 5-4 shows three words with two different melodies.

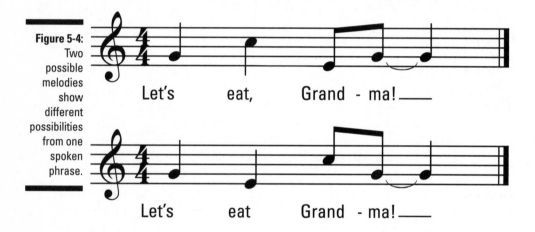

**Figure 5-4:**
Two possible melodies show different possibilities from one spoken phrase.

Let's    eat,    Grand - ma! ____

Let's    eat    Grand - ma! ____

The first version is an invitation to Grandma to join in the feast. The second one, though, sounds like an invitation for Grandma to *be* the feast. "Let's eat, Grandma" is very different from "Let's eat Grandma"!

Going further, we could make the second version even darker and more threatening by using a minor scale instead of a major scale (Figure 5-5).

**Figure 5-5:**
This is more a case of "Run, Grandma, run!"

Let's    eat    Grand - ma! ____

As you can see, your choice of scale can contribute to the mood messages you are trying to convey in your music.

In the examples so far, we've stuck to using short phrases of language to make a point. But there is no reason why you couldn't apply these ideas to an entire conversation — perhaps a musical transcription of your tape-recorded bus trip.

If you are writing a song, it is essential to be respectful of the way your lyrics fit rhythmically and melodically with your music, but you don't have to be a great lyricist to use a verbal idea as a source for your melodies. Maybe you will be the only one who knows that your famous composition started out as "Scrambled eggs, oh, baby how I love your legs" (Paul McCartney's original lyrics for "Yesterday").

# Finding Melody in the World Around You

Just about every composer has found inspiration for a song from walking outside and blinking at the world at one point or another. Nature is a great source of inspiration; city sidewalks and noisy factories are others. Sometimes it's just picking up the recurring rhythms of the environment and building a simple melody on top of that.

Other times, it can be as simple as stealing a bird's song for your melody — or the quiet humming or muttering of someone walking past you on the street, or the varying pitches of a concrete saw whining across the street. Some composers even claim that when they see the throat of a newly-opened flower, they hear singing in their heads. The inspiration for the greatest compositions in the world is all around you. Learning how to turn that inspiration into actual music is the challenge.

Sometimes composing a melody can be like creating a sonic dot-to-dot drawing. Many composers have attempted to recreate scenery, landscapes, cityscapes, and the activities of nature and humanity through their compositions, such as in George Gershwin's "Grand Canyon Suite." In fact, some melodies can be seen as literal landscapes on the musical staff. If you extract the basic melody from music, connect the notes on the staff, and hold it up in front of you, it looks like a dot-to-dot drawing of a scene.

If a melody is like a sonic painting of a landscape, the melody rises and dips into hills and valleys, sometimes quickly jumping up cliffs, and then just as suddenly diving into ravines.

Figures 5-6 through 5-9 show a few simple drawings. The first one has been transcribed into a melody for you. Pick a second one for you to do and write the notes on the blank staff at the bottom of Figure 5-9.

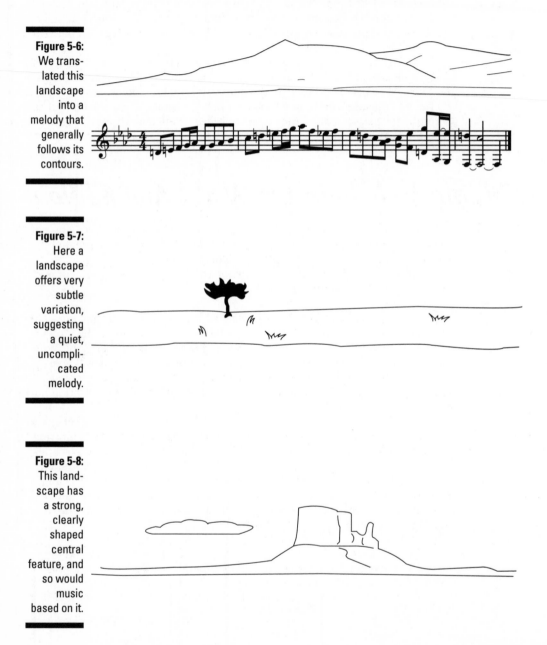

**Figure 5-6:**
We trans-
lated this
landscape
into a
melody that
generally
follows its
contours.

**Figure 5-7:**
Here a
landscape
offers very
subtle
variation,
suggesting
a quiet,
uncompli-
cated
melody.

**Figure 5-8:**
This land-
scape has
a strong,
clearly
shaped
central
feature, and
so would
music
based on it.

**Figure 5-9:**
This is a kind of abstract, sparse "land-scape," offering a more or less regular pattern.

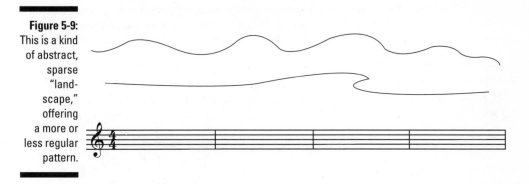

We don't expect you to be able to fully compose music yet. The preceding exercise is meant to show that you can draw inspiration and generally shape music around it.

If you were to stop and think about your choices of notes and rhythms to represent these scenes, you might also want to consider representing other *unseen* elements within them. For example, what other sounds — birds, waterfalls, insects — might be present, and how can they be represented musically? What sort of emotion does each scene convey to you? How can you represent and refine that emotion through tempo, choice of scale (also called mode), and instrumentation?

The visual realm is not the only one from which you can draw melodic inspiration. What does touch sound like? Soft caresses must sound different from a slap in the face, right? What about taste — can you represent taste through musical composition? What makes a piece of music bland or flavorful? And let's not forget the sense of smell. Can a musical composition smell sweet? We've certainly all heard a few that stink.

Music is the universal language, and language is descriptive by nature. Your job as composer is to describe an emotion through your choice of rhythm and melody — among other things.

# Helping Your Muse Help You

One can't overestimate the value of a good musical *imagination*. It is the single most powerful source for making music — *if* you can tap into it. The imagination is so powerful, in fact, that since long ago it has been personified as *the Muse*.

Because it is inside your head, though, your imagination is also the hardest source to put your finger on. Its timing is sometimes off, for one thing. The Muse can feed you melodies when you least expect them and are least prepared to do anything about them.

Always have a paper and pencil or a small recording device at hand, at all times, no matter where you go. They are a lot easier to carry around than a computer and keyboard.

You can do a few things to help your Muse work more effectively for you. Here are some things the Muse needs and ideas about how to do your part to help:

- **The Muse needs space to work in.**

  Turn off your TV and radio, log off the Internet, turn off your cell phone, and tell your family and roommates that you are indisposed for the next, say, hour or two.

- **The Muse likes to be nourished.**

  Every day, expose yourself to a variety of musical influences — *not* just the few favorites you keep cycling through. And if you want your Muse to get real exposure to different music, do it with full attention.

- **The Muse likes to be quiet.**

  Music as a background often silences or distracts the Muse. It is hard to focus on what you are hearing in the mind's ear when you're hearing things in your physical ear. The Muse is shy. Silence often causes her to come out of hiding.

- **The Muse needs you to follow where she leads.**

  The Muse can't do it all; you have to do your part. Once the Muse gives you something, run with it. Work it, play with it — above all, capture it. Write it down! Never think that you'll remember what the Muse tells you. No matter how impressive your melody seems at the moment, it will slip out of your head just as magically as it slipped in.

- **Your muse needs you to remember what she says.**

  Keep a pencil and paper or a simple recording device next to your bed. The first few seconds after you wake up provide the best opportunity to clearly recall your dreams. Discipline yourself to write them down, even if there is no music in them. And when you do wake up with a strangely unfamiliar and uncharacteristic Beatles song in your head, get it down on paper or tape. It is possible that it wasn't a Beatles song at all, but your muse playing hide-and-seek with you.

  (Of course, make sure it wasn't an actual Beatles song before you try to publish it! This is what happened with Paul McCartney when he wrote

"Yesterday" — he woke up with the tune in his head, but it sounded so familiar he couldn't believe he hadn't heard it somewhere before. He went around worried, for weeks, asking people if they had heard it before.)

✔ **The Muse works for you.**

If you sit at your keyboard, piano, guitar, computer, or pad and paper long enough in a patient, receptive state, your muse will show up more often than not. The muse lives in your subconscious mind, waiting for only one thing: your impassioned receptivity. Once you figure out how to turn that on, you will be on another level entirely as a composer. If you defend a routine time and place to work quietly, your muse will become trained to know when and where to make an appearance.

✔ **The Muse is fickle.**

Of course, even if you do all of this, it doesn't always work. That's why we call her the Muse.

# Finding Melody in Your Instrument

Once you have played an instrument for a while, you develop certain unconscious habits that are imbedded in your muscles and nerves. You can turn these habits to your advantage.

## Using scales in composition

Playing scales over and over on the piano, for example, trains your hands to behave in a certain way. This hand behavior becomes second nature, and you become better at grabbing the notes of a piece of actual music. In fact, many pieces of music have melodies that are not much more than scales.

Consider "Joy to the World" (Figure 5-10).

**Figure 5-10:** "Joy to the World" uses the entire descending major scale in its melody.

Joy to the world, the Lord has come.

The first eight notes of this incredibly famous piece are just a descending major scale — pretty easy notes to grab even for a novice musician.

So scales can definitely be used as melodies. We would get pretty tired of hearing *just* scales for melodies after a while, but there are tons of examples of scales, or pieces of them, appearing in melodies.

Any succession of notes that comes naturally from the mechanical skills of a musician can be used for melody. (Of course, ones that don't come so naturally can be used, too, but that is covered in the next section.)

Each musician has strengths and weaknesses in her playing technique. If you were to get two or three guitar players to improvise freely on the guitar, each of them would bring idiosyncrasies to the task. But because they have certain trained habits, just the act of grabbing a few seemingly random notes has the potential of generating excellent melodic ideas.

Improvisation is limited by skill sets, but style in some respects is a product of limitations as well as strengths. Mining the simple, intuitive, mechanical structure of your instrument can bring a wealth of melodic material, but many musicians toss aside melodic opportunities because they don't consider their improvisations to be anything but momentary bits of magic. Just because something is easy for you to play, it doesn't mean it would be worthless as a melody.

On the other hand, many musicians think everything they play is golden. Sometimes it's hard to evaluate your own work. Criticism is better than praise in this context most of the time. Find someone you can bounce ideas off. If you are receiving constructive criticism, and the criticism makes some sense to you, you are on the right track.

Learn to be a pack rat. Keep *all* your ideas.

## Using music theory in composition

With enough knowledge of music theory and a familiarity with the mechanics and languages of instruments, a composer can invent melodies. These melodies emerge from the possibilities within scales, modes, keys, and the techniques and limitations of the musicians who will be required to play them.

For example, a composer who knows how far a breath can get a musician on a clarinet — and the range of the instrument and its limits in terms of speed and versatility — can write melodies for that instrument largely out of theoretical abstraction. Just throw possibilities and challenges at the instrument based on a mode or mood that you are trying to convey. At one moment you can create fast-moving, frenetic phrases that jump about like grasshoppers, and at the next you can conjure pensive, provocative themes to be traded and danced around by the instruments.

This type of melodic composition demands an intimate knowledge of both music theory and the demands of playing each instrument. It can lead to many powerful results, although often the composer doesn't have such a clear idea of what the result will be until the music is played. It can be hard to hear these things in your head.

# *Exercises*

1. **Keep working with language.**

   Short or long phrases are rich sources of rhythms and melodies. See if you can fit a couple of different phrases together in a way that makes rhythmic or melodic sense. Take the melody you found in language phrases and see if you can fit a different phrase into the music. Write the phrase once and then write a variation. Read poetry for inspiration.

2. **While listening to a piece of music, draw freely.**

   Take a crayon, pen, or pencil and freely draw, moving your pencil along with the flow and contours of the music. You can draw abstract shapes, or if you prefer, something the music reminds you of. If you're using a colored pen or crayon, pay attention to the colors suggested and use them.

3. **Draw the landscapes suggested by the melodic movements of a piece of music.**

4. **Come up with a short melody to describe the scene outside your front door.**

   Add two or three more elements from the scene to it — a car driving by, a dog barking, a squirrel skittering past, the baby across the street screaming — and see how much of the individual parts of the scene you can put together. Your neighborhood has a soundtrack — what is it?

5. **Sit quietly with the TV and the radio turned off and listen to your breathing.**

   Does a rhythm or melody bubble up? Be prepared with paper and pencil. Keep a paper and pencil next to your bed. Force yourself to write something down every morning immediately after waking up. Even a single word or a measure of music could help you get in touch with your muse.

Have an instrument nearby that is ready to go. Take your guitar out of the case and leave it setting in a stand, ready to play. If you get a melody in your head, force yourself to write it in the key you heard it in inside your head. This will help keep your material from all sounding the same.

6. **Sit at your instrument and just let your hands land on the notes.**

If you don't come up with something good right away, keep repeating the mediocre things until they lead to something better. Trust your hands. If you hear something unusual or dissonant don't throw it away, work with it. How will you resolve the ideas?

7. **Try writing a few phrases of random notes keeping within a key or mode.**

Think of a specific instrument when you write. If it is a wind instrument, remember that the musician needs to breathe. If it is a stringed instrument, keep the bowing and picking in mind. Just fill up some measures without thinking too much about how it might sound. Then try playing what you wrote. Make adjustment where necessary.

# Chapter 6

# Scales and Modes, Moods and Melodies

Sometimes you have more of an idea about the direction you want your melody to move in than which notes you're going to use to create your melody. This is true of the melodies you may imagine building when you look at a landscape. Even more often, probably, you have an idea of the mood you want to convey with your music, without thinking about whether the melody should rise, fall, or take on any specific shape. If you are writing with a sense of directional movement — that is, up and down the staff — there are times you can benefit from limiting yourself to notes within a *scale* or *mode*.

There are twelve different pitches in the Western *chromatic scale*. That's the total number of notes that are available in any one octave. But there are many other combinations of those notes — other scales — and if you don't know at least several of them frontward and backward, you should work on that, because it can benefit your composing tremendously. The other scales have fewer than twelve notes, boiling them down to as few as five or as many as seven.

✔ Diatonic scales have seven different pitches in them.

✔ Pentatonic scales have five different pitches in them.

For our purposes in this chapter, the words *scale* and *mode* mean pretty much the same thing: a particular selection of successive notes within an octave. You will encounter both terms, so we use both here, too.

# Major and Minor Modes and the Circle of Fifths

Different modes and scales can evoke different moods. Major scales are good for happy, lively, calming moods. The minor ones are great communicators of sadness, seriousness, and introspection.

Figures 6-1 and 6-2 show two examples of nearly identical melodies in terms of directional movement.

**Figure 6-1:** This simple melody is in major mode.

Figure 6-1 is in a major mode, and Figure 6-2 is minor.

**Figure 6-2:** Here's the same melody in minor mode.

Play those pieces on an instrument, and you can easily hear the difference in mood between these two examples without even knowing what written key they're in (we deliberately left out the key signature). The melody in Figure 6-1 is actually in the key of F major, and the one in Figure 6-2 is in F minor.

Note that even though the directional shape of the notes on the staffs are identical, the pieces sound different because the first example is in a major mode and the second example is in a minor mode.

Figures 6-3 and 6-4 show them with their proper key signatures.

**Figure 6-3:**
Our melody in major mode is shown with the F major key signature.

**Figure 6-4:**
The same melody in minor mode is shown with the F minor key signature.

It's normally taken for granted that music students have memorized the Circle of Fifths, but sometimes a refresher may be called for (Figure 6-5). Remember that every time you move one letter clockwise from the C major/A minor position at the top, you add a sharp to the key signature. And at every point counterclockwise from C major/A minor, you add a flat. The major keys are given capitalized letters here, and the minor keys are in lowercase. Each position on the circle contains two keys: the major key and its relative minor, which share the same key signature.

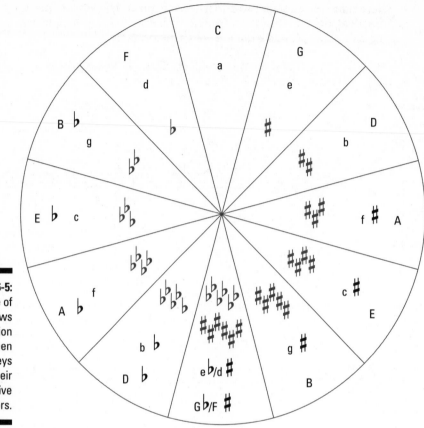

**Figure 6-5:**
The Circle of Fifths shows the relation between major keys and their relative minors.

It is useful to note that when you are writing something in a particular major key and you want to change the mood a little (maybe make it a little sadder or darker), you can use the relative minor scale of the key. For example, if your original melody was in G major, you could change to E minor for the sad parts. Doing this makes it unnecessary to change the key signature, though you may have to use a few accidentals here and there. Figure 6-5 shows you at a glance which major keys coordinate with which minor keys.

Another common practice in composition is to write the darker, sadder bits in the minor key of the original major. In other words, go from a G major scale to a G minor. As you can see from the Circle of Fifths chart in Figure 6-5, the parts written in G major would be written with the key signature for G, which has a single sharp (F sharp). The parts in G minor, then, would require the signature from *its* relative major, which is B flat. The key signature for B flat has two flats: a B flat and an E flat.

# Getting Moody

It's no big secret that playing a good song is an easy way to set the mood of a room. For some reason, that's doubly true in film. How many times have you watched a film with a wall-to-wall soundtrack of busy, unconnected pop songs and had it spoil the picture for you? How long does it take to get the creepy but incredibly simple soundtracks of films like *Halloween* or *Friday the 13th* out of your head after watching them?

The connection between music and mood isn't even confined to the human realm, either: Birds, bees, and four-legged animals of all sizes modulate their vocal utterances to try to attract mates or scare away competition. And if you think dogs barking isn't musical, then we must insist you take one more listen to the Jingle Dogs' *Christmas Unleashed.*

The ancient Greeks believed that not only did music itself invoke mood and even provoke certain behaviors, but that the *modes* the songs were written in were just as responsible. The original name for the Greeks' set of seven musical scales was échos, later renamed *modus* by the Romans who adopted the system.

Plato himself recommended that soldiers preparing for war should listen to music written in Dorian and Phrygian modes (more on these modes in the next section). In a modern context, that would mean that before heading off for any great confrontation, one should listen to songs like The Doors' "Light My Fire," Steppenwolf's "Born to Be Wild," Jefferson Airplane's "White Rabbit," and Yngwie Malmsteen's "Heavy E Phrygian." On the other hand, Plato discouraged these same soldiers from listening to songs in the Lydian or Ionian modes because it would interfere with their bloodlust. Therefore, putting on R.E.M.'s "Man on the Moon" is not a good idea before going off to war.

Plato and Aristotle also believed that an affinity towards certain musical modes were insights into a person's character, and that people who were fond of music in the Ionian, Aeolian, and Locrian modes were too relaxed and easygoing to do well in high-power political or military positions. After reading this chapter, you might want to take a look at the sort of music you yourself prefer listening to and see what musical modes most often pop up in your personal CD collection.

# Moods à la Modes

Just playing a mode or scale without any particular melody in mind can inspire you to come up with a melody. An easy way to start experiencing a few different modes is to play scales on all white piano keys, but starting on the different notes within the C scale. There are seven modes (often called *church modes*, although they're really ancient Greek) that you can make this way because there are seven unique white piano keys in an octave.

For example: Play a scale from F to F using only the white keys. Note that you will play the B natural instead of the B flat that is found in the key of F major. You just played a scale in the *Lydian* mode, and it sounds a little different from the old "Do Re Mi" that you learned as a kid.

You can try all seven modes by starting and finishing on other notes using only the white keys. Can you hear the interesting mood possibilities lurking in these modes? You can gain a lot of ideas by sampling the different modes and deciding which mode evokes which moods.

Let's look at all seven modes a little more closely now. It's true that for simplicity's sake we're illustrating the modes using only the white keys on the piano keyboard. But of course, each mode can be based on any note. It's the different pattern of the intervals between the notes that defines each mode.

## Ionian (major scale)

When you play seven ascending white keys starting with C, you get the Ionian mode (Figure 6-6). To build an Ionian scale on another note besides C, you use the whole-step (W), half-step (H) pattern: WWHWWWH.

Notice something familiar about this? You're right — this is the same pattern used to build major scales today.

**Figure 6-6:**
The Ionian mode should sound familiar, because it's the major scale.

## Dorian

Figure 6-7 shows the D Dorian mode. To build a Dorian mode on another note besides D, you would use the pattern WHWWWHW.

The Dorian mode is most commonly heard in Celtic music and early American folk songs derived from Irish melodies. Songs written in Dorian mode sound melancholy and soulful because the final note of the scale doesn't quite resolve itself, so it feels almost like a question left unanswered.

**Figure 6-7:**
The Dorian mode sounds melancholy and full of bittersweet longing.

## Phrygian

Figure 6-8 shows the E Phrygian mode. To build a Phrygian mode on another note besides E, you would use the pattern HWWWHWW.

Most flamenco music is written in the Phrygian mode, which has a bright, Middle-Eastern sound to it that works well with folk and traditional dance music. Many modern composers and guitarists commonly use Phrygian modes with major scales (instead of minor scales) because it sounds brighter and less melancholic than the minor scale.

**Figure 6-8:**
The Phrygian mode can give your music a bit of exotic spice.

# Lydian

Figure 6-9 shows the F Lydian mode. To build a Lydian mode on another note besides F, you would use the pattern WWWHWWH.

The Lydian mode is the complete opposite of the Ionian mode/major scale, so it feels as solid and bright as a major scale but the intervals are surprising and unexpected. This is a popular mode among jazz musicians who enjoy using a mixture of major and minor chord progression in inventive ways.

**Figure 6-9:**
The Lydian mode has something of a surprising, jazzy feel to it.

# Mixolydian

Figure 6-10 shows the G Mixolydian mode. To build a Mixolydian mode on another note besides G, you would use the pattern WWHWWHW.

Mixolydian is similar to Lydian in the sense of having a major-scale feel with minor intervals, and it's a great mode to work within to give a bluesy feel to your compositions. Mixolydian mode is another popular scale for solo musicians looking for a counterpoint to the Ionian key of the song.

**Figure 6-10:**
The Mixolydian mode is often used for blues and bluesy rock music.

## Aeolian (natural minor)

Figure 6-11 shows the A Aeolian mode. To build an Aeolian scale on another other note, the pattern you'd use is WHWWHWW.

This should also look familiar to you — it is the whole-step, half-step pattern we use to build minor scales today.

The intervals of Aeolian mode create the same feel as many modern blues songs. Songs composed in Aeolian mode have a strong sense of sadness. The final note of an Aeolian scale feels resolved in a completely different sense than the final note of the Ionian. If the Dorian mode reflects melancholy, the Aeolian reflects despair.

**Figure 6-11:**
The Aeolian mode can convey great sorrow, regret, and despair.

## Locrian

Figure 6-12 shows the B Locrian mode. To build a Locrian scale on any other note, you would use the pattern HWWHWWH.

Locrian mode is considered to be so unstable that most composers consider it unworkable. There are few songs written in the Locrian mode, which has led some music theorists to label it a "theoretical" mode. You find it occasionally used in heavy metal. This mode exists because all seven notes of the Ionian scale could form it in a mathematical sense, but the relationship between intervals in the Locrian mode is difficult for many composers to work with. Music that is composed within this mode sounds unsettling, disturbing, and just a little bit off. Listen to the synthesizer melody at the beginning of Rush's "YYZ" for an example, or try playing "Three Blind Mice" in a Locrian mode — it sounds like incidental music from a Tod Browning film.

**Figure 6-12:**
The Locrian
mode
sounds a bit
twisted and
wrong.

These modes are good tools for writing *tonal* music (music that conforms to a scale or mode and adheres to a tonal center or key). By limiting yourself to notes within a particular mode — that is, notes that make some harmonic sense together — you may find it easier to write something engaging for most listeners. As we've said, your composition style is partly a product of your limitations, and modes are limitations. Working within limitations can help you define your style. It's like tennis: It wouldn't be as fun without the net and the lines that define the court.

When working with scales, keys, and modes, be aware of the character of the mode choices you have made. Some modes and scales sound happy and simple, and others sound foreign to the unexposed ear.

There are also quite a few other scales and modes that are not used much at all in Western music — and by *Western* we don't mean cowboy campfire songs, we mean European music and its descendents. Some non-Western scales have pitches between our half steps called *quarter tones*. Some use intervals that sound odd, or even out of tune to the Western ear. The subject of modes and scales is a huge one, but if you intend to compose music where a keyboard of some kind is involved, you probably won't have any way of conveying pitches in some of these exotic modes.

# The Pentatonic Scale

There is one kind of scale that is fairly common throughout the world — despite all the other musical differences among various cultures. That would be the *pentatonic scale*, also called the *five-toned scale*. One can refer to a major pentatonic scale or a minor pentatonic scale, but the notes of the major scale are shared with the relative minor key.

For example, Figure 6-13 shows a G major pentatonic scale, and Figure 6-14 shows the pentatonic scale of its relative minor, E minor.

**Figure 6-13:**
The pentatonic scale is found all over the world.

**Figure 6-14:**
The E minor pentatonic scale, G's relative minor.

Notice that although these two scales have a different *tonic* note, they share the same five notes: G, A, B, D, and E (which are the first, second, third, fifth, and sixth tones of the diatonic scale). Many of the other scales and modes around the world seem to revolve around this simple scale formula. Every rock-and-roll guitar soloist on the planet can play a pentatonic scale without even thinking about it (though many of them might not know what it is called). There is a pentatonic scale lurking behind most tonal music.

# Harmonic and Melodic Minor

Two commonly used scales that aren't listed in the above modes and scales are the *harmonic minor* and the *melodic minor* scales. These scales differ from the *natural minor* scale (Aeolian mode) — which is basically a scale taken directly from a relative major — in small, but important ways.

Harmonic minor sharps the seventh note in the scale (Figure 6-15). This note brings the scale a little closer to the A major scale, but other notes in the scale prevent it from sounding too happy.

**Figure 6-15:**
The A harmonic minor scale contains a G sharp, unlike the A natural minor scale.

The melodic minor scale has different notes when the scale ascends than it does when the scale descends (Figure 6-16).

**Figure 6-16:**
The A melodic minor scale is different going up than it is coming down.

It is like a major scale with a flatted third on the way up, and it is a natural minor on the way down. This is so that it fits better with the movements of chords in *cadences* (see Chapter 10 for more on cadences).

# Exercises

1. **Try to write a melody using notes from the C major scale while playing a G major chord underneath.**

   The scale from G to G is G Mixolydian mode now. If you want, you could add a flat 7th (F natural) to the chord you are playing for a more playful-sounding combination.

2. **Write a short melody in a major mode (it could be your own or some-one else's).**

3. **Rewrite step 2's melody in a minor mode.**

4. **Write a short melody in a minor mode.**

5. **Rewrite step 4's melody in a major mode.**

6. **Improvise using notes in the C major scale while playing an F major chord.**

   Sound mysterious? You're in the Lydian mode.

7. **Pick a different mode among the ones we discuss in this chapter, one that sounds interesting to you, and try to write a melody that fits its mood.**

8. **Find the pentatonic scales for all major and minor keys.**

   Hint: Once you find the major, you can apply it to the relative minor.

# Chapter 7

# Building Melodies Using Motifs and Phrases

## In This Chapter

▶ Exploring motifs

▶ Building a melodic phrase

▶ Avoiding boredom by varying the theme

▶ Changing up the rhythm

▶ Truncating and expanding your melodies

▶ Exercising your phrase- and motif-building

*I*f you wrote melodies for the landscape drawings in Chapter 5, you may have noticed that some of the landscapes suggested *repetitive* themes and some didn't. Some lent themselves to the use of a few short statements, whereas others seemed to demand more of a single, long narrative. Musical themes in composition are characterized by three main categories:

✔ **Motif:** A motif is the smallest form of melodic idea. It can be as short as two notes, like "cu coo," or the first two notes of the theme from *Star Wars*.

✔ **Melodic phrase:** A melodic phrase can be up to four or more measures in length. Often a phrase is not really a complete musical idea. Phrases are usually separated by slight pauses, breaths, or rests. You can think of them as being similar to a single line of poetry. Several phrases make a *period.*

✔ **Period:** A period is a complete melodic idea. It can be 4, 8, 16, or even more measures long. It constitutes a musical completeness and can contain motifs or short or long phrases. When we refer to musical forms using letters (ABA and so on), each letter usually represents a period.

You use these three kinds of melodic elements to build your compositions.

# The Long and Short of Musical Themes: Motifs and Phrases

Often a composer's entire body of work belies a tendency towards melodic long-windedness — using long, elaborately developed phrases — whereas other composers are more at home with shorter, choppier motifs.

Take a look at Maurice Ravel's long and winding opening phrase in his famous one-movement orchestral piece, *Boléro* (Figure 7-1).

If you're not familiar with *Boléro*, and you have a high tolerance for prurience, go out and rent the film *10*, starring Dudley Moore, a heavily be-braided Bo Derek, and lots of jogging. You'll be glad you did.

Now, compare *Boléro* to Figure 7-2: Beethoven's four-note exclamatory motif in his Symphony No. 5 (Opus 67).

**Figure 7-1:**
The first
and most
recognizable
phrase, or
theme, of
Ravel's
*Boléro*.

**Figure 7-2:**
Da-da-da-
DU —
perhaps
the shortest
and most
famous
motif ever.

If you don't know *that* one, you must have just crawled out from under the rock where you've been hiding for at least 200 years.

In the Ravel piece, he weaves his melody up and down for sixteen measures before he gets us to the end of a period, whereas Beethoven doesn't even need four beats to state his motif. There is no question that both these compositions were successes for their composers, but their approaches are obviously very different. There are similarities as well: Each repeats his theme and explores variations throughout the piece, giving the theme to different instruments and throwing it at the listener from various perspectives.

With Ravel, our fascination springs from seeing how far he can take a single, long theme while keeping it within a very repetitive rhythmic framework. Or is it seeing how far he can push a repeating rhythmic idea by leading us through it with his melodic narrative? The rhythm helps us hold our place as his long narrative expands. The long melody line keeps us from getting bored with the rhythm. Of course, the long, slow build-up of magnitude and intensity creates tension and keeps us interested, too.

Beethoven's melodic repetitiveness holds our interest because we are fascinated and surprised by the variations he is able to bring to such a short, powerful motif, and the uses to which he puts such a simple idea. How many ways can you say, "I love you"?

It's okay for your melodies to speak through short melodic ideas or long ones. The danger lies in losing the listeners' interest. If your melody goes around the block a few times before reaching its destination, then maybe you should support it with a framework that allows your listeners to keep track of where they are, and where they are headed. A strong, repetitive, supporting rhythmic phrase or motif could be a good choice. And if your melodic ideas are short and sweet, it is important not to let them get boring. You have to get pretty inventive with the various uses of a short motif or phrase to make it hold interest for very long.

Remember that a motif is not particularly useful unless it is somewhat self-contained. If you imagine Beethoven's Fifth without the fourth note, it would be very weak and we probably wouldn't be able to remember it very well. And Beethoven still needed more development around his motif in order to drive the idea home without driving the listener crazy. The whistling part from the movie *The Good, The Bad, and The Ugly* is another good example of a motif that is complete and sticks in your head as a result.

Similarly, a good melodic phrase is one that carves a place easily in a listener's memory. If the phrase is too much like another one, it might be as easily forgotten as if it were too complicated to make sense out of. Walking the line of originality, accessibility, and familiarity is the trick to writing a lasting, memorable musical composition.

Of course, it is not uncommon to hear compositions in which a long melody line seems almost suspended in timelessness, like *Pavane for Une Infante Defunte* by Maurice Ravel. In this composition the composer leads the listener through several different melodic periods that are almost complete enough and different enough from one another to have been the basis for three different compositions.

It is all about mood, and few things are as tricky as sculpting time into a sense of temporal stasis where time itself seems to stand still.

# Building a Melodic Phrase

Let's step back from motifs for a minute and examine phrases — the most basic building blocks of melody. How do we turn a couple of bars of melody into a musical composition? Consider the very simple melody line shown in Figure 7-3.

**Figure 7-3:**
A very straight-forward, hummable melody line can be your foundation.

Now, let's make the piece longer than the three measures it already is by employing repetition. *Repetition* is just like it sounds — repeating a musical theme in a piece of music, either immediately after the first time it's played, or somewhere later on in the song.

Figure 7-4 shows what it looks like if you repeated the melody immediately after the first time it's played.

**Figure 7-4:**
Repeating a melodic phrase reinforces it in the listener's mind.

In Figure 7-5, we employ repetition again, this time adding a few additional phrases, sticking them in between the repeated parts.

**Figure 7-5:**
You can vary your use of repetition by adding other phrases to it as you repeat.

Another way to employ repetition is to have multiple instruments take turns playing the same phrase. You could give the music in Figure 7-6 to one instrument and that in Figure 7-7 to another, and the result would be a "round" kind of effect.

**Figure 7-6:**
Instrument number one could play this melody . . .

**Figure 7-7:**
. . . While
instrument
number two
plays this
melody.

Another way to spread the phrase across the instrumentation would be to have the two instruments take turns "soloing," as shown in Figures 7-8 and 7-9.

**Figure 7-8:**
Instrument
number one
plays the
phrase while
instrument
number two
rests . . .

**Figure 7-9:**
. . . And
instrument
number
two picks
up where
instrument
number one
leaves off.

# Spicing It Up by Varying the Phrase

If you were a minstrel living in the Middle Ages, the information provided so far in this chapter would probably be all you would need to know to make your compositions minimally palatable to an audience. However, modern audiences want more from a composition than the same musical motifs and phrases repeated over and over.

Three ways to give them what they want would be to use the following tools:

- Rhythmic displacement
- Truncation
- Expansion

These three methods are all ways to help make your short or long phrases expand into full-fledged compositions.

## Rhythmic displacement

You can expand a rhythmic idea by changing the meter of the phrase. *Rhythmic displacement* is a favorite tool of jazz players. They pass around a theme, with the rhythm of each solo differing just enough to make it sound like they're not all playing the same piece of music — even though they pretty much are.

In the example shown in Figure 7-10, we've taken our original theme and expanded on it by changing the rhythm of the repeated theme.

**Figure 7-10:**
Here is our phrase after employing some good old rhythmic displacement.

By changing the values of some of the notes, we've changed the tempo and even the mood of the repeated phrase.

## Truncation

When you *truncate* a verbal phrase, you cut it short (for example, Jefferson Starship truncated their name to Starship after guitarist Paul Katner left the band). When you truncate in music, you're cutting a repeated musical phrase short, as shown in Figure 7-11.

**Figure 7-11:**
Here is our
phrase, this
time with
the first
repeat
truncated.

It's completely up to you where and when you want to make the cut-off.

## Expansion

*Expansion* is, of course, the opposite of truncation. In expansion, you add new material to the original phrase to make it last longer. You typically do this at the end of the phrase, as shown in Figure 7-12.

**Figure 7-12:**
Using
expansion
to fill out
our phrase.

Expanded phrases are found at the end of many classical music pieces, including Beethoven's "Moonlight" Sonata and, especially, his Symphony No. 5.

## Exercises

1. Write 16 measures of melody based on a three- or four-note motif.

2. Write a 16-measure melody (period) in which there are no repeating motifs.

3. Write a 16-measure melody (period) that contains the smaller repeating motifs of Exercise 1.

4. Write 16 measures using small pieces from Exercise 2.

5. Take one of the phrases resulting from the previous exercises and build on it, using repetition and rhythmic displacement.

6. Take one of the phrases resulting from the previous exercises and build on it, using repetition and truncation.

7. Take one of the phrases resulting from the previous exercises and build on it, using repetition and expansion.

# Chapter 8

# Developing Your Melodies

• • • • • • • • • • • • • • • • • • • • • • • • • • • • • • • • • • • • • • • • • • • • •

## In This Chapter

▶ Finding your structural tones

▶ Using step-wise and skip-wise motion

▶ Fleshing out your melody with passing tones

▶ Visiting the neighborhood with neighboring tones

▶ Exercising with musical bridges and solos

• • • • • • • • • • • • • • • • • • • • • • • • • • • • • • • • • • • • • • • • • • • • • •

K eys, modes, meters, tempi, and orchestration can all change within a composition to express changing moods. A good composer must not be afraid of using repetition *or* change to express an idea. Sometimes a change can be startling, and sometimes it can sneak up on you and happen with a great deal of subtlety.

A mastery of transitions in music is the mark of a good composer.

In this chapter we give you some helpful ideas to move you from one melodic theme, or motif, to another.

## Structural Tones

One way to introduce change to a piece of music is by reducing your melody to its *structural* (central, essential) tones and then building it out again. This way, you can keep the skeleton of your theme but not sound like you're just playing the same melody line over and over. Also, by re-examining your melody and reducing it to its structural tones, new possible ways to present the melody line can be opened up to you.

For example, take a look at the melody shown in Figure 8-1.

**Figure 8-1:**
We'll use this simple melody to reveal structural tones.

If we boil down that melody to only the most important pitches on the most important beats, we come up with something like Figure 8-2.

**Figure 8-2:**
The structural tones are the most important pitches of our simple melody.

The structural tones shown in Figure 8-2 are the heaviest, most significant notes of the melody line, and the ones that carry the beat. All the other notes hinge on these.

# Step-wise and Skip-wise Motion

When notes are placed on the staff in alphabetical sequence, in intervals of one whole or half step, the succession of pitches is said to be *step-wise*, or *conjunct*. Step-wise motion happens when moving from one pitch to the next in either an ascending (upward in pitch) or descending (downward) direction.

If you were to take the structural notes of our melody and apply step-wise motion to it, it would look like Figure 8-3.

**Figure 8-3:**
Our melody
is changed
using step-
wise motion.

And, voila, we've got a brand-new melody line!

Unlike step-wise motion, *skip-wise* or *disjunct* motion is when the melodic line jumps all over the musical staff. Instead of moving predictably from one tone or semitone to another, any interval can exist between notes in a piece with disjunct motion.

If you were to take our structural tones and apply skip-wise motion to them, one possibility would look like Figure 8-4.

**Figure 8-4:**
Our melody
is changed
using skip-
wise motion.

# Passing Tones

*Passing tones* allow smooth, scale-wise motion in tonal music by "filling in" the space between two structural tones. Whenever the structural tones are at least a third apart, the passing tone is a diatonic scale degree in between — meaning that if the two notes in question in the key of C, are C and E, then the passing tone would be a D.

However, other intervals may also have passing tones between them. Two or more passing tones might be used to smooth over a leap of a fourth (from C to F, for example, the passing tones would be either D or E, or both), or a single, chromatic passing tone may be used to strengthen the movement of a major second (from C to D, the passing tone would be a C sharp/D flat).

Passing tones are often found above and below the melody, connecting two notes from the basic melody line together.

You can use passing tones to make a boring chord interesting, to point to the melody, and/or to just add to the flavor of the song as you make your music flow.

Now, if we color in the spaces between the notes with passing tones, we could end up with something like this Figure 8-5.

**Figure 8-5:**
Adding passing tones to our melody.

Can you tell in Figure 8-5 that the structural notes are still there?

Passing tones are always used on the weak beats of a measure, and the structural tones are used on the strong beats. Paying attention to whether a note falls on the strong or the weak beats is important, because this deeply affects the music.

# Neighboring Tones and Appoggiatura

*Neighboring tones* are notes that are visited briefly (like your neighbors) before returning home. That is, you start with your structural tone, move up or down a step or half step, and then return to your original note. It's a cool little embellishment that's used a lot in kids' piano books, simply because it sounds much more complicated to play than it actually is. If you rapidly repeat neighboring tones, as in Figure 8-6, it makes for a neat little *trill*.

**Figure 8-6:**
Adding neighboring tones to our melody. Note the trill in the first measure.

If we take a disjunct leap from a structural tone to a note neighboring the next structural tone and then step to that tone, we have an *appoggiatura*, an example of which is shown in Figure 8-7.

**Figure 8-7:**
The appoggia-tura here is in measure 2.

C. P. E. Bach (Carl Philipp Emanuel, son of J. S. Bach) was a great lover of using the appoggiatura in his musical arrangements. He wrote a good deal of theory-related material on what exactly should be the requirements for using appoggiatura in music.

First of all, when a short appoggiatura is written —symbolically, as a small note — it is ignored when summing up the time values in a bar, as seen in Figure 8-8.

**Figure 8-8:**
Here are two examples of short appoggia-turas.

Second, the appoggiatura is always written on the left of a note, and is slurred into a principal note — a note normally played on the beat. Third, the appoggiatura is also always played on the beat, with the principal note fol-lowing. Basically, the two notes are played *almost* together, with the appog-giaturas slurring into the principal note quick enough that both notes carry the beat.

Appoggiaturas are now more normally known as *grace notes*, meaning that they're extra notes that are "forgiven" for making a measure's total note value equal just a little more than allowed.

# Other Melodic Techniques

Numerous other neat little tricks are available to help you develop your melody.

## Escape tones

An *escape tone* is kind of the opposite of an appoggiatura (say that five times fast). You first step away from your tone — and then leap in the other direction to the next chord tone, as shown in Figure 8-9. Instead of slurring into the principal note with the beat, an escape tone slurs into the tone <u>note</u> carrying the beat.

**Figure 8-9:**
Escape tones are the anti-appoggiatura.

## Suspension

If you hold a tone out longer than the chord and then drop the note down a step to your new chord tone, it is called a *suspension*. Figure 8-10 shows an example.

**Figure 8-10:**
The suspension is in the last two measures.

# Retardation

The opposite of suspension is to stay on your tone and then step up to the next tone. This is known as a *retardation*, and an example is shown in Figure 8-11.

**Figure 8-11:**
Retardation
is introduced
to our
example.

# Anticipation

If you arrive at the next tone before the chord changes, it is called an *anticipation*. You'll see two of these in Figure 8-12: one across the second measure line, and one across the third.

**Figure 8-12:**
Anticipation,
unsurpris-
ingly,
anticipates
the next
chord.

# Pedal point

If you stay on or repeat the same note, despite (or because of) the dissonance with the next chord, and keep playing it till the harmony of your chord progression allows it to resolve, it is called a *pedal point*.

The pedal point technique is usually used in the bass. If used for an upper part, such as a soprano, it is called an *inverted pedal,* and in the middle voices (tenor or alto) it is called an *internal pedal*. The name comes from the bass register pedals of the organ. The organ is capable of sustaining long notes, and a lot of organ music takes advantage of this fact.

Figure 8-13 shows an example of a pedal point.

**Figure 8-13:**
A pedal point stays on a note until it resolves with the chord.

There are a few more obscure names for techniques for moving between chord tones, such as *cambiata*, a sort of escape tone that moves in the same direction as the chord tone. All of the ones we discuss in this chapter can lend interest, tension, and variety to your chord movements.

You can move any way you like, of course, if it sounds good to you. Now you know what to call it when you do.

In most of the examples used in this chapter we have stuck to the essence of the original melody, but you could use the same structural notes and depart quite a bit from the original, as in Figure 8-13.

One last reminder here is in order: If you massage your melodies with repetition and the types of techniques that you are comfortable with, and if you keep a sensitive ear, your melodies will naturally arrive at variations, climaxes, and new themes in just the right way and at just the right time. You've got to roll them around in your head for them to mature and move on, and for your muse to get a handle on them. Trust this.

# Exercises

**1. Build a musical bridge between your different melodic themes.**

Your building materials are rhythm, melody, harmony, and above all, time. You don't necessarily have to slam one idea into another. You can

## Less is more

Many composers are guilty of trying to write too much into their compositions. The old adage "Less is more" is worth remembering. If you find yourself doing this (and you realize it), cut your melodies up at breathing points and make separate melodies out of them.

When we say "breathing points," we're referring to the places in a good melody where the natural cycles occur. If you can't find these in your music, maybe you aren't writing melodies

that breathe. It doesn't necessarily mean that a person singing your melodies wouldn't have any places to breathe (although that is an essential consideration when writing for any instrument that uses breath power), but that the cycle of tension and release that should run through your music may not be there.

You can read more about creating tension and release in music in the sections on cadences in Chapter 10.

compose a transition that makes its own demands regarding the number of measures required for your musical metamorphosis. How about an entirely new melody just for the transition?

Build one theme up and up to the breaking point and let the next theme coalesce from the fallout.

If you can create enough of a ruckus, you will have plenty of musical material floating around as the dust settles. This is a good way to go from a fast-paced, exciting mood to a calmer, more serene one.

2. **Write an instrumental solo that wanders from the end of one theme to the beginning of the next.**

Throwing a solo into your compositions is often a good way to break up the scenery. If you are writing in a popular genre, you will probably want to let the soloist improvise over some chord changes, but if you are able to write the solo out for the musician, you have an opportunity to create a bridge between almost any two melodic themes. You need to be especially knowledgeable about the instruments you are writing for when you write solos.

It is worthwhile to note that some themes probably don't belong together in the same composition, and no amount of massaging them will reconcile their differences. This doesn't mean that you should discard one of them. Save it for another piece.

# Part III
# Harmony and Structure

## In this part . . .

*N*ow that you have your melody going, you can begin to figure out what the harmonic components of the music will be. In this section, we show how studying the melody itself can help tell you what the harmony needs to be. We also give you lots of hints for where to get your compositional ideas from, how to get the most out of chords, and how to use structure and form to your advantage.

# Chapter 9

# Harmonizing with Melodies

A melody floating around in space is nice, but a good melody deserves a framework in which to bob and weave. At least it deserves some company. Where can we find good harmonizations for our melodic ideas?

A simple melody can suggest a harmony, which in turn can suggest chords. After all, a chord is nothing more, or less, than a harmonic cluster. So harmonic composition can mean anything from a melody and a single harmony to a progression of chords that supports a melody, or from which a melody can be extracted.

This chapter begins the search for harmonies to go with your melodies. And we begin by trying to define why some notes sound better together than others.

## Harmonizing Using Consonance and Dissonance

One good source for harmony is the melody itself. Melodies often suggest harmonies, and vice versa. Even a single note can suggest harmony.

A single note played on an instrument can generate enough harmonic overtones to define an entire scale. *Harmonic overtones* happen whenever you play or sing a note. For example, when you play an open A string on the guitar, the string vibrates along its entire length, but it also makes smaller vibrations along two equal halves of its length, three equal thirds, and so on. Each of these smaller vibrating subdivisions of the string produce pitches that are related harmonically and mathematically to the fundamental A that you are playing. We hear these overtones as part of the *timbre* of the instrument, and don't usually think of them as separate pitches — but that A you play actually generates (albeit quietly) all the pitches of the A major scale and beyond. This is why a brass instrument like a trumpet can play so many different pitches with only eight possible valve combinations, which relate to tubing lengths.

Added to this is the fact that it is quite possible (if not likely) that the melody in your head is already *diatonic,* meaning that it has a key center (making it a *tonal melody* as opposed to an atonal one). This means that there is a particular musical scale or set of related pitches from which your melody is drawn, or with which your melody will feel conformable. This has to do with the way in which our ears work, along with the musical exposure to scales and modes that you may have had.

So, without our realizing it, tonal melodies do tend to make their own demands regarding harmony. You just have to be paying attention and have the proper tools at hand, such as a pencil and paper or a keyboard and computer, to capture what you hear in your head.

Harmony in music can be defined as any combination of notes that are played together at the same time. If you play a C and a G together, they sound pleasant, or *consonant* (Figure 9-1).

**Figure 9-1:**
C and G are consonant because they are a perfect fifth apart.

Intervals that produce *perfect* consonant notes include unisons, octaves, and perfect fourths and fifths. *Imperfect* consonants include major and minor thirds and sixths. But basically, if a harmony is consonant, it sounds at least okay.

Not all harmony is easy or pleasant to the ear, though. If you substitute a G flat for the G, the resulting harmony is *dissonant*, meaning not so sweet-sounding (Figure 9-2).

**Figure 9-2:**
C and G flat
(a tritone)
sound
terrible
together.

## Tritone: The devil's interval

All the way through the 10th century and beyond, the dissonant augmented fourth (or flat fifth), also known as a *tritone*, an example of which is shown in Figure 9-2, was actually forbidden in music by the Catholic Church. It was known as the devil's interval, *diabolus in musica*, or *mi contra fa* (all of which mean roughly the same thing). Play it a few more times to get the sense of evil that lurks there. Spooky, huh?

Nowadays, tritones are used in heavy metal. This is partially thanks to Black Sabbath's Tony Iommi's heavy use of the interval. Iommi mostly started using it after the tips of two fingers on his fretting hand were cut off in a machine cutter. His homemade prosthetic wouldn't form power chords as easily as it would the tritones. This use of tritones, and the band's eventual discovery that they had been playing the devil's interval all along, led to the tritone being a standard in metal music well into the present.

Without getting too scientific, our ears interpret combinations of pitches as *consonant* when the pitches and their overtones are either in unison, or are at least a minor third apart. Pitches that are either closer together than a minor third or have overtones that are closer than a minor third are perceived of as *dissonant*. This is why the interval of a minor second (B and C, for example) is dissonant, and so is the interval of a tritone, or flat fifth (B and F).

It is interesting to note that the differences in music from different cultures round the world do not lie in the acceptance or usage of consonance, but in the uses and general acceptance of dissonance.

It was J.S. Bach who brought tritones into acceptance through his music. So really, you could say that Bach was the father of death metal — or at least hair metal. Take a listen to Bach's "The Goldberg Variations" to see if you can hear the seeds of "War Pigs" in there. You probably won't, but you should be able to hear the masterful use of dissonant tritones in the piece.

## Conflict and resolution

Aside from scaring people and suggesting darkness, of what use is a dissonant harmonic interval? Dissonance creates a feeling of instability, tension, and conflict. In music composition — just as in literature, the cinema, and the theater — the concepts of conflict and resolution are extremely important. Conflict and resolution keep the plot moving and keep your audience interested.

In music, conflict can be represented by dissonant tones, with resolution represented by consonant tones.

Try playing the set of notes in Figure 9-3 to see what we mean.

**Figure 9-3:**
Conflict and resolution accomplished in just two measures.

Don't you feel a mild sense of aural relief when the dissonant tones logically progress to consonant tones? It's very much like the feeling of coming home. The musical conflict inflicted on our ears by the dissonant interval is resolved, and you can rest easy (until the next conflict arises). In fact, we can now tell what key the music is in because it has clearly arrived at a resolved state and we can sense that G is the tonic, at least for the moment. Now we can write the key signature for G (Figure 9-4).

**Figure 9-4:**
Our melody, now har-monized into the key of G major.

Even though what you play in Figure 9-4 only uses two voices playing three notes, both melody and harmony are present. You can look at it also as being really two melodies: one melody being played with the upper register (G, F sharp, G) and the other being played with the lower set of notes (C, C, B).

There is also a suggestion of full chords implied by these intervals. Try the obvious first (Figure 9-5).

**Figure 9-5:**
Perhaps the most obvious set of chords implied by the melody.

But with a little knowledge of chords and a sense of melody (or a little experi-mental mucking around), you could come up with something like Figure 9-6.

**Figure 9-6:**
A less obvious set of chords implied by the melody.

This second chord progression (in Figure 9-6) is based on the relative minor of the first one (in Figure 9-5): The key of E minor is the relative minor of G major. You could think of this minor version as a *substitution* — a chord used instead of the one you would normally use — for the more obvious major version.

It is important to realize that there are many other possible ways that you could harmonize a simple melody. Our melody could be harmonized into other keys. It could even exist outside of a diatonic framework. The second melody here (in Figure 9-6) defines the key signature by presenting some definition harmonically. It only takes two notes sounding together to imply a harmonic framework in which a particular melody exists.

Many substitutions for chords are implied by melodies and harmonies. A large portion of what jazz is all about is being aware of these substitutions and incorporating them — and the scales attached to them —improvisationally. But before we start playing around with substitutions, it's a good idea to tune into the more usual, mainstream harmonies available.

# Harmonizing Using the Circle of Fifths

Take another look at the Circle of Fifths (Figure 9-7). We have talked about the fact that as you go clockwise around the Circle, you move through the key signatures by the interval of a perfect fifth. But did you notice that going counterclockwise moves you in perfect fourths?

So what? Well, consider that if you start on any slice of the Circle of Fifths pie, the fifth of the selected key is on its right, and the fourth of the selected key is on the left. For example, select G. The next one clockwise is D, and counterclockwise is C. D is the fifth tone (dominant) of the G major scale, and C is the fourth tone (subdominant) in the key of G. The fourth and the fifth are the most important tones in a scale, next to the tonic, and there they are huddled snugly against the chosen key. The IV chord and the V chord are the most important chords after the I chord.

A musical composition, as we have said many times, is like a good story; it has a beginning, a middle, and an end. In music, we use the terms *statement*, *development*, *departure*, and *resolution* (or *recapitulation*).

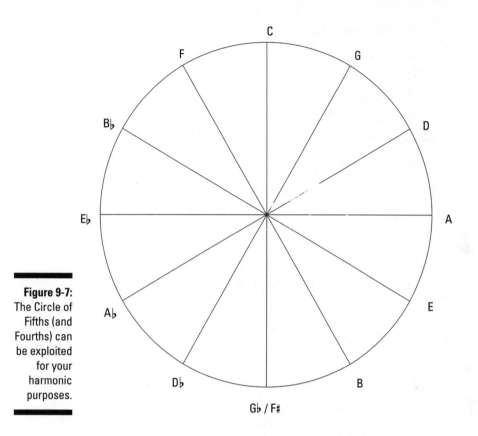

**Figure 9-7:**
The Circle of
Fifths (and
Fourths) can
be exploited
for your
harmonic
purposes.

The IV chord often can be used for a sense of departure, while the V chord gives a sense of anticipation, which itself is a kind of tension, and the I chord brings us resolution. After you pick a key to write your composition in, you can look at the circle of Fifths (and Fourths) and easily find the chords that are in the family of the chosen key. You can start to develop musical ideas around this family of chords.

Whereas I, IV, and V chords can go a long way (blues and most of rock and roll are totally based on these three chords), sooner or later we are going to need more colors in our crayon box to keep our listeners' attention.

The other *diatonic triads* (chords with three notes in them) that are in a given major key's family are as follows, including which tones of the scale they include:

✔ **The 1 (tonic) major:** 1, 3, 5

✔ **The 2 minor:** 2, 4, 6

✔ **The 3 minor:** 3, 5, 7

✔ **The 4 major:** 4, 6, 1 (or 8)

✔ **The 5 major:** 5, 7, 2

✔ **The 6 minor (relative minor):** 6, 1, 3

✔ **The 7 diminished:** 7, 2, 4

See Figure 9-8 for examples in the key of C major.

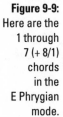
**Figure 9-8:**
Looking at the 1 through 7 (+ 8/1) chords in the key of C major.

All of these chords work within the melodic confines of a major scale. They shift along with the modes (Chapter 6 has more on modes). For example, if you were working in the Phrygian mode, you would count the third chord example in Figure 9-8 as the I chord, and all other numbers would shift accordingly, as shown in Figure 9-9.

**Figure 9-9:**
Here are the 1 through 7 (+ 8/1) chords in the E Phrygian mode.

For most composers, staying within the confines of a major scale is too confining. The chord families shown in Figures 9-8 and 9-9 represent places to start if you are working up a tonal composition in a set key.

# Harmonizing Using Pivot Notes

A good way to escape the comfort and predictability of accepted chord progressions (see Chapter 10 for more on chord progressions) is to use a note or two in the melody as a *pivot*.

What's a pivot? Find a chord that is related to your melody notes, but *not* to the key. Build into a new key center from there, or just depart from the constraints of your current key center for a surprising moment and return home right away if you like. Figures 9-10 and 9-11 provide examples. First, we have a melody, accompanied by chords that stay within the chord family. Play the piece in Figure 9-10 accompanied by the chords labeled above the staff lines.

**Figure 9-10:**
Our melody, accompanied by the most obvious chords.

Now let's try the same melody, only pivoting the tonality with a chord that is related only to a pair of notes in the melody rather than to the whole key. Play the piece again, but with the Fmaj7 chord as accompaniment to the second measure instead (Figure 9-11).

**Figure 9-11:**
Our melody,
with the
harmonic
accompani-
ment slightly
altered via
a pivot.

The music in Figure 9-11 sounds a little more interesting, doesn't it?

How did we choose the pivot? Well, the Fmaj7 chord contains the E and the A, but isn't a close relative to this key signature, so it pulls us out of the key center for a second. In this case, it actually fakes us out as to what key we are in, because it is the first chord we hear. This sort of harmonic opportunism makes the resolution to the tonic even more satisfying because the distance home is greater than it would be if we were traveling from a closer relative chord.

# Exercises

1. **Re-harmonize any familiar song.**

   Try "Yankee Doodle" in a minor key, for example, or anything you like.

2. **Write a chord chart using randomly selected chords from within a key's chord family.**

   Start anywhere, but return to the I chord at the end.

3. **Write two alternative melodies for the chord chart you wrote for Exercise 2.**

4. **Re-harmonize one of the melodies you just wrote for Exercise 3.**

   Try to use some pivot chords to escape from the monotony of your tonal center.

5. **Pick two or three unrelated chords and try to string them together with a melody.**

6. **Try the same melody with the relative majors or minors of the chords from Exercise**

# Chapter 10

# Composing with Chords

. . . . . . . . . . . . . . . . . . . . . . . . . . . . . . . . . . . . . . . . . . . . . .

## In This Chapter

▶ Getting moody with chords

▶ Combining chords

▶ Making progress with chord progressions

▶ Ending up with cadences

▶ Getting harmony from melody

▶ Considering chord changes

▶ Exercising your chord harmonization

. . . . . . . . . . . . . . . . . . . . . . . . . . . . . . . . . . . . . . . . . . . . . .

*O*ne major point you should have gotten from your experience with music theory is that the *key signature* of a piece of Western tonal music governs the main notes within that piece. When you want to escape the key signature within that piece of music, you have to use *accidentals* (sharps, flats, and naturals) to indicate notes outside the key.

You can have several octaves' worth of notes on an instrument, but only the notes allowed by the key signature can be used without accidentals in that piece of music. The *scale* of the piece governs the music's tonality — which means breaking free from the original key is a good way to add spice.

Therefore, if you have a song written in C major, the main eight notes that will appear in the song are C natural, D natural, E natural, F natural, G natural, A natural, and B natural. If your song is written in A major, the only notes appearing in that song will be A natural, B natural, C sharp, D natural, E natural, F sharp, and G sharp. In either of these keys, the chords are also made of some combination of the seven notes in each key.

There are two types of major chords:

 ✔ **Diatonic chords** are built from the seven notes of a major key signature. The letter name of a diatonic chord (such as A Major, A minor, or A augmented) comes from the major scale the chord is built on.

 ✔ **Chromatic chords** are built from notes *outside* the major key signature, such as chords built on minor scales. Chords found within minor keys are a little trickier, because nine notes potentially can fit under a single minor key signature, when you take the melodic and harmonic minor scales into consideration.

Because the natural, melodic, and harmonic scales are taught as separate scales for musicians to practice, there a misconception that you have to stick to *one* of these types of minor scales when composing music. But really, you can draw from all three types of minor scales within the same piece of music.

# Chords and Their Moods

You can let your melodic ideas suggest different chords, as we have seen in previous chapters. This can be a very good way to open up possibilities — by suggesting departures from your key center and adding color to your work. But you could just as easily start with a chord progression and build a melody up from there. Thousands of compositions began with a sense of harmonic movement first, followed by melody.

Here is an opportunity for your Muse to step in. Or maybe you could just plunk your hands down on your piano and listen for the possibilities. To excel at chordal composition you should have a strong knowledge of chords. You should, at very least, have a working familiarity with following chord qualities in every key:

 ✔ Major and minor

 ✔ Major and minor seventh

 ✔ Dominant seventh

 ✔ Major and minor sixth

 ✔ Suspended fourth

 ✔ Ninth

 ✔ Diminished

 ✔ Augmented

> ✔ Minor ninth
>
> ✔ Minor seventh flat fifth

No matter which key you're in, each of those specific chords comes with its particular sonic character, called its mood, or quality. Therefore, if you know how minor chords are constructed, and you sit at that same piano and play some minor chords, chances are the sound that comes from that set of chords is closer to what you're looking for than if you just started playing random chords.

Certain chords express certain moods. It's really up to you what sort of mood is to be implied by each chord, but in the following sections we include a short list of our own observations, based on asking students to describe the feelings conveyed by these chords.

# Major

Major chords are "happy, simple, honest, bold."

To build a major chord using half and whole steps, remember: root + 4 half steps + 3 half steps (Figure 10-1).

**Figure 10-1:**
C major.
Major
chords are
made from
the 1, 3, and
5 tones of
the major
scale.

# Minor

Minor chords are "sad, serious."

To build a minor chord using half and whole steps, remember: root + 3 half steps + 4 half steps (Figure 10-2).

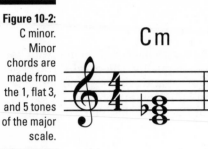

## Major seventh

Major seventh chords are "pretty, delicate, sensitive, thoughtful."

To build a major seventh chord using half and whole steps, remember: root + 4 half steps + 3 half steps + 4 half steps (Figure 10-3).

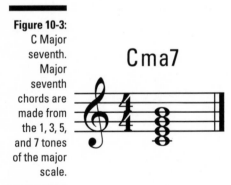

## Minor seventh

Minor seventh chords are "pensive, moody, introspective."

To build a minor seventh chord using half and whole steps, remember: root + 3 half steps + 4 half steps + 3 half steps (Figure 10-4).

**Figure 10-4:**
C minor
seventh.
Minor
seventh
chords are
made from
the 1, flat 3,
5, and flat 7
tones of the
major scale.

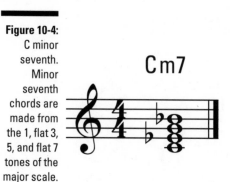

# Dominant seventh

Dominant seventh chords are "sassy, outgoing, strong."

To build a dominant seventh chord using half and whole steps, remember: root + 4 half steps + 3 half steps + 3 half steps (Figure 10-5).

**Figure 10-5:**
C dominant
seventh.
Dominant
seventh
chords are
made from
the 1, 3, 5,
and flat 7
tones of the
major scale.

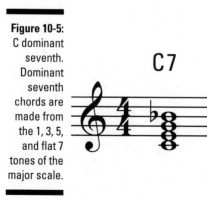

# Major sixth

Major sixth chords are "playful."

To build a major sixth chord using half and whole steps, remember: root + 4 half steps + 3 half steps + 2 half steps (Figure 10-6).

**Figure 10-6:**
C Major
sixth. Major
sixth chords
are made
from the 1,
3, 5, and 6
tones of the
major scale.

## Minor sixth

Minor sixth chords are "dark, sensuous, troubled."

To build a minor sixth chord using half and whole steps, remember: root + 3 half steps + 4 half steps + 2 half steps (Figure 10-7).

**Figure 10-7:**
C minor
sixth. Minor
sixth chords
are made
from the 1,
flat 3, 5, and
6 tones of
the major
scale.

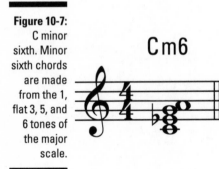

## Suspended fourth

Suspended fourth chords are "regal, martial."

To build a suspended fourth chord using half and whole steps, remember: root + 5 half steps + 2 half steps (Figure 10-8).

**Figure 10-8:**
C suspended
fourth.
Suspended
fourth
chords are
made from
the 1, 4, and
5 notes of
the major
scale.

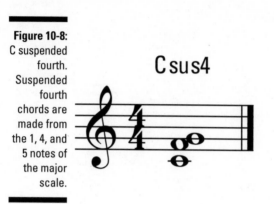

## Ninth

Ninth chords are "energetic, lively."

To build a ninth chord using half and whole steps, remember: root + 4 half steps + 3 half steps + 6 half steps. To build a minor ninth (see Figure 10-9), it's root + 3 half steps + 4 half steps + 6 half steps.

**Figure 10-9:**
C ninth.
Ninth
chords are
made from
the 1, 3, 5,
and 9 tones
of the major
scale.

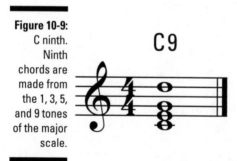

## Minor ninth

Minor ninth chords are "sad, tender, complex."

To build a minor ninth chord using half and whole steps, remember: root position + 3 half steps + 4 half steps + 6 half steps (Figure 10-10).

**Figure 10-10:**
C minor
ninth. Minor
ninth chords
are made
from the 1,
flat 3, 5, and
9 tones of
the major
scale.

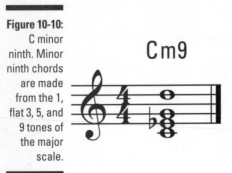

## Diminished

Diminished chords are "dark, strained, complex."

To build a diminished chord using half and whole steps, remember: root, 3 half steps + 3 half steps (Figure 10-11).

**Figure 10-11:**
C diminished.
Diminished
chords are
made from
the 1, flat 3,
and flat 5
tones of the
major scale.

## Augmented

Augmented chords are "anticipatory, full of movement."

To build an augmented chord using half and whole steps, remember: root position + 4 half steps + 4 half steps (Figure 10-12).

**Figure 10-12:**
C aug-
mented.
Augmented
chords are
made from
the 1, 3, and
sharp 5
tones of the
major scale.

# Minor 7, flat 5 / half-diminished

There are two different names for the same chord. The chord is "despairing, sorrowful, difficult, deep."

To build a minor seventh, flat fifth chord using half and whole steps, remember: root + 3 half steps + 3 half steps + 4 steps (Figure 10-13).

**Figure 10-13:**
C Minor 7,
flat 5. Minor
7, flat 5
chords are
made from
the 1, flat 3,
flat 5, and
flat 7 tones
of the major
scale.

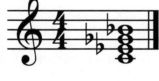

There are many, many more chord configurations than just these, but the ones we list in this section are a good start. As we said before, you have to decide for yourself how each of these chords makes you feel.

It is also important to note that the character of a chord is strongly dependent upon its surroundings. For example, a dark and dissonant chord like a minor 7, flat 5 sounds dark and dissonant when out there on its own, but if used to pass from one chord to another, it doesn't have the same feeling (Figures 10-14 and 10-15).

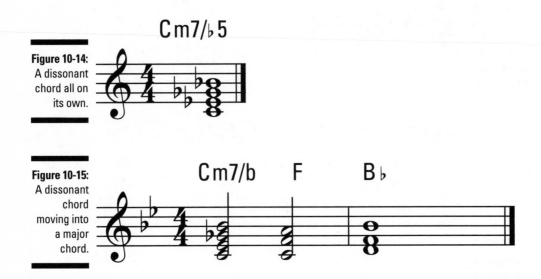

**Figure 10-14:** A dissonant chord all on its own.

**Figure 10-15:** A dissonant chord moving into a major chord.

# *Putting Chords Together*

Once you have decided on a chord progression for a section of your piece, you might find it useful to experiment with different chord *voicings,* or all the different ways the same chord can be put together. A simple *triad* (a chord with three different pitches in it) has three different arrangements of its notes within an octave.

A chord's voicing can be arranged in the following ways:

✔ Root voicing has the root as the lowest note: C (root), E, G

✔ First inversion: E, C, G

✔ Second inversion, G, C, E

The examples in Figures 10-16 through 10-18 use the C major chord to illustrate.

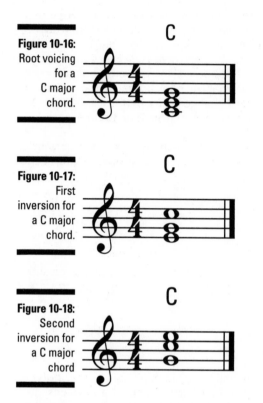

**Figure 10-16:**
Root voicing for a C major chord.

**Figure 10-17:**
First inversion for a C major chord.

**Figure 10-18:**
Second inversion for a C major chord

If you already have a melody, you will find the melody useful in determining your chord voicings. Most often you will want the melody to represent the top notes in your chords. This will dictate which voicings sound best. If you don't have a melody yet, choosing your chord voicings can help you write one. Try a few chord voicing changes and have your melody grab the top notes. If you don't like the results, invert some chords and try again. Don't forget to use some passing tones while you are at it.

# Rhythmic Movement

When composing with chords, determining a rhythmic movement for your chord changes may help. What this means is that you will decide how often, and on which beats or accents, your chords will generally change. You could have a chord change every measure, every four measures, every two beats, or even every beat within a measure. The choice is yours, but remember that fast-moving melodies can sound awkward if the chords change too quickly. A general rule is that more frequent chord changes work better with slower melodies, but this, like most rules, can be broken from time to time.

Of course, the rhythmic movement of your chord changes can vary as your composition moves along. You don't need to keep the chords changing at the same rate throughout the section of your piece (Figure 10-19).

**Figure 10-19:**
Different melodic rhythms in the same piece of music.

The chords you write might not be played by a guitar, piano, or other polyphonic instrument. They might be played by a string quartet, a horn ensemble, or any other combination of instruments. Writing chord changes out first is just one way to create some underlying structure for your composition.

You may want to find some locations in the rhythmic structure of your composition that lend themselves to pivoting your chords out of the key center. It is not difficult to hear in your head where a surprise or a change harmonically would be good.

Just don't overdo the surprises and departures. If you are driving down a bumpy road and you hit another bump, it doesn't mean much. Lead the listener into your changes. Build drama, tension, and release.

# Chord Progressions

One way to easily build tension and release in your music is to follow some of the simple rules already laid out for you hundreds of years ago by people like Christiaan Huygens and Nicola Vicentino. According to them — and the thousands of musicians who followed — certain sequences of chords, called *chord progressions*, sound nicer than others. Over time, a consensus about the "rules" of chord progressions has come about.

In the following sections, capital Roman numerals indicate major chords, and lowercase Roman numerals stand for minor chords. The numeral itself stands for the note on the major scale the chord is built on. For example, in C major, the I would be a C major chord, the ii would be D minor, the iii would be E minor, and so on. The ° symbol indicates a diminished chord, and the + symbol is used for augmented chords.

## "Rules" for major chord progressions

- I chords can appear anywhere in a progression.
- ii chords lead to I, V, or vii° chords.
- iii chords lead to I, ii, IV, or vi chords.
- IV chords lead to I, ii, iii, V, or vii° chords.
- V chords lead to I or vi chords.
- vi chords lead to I, ii, iii, IV, or V chords.
- vii° chords lead to I or iii chords.

## "Rules" for minor chord progressions

- i chords can appear anywhere in a progression.
- ii° or ii chords lead to i, iii, V, v, vii°, or VII chords.
- III or III+ chords lead to i, iv, IV, VI, #vi°, vii°, or VI chords.
- iv or IV chords lead to i, V, v, vii°, or VII chords.
- V or v chords lead to i, VI, or #vi° chords.
- VI or #vi° chords lead to i, III, III+, iv, IV, V, v, vii°, or VII chords.
- vii° or VII chords lead to the i chord.

As far as these rules go, they just mean (in the case of major chord progressions) that a ii chord (such as D minor if you're playing in the key of C major) sounds most natural when it leads to I (C major), V (G major), or vii° (B diminished). However, there's absolutely no reason why you can't go from a ii chord to a IV chord, for example — but you have to bear in mind that it won't be what listeners are expecting.

When it comes to departing from the rules, a little goes a long way. You may have to back off after using a couple of unconventional chord changes and play more conventional ones to satisfy your audience. Pop music especially adheres to the rules regarding chord progressions, and is even more didactic than classical music about what sounds "good" and what sounds "strange."

Try the above chord progressions with an added seventh to the triads to see if they sound acceptable to you. You will probably find that some sound good — and some, not so good.

# Coming Home with Cadences

An important part of making your music (and audience) breathe is through the use of *cadence*, or a return to the I/i chord from a iv or a V chord.

The longer you take to reach this point of cadence, the more tension you can build in your music.

A musical phrase can come to an end by simply stopping, of course, but if that stopping position doesn't make "sense" to the listeners, they may not be very happy with you. Ending your song on the wrong note or notes is like ending a conversation with a non sequitur, and you may leave your listeners a little uncomfortable. Some audiences are absolutely delighted to hear music that confounds their expectations, however, and this may be exactly the audience you're trying to reach.

This section covers the four main types of cadences:

✔ Authentic

✔ Plagal

✔ Deceptive/Interrupted

✔ Half-cadence

## Authentic cadences

*Authentic cadences* are the most obvious-sounding cadences and are therefore considered the strongest. In an authentic cadence, the harmonic goal of the phrase is the 5 chord, (V or v, depending on whether the piece is in a major or minor key). The cadence occurs when you move from that V/v chord to a I/i chord, as shown in Figure 10-20.

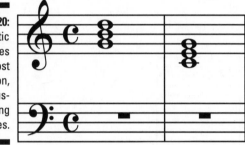

**Figure 10-20:**
Authentic cadences are the most common, obvious-sounding ones.

## Plagal cadences

The harmonic goal of a *plagal cadence* is ultimately the 4 (IV or iv) chord, with cadence occurring when the 4 chord moves to the 1 chord. The progressions IV-I, iv-i, iv-I, and IV-i are all possibilities. The plagal structure originated with Medieval Church music, which was mostly vocal, and is therefore often referred to as the *Amen cadence*. If you're familiar with Gregorian chants at all, or even many modern hymns, then you've heard the Amen cadence in action. It usually happens (no surprise here) at the point where the chanters sing the two-chord "A-men."

Despite the "amen" label, plagal cadences are usually used within a song to end a phrase, and not at the very end of a song, because they're not as decisive-sounding as a perfect cadence (Figure 10-21).

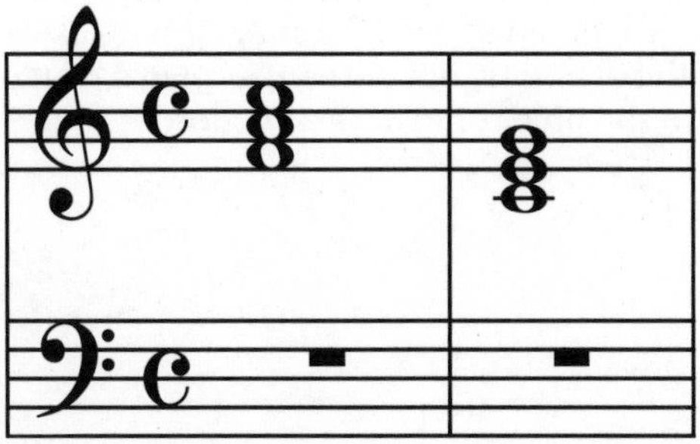

**Figure 10-21:**
Plagal cadences are not as conclusive as authentic cadences.

## Deceptive or interrupted cadences

A *deceptive cadence*, or *interrupted cadence*, essentially reaches an ultimate point of tension on a V/v chord, just like the authentic cadence, but it resolves to something *other* than the tonic (I/i) chord — hence, the name *deceptive*. The most common deceptive cadence out there, used 99 times out of 100, is the V/v chord that moves up to a VI/vi chord. The phrase looks and feels like it's about to end and close with the 1 chord, but instead it moves up to the 6 instead, as shown in Figure 10-22.

**Figure 10-22:**
Deceptive cadences are nice to use when you want to fake the audience out.

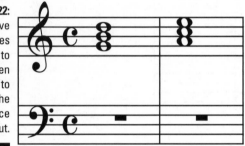

Other deceptive/interrupted cadences include moving from the V chord to the IV chord, the V chord to the ii chord, and the V chord to the V7. Deceptive cadences are considered one of the weakest cadences because they invoke a feeling of incompleteness.

## Half-cadences

Half-cadences are a little more confusing. The authentic, plagal, and deceptive cadences all occur in musical phrases that resolve before the phrase is complete. In other words, with the other cadences the phrase starts at a point of rest (I/i) and moves through a series of chords to reach either a iv/IV or a v/V chord. It could be as easy as the I/i chord going straight to the V/v chord and back to the I/i, or it could spend 20 hours circling like a plane in a holding pattern between those points, but authentic, plagal, and deceptive will all musically release to the point of rest: the I/i chord.

Half-cadences are the only ones that don't end this way. With a half-cadence, the musical phrase ends at the point of tension — the V/v chord itself. It basically plays to a chord that is not the I/i and stops, resulting in a musical phrase that feels unfinished. Examples would be a V-IV progression, a V-vi progression, a V-ii progression, and a V-V7 progression. It's called a half-cadence simply because it just doesn't feel like it's done yet.

# Fitting Chords and Melodies Together

Often, when you're working with just a melody, the basic accompanying harmony is already there in your subconscious. The melody lends itself to the harmony so obviously that accompanying the melodic line is the easiest part of writing the music. You may be aware of which note in your melody represents the tonic note right away, and you might even be aware of very specific chord movements that are screaming out at you from your melody.

Likewise, that cool chord progression you came up with last night is eager to provide you with *structural tones* (also sometimes called *chord tones*) from which a melody can magically emerge (see Chapter 8 for more information on structural tones).

## Extracting harmony from melody

If you take a simple major scale and consider only the I chord (also called the *tonic*), the IV chord (the *subdominant*), and the V chord (the *dominant*), you can hear fairly simple and obvious suggestions of relationship between notes in the given key that might be used to accompany them.

There are, of course, many other possibilities and substitutions, but here we stick with the I, IV, and V chords in the example shown in Figure 10-23.

**Figure 10-23:** Seeing the scale in I, IV, and V chords.

You can use tones from within the chords (called, as we mentioned, chord tones) and string these tones together in various ways using *non-chord tones*. Some of the techniques for stringing together different melody notes are covered in Chapter 8. Here we cover some more techniques.

First, let's give an example of a simple chord progression that we can use to extract some structural tones from (Figure 10-24).

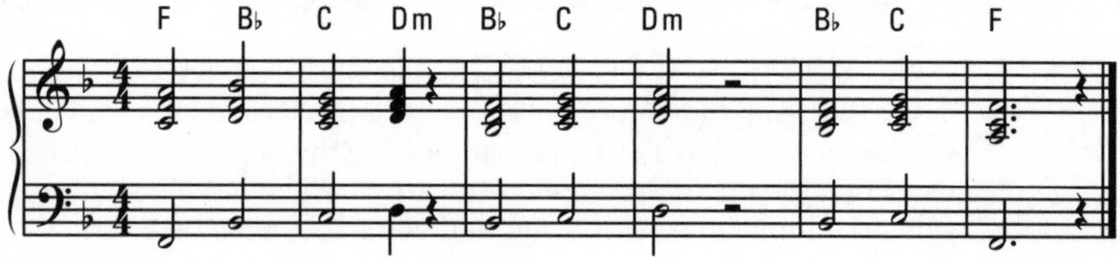

**Figure 10-24:**
Seeing structural tones in a simple chord progression.

Now we extract a melody from these chords using only notes from within each chord — the chord tones (Figure 10-25).

**Figure 10-25:**
Extracting chord tones from a chord progression.

Now let's add some passing tones. Remember that *passing tones* close the gaps between structural tones. They make *disjunct* melodies more *conjunct*. Passing tones go in steps and end up stepping into the next structural tone (Figure 10-26).

**Figure 10-26:**
Adding
passing
tones to fill
in the
structural
tones.

If you step away from the tone before stepping back to it, it is called a *neighboring tone* (Figure 10-27).

**Figure 10-27:**
Having a
little visit
with
neighboring
tones.

## Using chord changes

A chord change is a powerful thing. It is hard to take a chord change lightly. That is why you need to be picky about the choices you make regarding where in the rhythm of your music the chords change.

If your chords change every measure on beat one, that beat will be strengthened. If instead you place the chord changes on beats four *and* one, both of those beats will gain some gravity. A chord change brings some attention to any rhythmic subdivision. It is a good idea to place chord changes strategically to emphasize the rhythmic feel, or groove, of your piece.

Often your music will benefit from adding more chords in between the structural chords you started off with. For this you can go back to your non-chord tones, as shown earlier in this chapter. Some of the non-chord tones you added while stringing together your chord tones may provide rhythmic accents. Or maybe you just like these notes and want the listener's attention drawn to them. So why not add chord changes at those same moments? Let's call these *passing chords*.

Figure 10-28 shows the example again with all the non-chord tones we added.

**Figure 10-28:**
Adding all
the non-
chord tones.

Now let's add some passing tones to go along with the non-chord tones
(Figure 10-29).

**Figure 10-29:**
Adding
passing
tones again.

That makes for a richer, more colorful phrase, doesn't it? The possibilities are
limitless. You could have a chord change every beat, every half beat, or whatever suits your intentions. This would be a good time to go back and study
the table we gave you, earlier in this chapter, regarding chord progressions.
Knowing which chords flow into which can be helpful here. And don't forget
about the moods you evoke with your choices. A study of jazz can provide
you with some ideas about chord substitutions as well.

On the other hand, there are times when a chord change is distracting and
pulls away from the hypnotic, trancelike mantra of your groove. As an example, Ravel's *Boléro* (which was written intentionally as a piece with no structural development) pulls us along and drives us deeper and deeper into its
feel. When Ravel exhausts the dynamic headroom of his orchestra, he surprises us and wakes us up into a new realm by changing the chord and the

tonality all at once, near the very end. This alerts us that the climax is on its way (it also puts the orchestra in a range where there is some additional dynamic power to be tapped into). It is totally unexpected and somewhat disconcerting, but he had to launch an ending somehow.

You're okay when you can use an unexpected wake-up chord change as powerfully as Ravel, but in the meantime be careful not to loosen your hold on the listener with too many chord changes if you've got a good groove on.

You can have more than one musical idea going on at the same moment in the same piece. Three or more are perhaps too many, because confusion ensues and the listener doesn't know where to turn. You always want to retain a sense of focus, even when your music gets chaotic.

You could have your chords change in one rhythmic pattern and have the melody move in another pattern. Mixing it up like that would convey two different rhythmic statements. You might think of it as keeping the non-chord tones and the chord structure and throwing out some of the structural chord tones in your piece.

Figure 10-30 shows an example with a tiny bit of polishing.

**Figure 10-30:**
Melody and harmony, together in perfect . . . well, harmony.

From what we have discussed in this chapter so far, it should be easy enough to reverse these processes if you had a melody to start with and were looking for the right chords to go along with it. You have to decide which notes in your melody are structural, as we discuss in Chapter 8. Then you can determine the key of your piece and where you feel you need to accentuate your melody with chords. The challenge here is to be aware of the many harmonic possibilities available to you for harmonizing your melody.

## Jonathan Segel of Camper Van Beethoven

A lot of what I do when I'm teaching people to play instruments is to show people the relationships between notes and how they relate to each other. For instance, if you're showing a person how to play a song, say on guitar, you show them which chords they need to play, and then you ask, "Okay, which are the common notes in these chords, and how are they related to each other? What note changes do you need to make this chord into the next chord?" And then the melody, you know, the melody is notes that are also in the chords, or around the notes that are in the chords. So people ultimately learn how all the notes in a song are related to one another.

There are more harmonic possibilities in a single note than there are melodic possibilities in a chord.

# Exercises

1. **Harmonize an ascending fifth (one letter name clockwise around the Circle of Fifths).**

   Find chords that fit with a D note held for two beats followed by an A above held for two beats. Ideas:

   Start with a D major chord.

   Start with a B flat major chord.

   Start with an E minor 7 flat 5 chord.

   Start with a G major chord.

2. **Try chord progressions at random.**

   Write the names of a dozen or so chords on small pieces of paper. Make sure you include some of the ones that sound strange to you. You can use any chord in any key. Put them in a hat and shake them up. Pick out four or five of them and write them down in the order you picked them on some staff paper. Compose a melody that makes sense of this chord progression. You can add some passing chords if you like.

3. **Lead Exercise 2 to a perfect cadence.**

   Add chords and melody where needed. Give it a key signature.

4. Take any two notes and explore the chord combinations available.

5. Take any two chords and explore the melodic possibilities between them.

6. Listen to some familiar music and see if you can identify the non-chord tones by ear.

7. Write a chord progression and extract the structural tones.

8. See how many different non-chord tones you can add and determine which ones work well for your style of music composition.

9. Invent a whole new melody by removing some of the original structural tones and leaving the non-chord tones.

# Chapter 11

# Composing from the Void

· · · · · · · · · · · · · · · · · · · · · · · · · · · · · · · · · · · · · · · · ·

· · · · · · · · · · · · · · · · · · · · · · · · · · · · · · · · · · · · · · · · ·

*T*here's going to be a time in your life when you want desperately to sit down and write a song or a piece of instrumental music, but you find you just can't come up with anything. Nada. Zip. A complete and seemingly insurmountable case of composer's block. So, does that mean you should admit you've got nothing left and quit? No way!

Never, *ever* give up.

One of the keys to being a successful and prolific musician is getting through these creative dry spells and coming out the other end with either a piece of finished music, some song lyrics and a melody, or even just a solid beginning, middle, or ending you can work on in the future. There are many ways to coax your creative juices out from hiding, including beating your head against the piano over and over again, a la Guy Smiley from *Sesame Street*.

In this chapter we discuss two ways of squeezing blood from a turnip: using the environment around you and using a strange science called effort shapes.

# Composing Using the Movement Around You

Many musicians, especially pianists, have a secret weapon in their composition arsenal that they almost never discuss with non-musicians, because it seems either too matter-of-fact or just silly. When they're having "dead" periods of no inspiration, they work on writing mini-soundtracks for the activities going on around them. For example, a cat walks into the room. What sound would the cat's footsteps make if you were trying to capture the image in music? How about the cat's voice? Let's call the cat's soundtrack Part A.

Now, what if the cat continued on into the kitchen, where your mother, or brother, or a1950s housewife was cheerfully washing dishes? What would that soundtrack be? What if the dishwasher was actually your tired, stubble-faced roommate, who was rather unhappy about washing the dishes? What would his music sound like? How would both or either of those people react to the cat? There are your Parts B (the dishwasher) and C (the dishwasher and the cat) — practically a whole composition waiting for you in this scenario.

 Look and listen around you. What did you do last night, this morning, whom did you see, what stories were told? What happened in your dream? Almost anything can serve as a starting point for some kind of soundtrack. Make a movie in your head out of the action in your life and then score that movie.

Your soundtrack can be a simple melody line that deftly "haikus" and condenses each character — or it may be a full melody with accompaniment. Capturing the essence of the activities around you in music can actually result in full-fledged compositions. On the other hand, they can end up as pieces of music you'll never use in the real world. The purpose of this idea, however, is to get you to *start* playing and writing music again, to work past your composer's block. Plus it's fun, too, and playing music for the fun of it is a great way to get your mind to relax and open itself up to new musical possibilities.

If you think this all sounds too silly to try yourself, try to wrap your head around this one: Much of Pyotr (Peter) Ilyich Tchaikovsky's famous score for the *The Nutcracker Suite* was composed *after* the ballet had already been choreographed. He came in after all the "footwork" was already done and wrote music to accompany the physical movements of the dancers. The dancers were his "movie," and he wrote their soundtrack.

As helpful as this everyday soundtrack idea can be, there is a more systematic approach available to you: effort shapes.

# *Introducing Effort Shapes*

A more precise and useful way to describe movement than just walking and washing dishes is through the language of effort shapes (also called Laban Movement Analysis or Eukinetics). An *effort shape* is a style of movement that incorporates particular uses of weight, time, control, and space. When we use effort shapes to compose music, we're trying to capture the emotion and feel of those movements in the music itself.

Effort shapes have been used by choreographers since the 1930s, after choreographer Rudolf von Laban published his treatise *Kinetographie Laban* in 1928, which detailed a system of dance notation that came to be called *Labanotation*. Labonation is still used as one of the primary movement notation systems in dance.

During World War II, Laban fled from Germany to England. The British government hired him to observe factory and farm workers, analyze their movements, and devise more efficient procedures for them to follow to improve productivity. Laban broke down human movements into eight effort shapes. Used as a tool by dancers, athletes, and physical and occupational therapists, it is one of the most widely used systems of human movement analysis. His eight effort shapes are also used by acting teachers to help actors define the behaviors of characterizations they wish to portray, and in the area of behavioral analysis.

*Effort*, or what Laban sometimes described as *dynamics*, is a system for understanding the more subtle characteristics about the way a movement is done with respect to inner intention. The difference between punching someone in anger and reaching for a glass is slight in terms of body organization — both rely on extension of the arm. However, the attention to the strength of the movement, the control of the movement, and the timing of the movement are very different.

Effort has four subcategories, each of which has two opposite polarities:

- **Weight:** Heavy and light
- **Time:** Sustained and staccato
- **Flow:** Bound and free-flowing
- **Space:** Direct and indirect

Laban named the combination of the first three categories (space, weight, and time) the *effort actions*, or *action drive*. Flow, on the other hand, is responsible for the continuousness or ongoingness of motions. Without any flow effort, movement must be contained in a single initiation and action, which is why there are specific names for the flowless action configurations of effort. In general, it is very difficult to remove Flow from much movement, and so a full analysis of effort typically needs to go beyond the effort actions.

So, how does this all relate to composing music? Read on.

## Weight: heavy versus light

The ideas of *heaviness* and *lightness* are easy enough to translate into musical terms. Something light is usually played softly or gently. Often light, melodic phrases are played by instruments with higher pitch ranges, but not always. A French horn can be played lightly or heavily in the low register, for example.

Light and heavy are also related to loud and soft. You might feel like a minor melody at a slow tempo is heavy by nature, but slow pieces in minor keys can have either light or heavy qualities. We are talking about light or heavy — not light or dark. With strings, light and heavy can be communicated through bowing. The specific articulations of other instruments convey light and heavy also.

Light and heavy can be expressed through choices of instrumentation as well. A violin or flute is inherently lighter than a saxophone or a trumpet. A string quartet may be lighter than a brass ensemble. Of course the composer can control a wide range of weights within any of these instruments or instrument groupings.

## Time: Sustained and staccato

Laban's terms *sustained* and *staccato* mean almost the same things as the musical terms *legato* and *staccato*, but the musical terms refer more exactly to the general perceived flow of a melody. The notes may not be written exactly with legato or staccato indications in the sheet music. They may just come across as more or less smooth and connected or separated and quick. Writing indications in the actual sheet music works, too, but you don't always have to go to this extreme to get the feeling across.

When staccato is light and direct it can result in *Dab*, and when it gets heavy and bound, it might become *Punch*. Or if the energy is indirect, the light staccato becomes *Flick* and the heavy becomes *Slash*. (More on these terms later in this chapter.)

# Flow: Bound and free-flowing

Bound and free-flowing are a little harder to grasp. A melody that is *bound* might be one that has very few trills or other ornaments. It would be fairly controlled and might be played by more than one instrument in unison or harmony, one instrument "binding" the other to the task of melody making.

A *free-flowing* melody is a little looser in construction. This is not to say that it jumps all over the place (that would make it free-flowing *and* indirect), but it might make more use of a single instrument's virtuoso capabilities and not be so apt to stay a straight and narrow course. A bound melody might seem ponderous and deliberate, whereas a free-flowing melody rises and falls with ease and abandonment. In a sense, bound energy doesn't communicate happiness as well as free-flowing energy does. Bound energy often conveys sorrow, pride, and determination. Some instruments are more bound or more free-flowing in general: The clarinet and piano are capable of free-flowing passages, but the baritone saxophone and bass viol are a bit more bound by nature.

# Space: Direct and indirect

A *direct* melody doesn't get diverted or sidetracked on its way to conclusion. It might be peppered with *trills* (playing two adjacent notes of a scale quickly), *mordents* (playing three adjacent notes of a scale quickly), and all manner of nuance, or it might move straight and simply, but it is headed from the beginning to the end without changing course or getting confused. It doesn't beat around the bush. If I want you to give me a ride home, I can say, "Do you think you could give me a ride home?" Or I could say, "I wonder how I am going to get home later. I suppose I could walk or take a cab. Is there a bus that runs later?" That's the difference between direct and indirect. Eventually I get home, but the indirect example is a roundabout journey just to get the ride.

Many composers make efforts to ensure that their melodies are always a little indirect. Bela Bartok was a great example of this. Mozart was very direct, on the other hand. At a time when listeners demanded that their expectations be fulfilled musically, it was difficult for composers to write much in the way of indirect melodies. Direct melodic choices are always the ones that get stuck in your head. Indirect melodic choices demand your attention and are interesting, but often are soon gone from memory — or rather, they are remembered indirectly. You remember the *sense* of them without remembering the exact notes.

Now that you have some sense of what the effort shapes mean, let's connect them more directly to composing music.

# Composing Using Effort Shapes

Basically, as we have tried to establish, effort shapes are natural human styles of movement, and they convey moods and emotions. They are body language. Any musical phrase or passage can also be broken down into Laban's four components and resolved into his eight effort shapes.

The eight effort shapes have been given names, and here we attempt to describe each shape musically. For the most part, the names of the effort shapes speak for themselves. It is also easy to see how you can use these names as a guide for composing music that conveys certain moods.

## Dab

*Dab* is light, direct, staccato, and free-flowing.

Imagine you're dabbing something with a paintbrush, or the tip of a washcloth. When you dab, you're not striking it hard, and you're not squishing it flat. You're gently and quickly poking it.

When you want to capture the feeling of dabbing in your music, you're going to play it lightly and quickly — like you're softly and quickly poking the exact center of a piano key. You have a musical idea you want to quickly get across to your listeners, and you're not going to dance around things to get it across. But you're not trying to hit your listeners over the head with it, either.

Mozart wrote a lot of dab music, as do contemporary composers like Toog, Momus, Henry Purcell, Mr. Wright, and Belle & Sebastian.

# Flick

*Flick* is light, indirect, staccato, and free-flowing.

Imagine you're flicking an eyelash off of someone's cheek with your finger. You're not pouncing on that little stray hair to remove it — instead, you're aiming at the general direction of the hair, just brushing against the cheek of the person and the area around the eyelash as well. When you're trying to capture the feeling of flicking in your music, you're quickly and gently hitting the notes you want to hit, but you're also playing with the notes around your core musical idea as well.

Serialism and fugue counterpoint use the concept of flick in their construction, as do artists such as J. S. Bach, Elf Power, Philip Glass, and Can.

# Glide

*Glide* is light, direct, sustained, and bound.

Imagine a bird gliding, and make your music take on that sound. When you're writing music that glides, keep in mind that you're trying to make music that soars, just like that bird.

Tchaikovsky's *Nutcracker*, Brian Eno's atmospherics, and Arvo Päart all manage to convey glide.

# Press

*Press* is heavy, direct, sustained, and bound.

Press music does just that — it presses down hard on the listener. This is you, the composer, pressing down hard on the fly that landed on your keyboard, slowly and with great intent. There's no misconstruing your musical concept when you compose in press, which is why almost all heavy goth music and slowcore fit under this heading.

Wagner, Low, Nick Cave, Sonic Youth, Canadian folk artist Hayden, This Mortal Coil, Mogwai, Popol Vuh, and Joy Division all are into press.

# Float

*Float* is light, indirect, sustained, and free-flowing.

Float is a lot like glide, except that it is less direct.

Think Claude Debussy and Stereolab.

# Punch

*Punch* is heavy, direct, staccato, and bound.

This is the most direct and aggressive-sounding music of the bunch. When you write music with punch, you're telling your audience that you have a message and you want them to hear it right now. You're punching out the notes on your instrument — if you're playing the piano, you're hitting the keys directly and with force.

Music with punch includes Stravinsky, The Ramones, Sir Mix-a-Lot, P. J. Harvey — and basically, for that matter, most rock and rap music.

# Slash

*Slash* is heavy, indirect, staccato, and free-flowing.

Slash is a lot like punch, except that the message and the sound aren't hammered so much into the audience. You're toying with the audience a bit, putting them just a bit on edge and catching them by surprise with your musical and rhythmic choices.

Think Stravinsky, The Swans, *Ziggy Stardust*-era Bowie, Jarboe, and Akron/Family.

# Wring

*Wring* is heavy, indirect, sustained, and bound.

Think of wringing out a washcloth, and you've got the basic idea behind what you're trying to do to your audience when you use this effort shape. You're slowly wringing them out emotionally while moving to your musical climax, potentially exhausting them with the sheer effort of moving to the end of the song or the section of music.

Think Holst, Bartok, Legendary Pink Dots, The Swans, Throbbing Gristle, Popol Vuh, and Godspeed You Black Emperor.

## *Shaping story and mood by combining effort shapes*

Your composition tells a story. Using effort shapes, you can decide on the moods of your story and the order in which you want to present them, and then you can write heavy, light, direct, indirect, and so on to get the moods across to the listener. You can use a change of effort shape to develop or restate a motif or melodic phrase.

Just as there are a lot of ways to say, "I love you," there are also many ways to present any melodic idea. A single phrase can be arranged to sound sustained or staccato. You can take any musical idea and frame it into an effort shape with surprisingly little difficulty using choices of orchestration, tempo, the octave in which the melody is played, or almost anything else you like. The effort shapes just give you handy, pre-packaged combinations of ingredients to get your message across.

A good way to get a grasp on composition is to listen for these effort shapes in the music of others. They are everywhere. Although composers don't often use them consciously, it is difficult to find a single moment in music that can't be assigned one or more effort shapes. Most musical compositions move back and forth between a couple different effort shapes. Some music stays pretty much on a single one. And some compositions run almost the entire gamut of them. This is true for tonal music, atonal music, popular, hip-hop, jazz, metal, classical, and so on. Some genres of music are almost entirely characterized by single effort shapes. There is a good deal of Punch and Dab in hip-hop, a lot of Slash in metal, and Press in rock and roll. Jazz uses a lot of Glide, Float, and Flick energy.

Consider Gustav Holst's *The Planets* (op. 32). To follow along, you may have to go out and get a recording of this orchestral suite. But if you don't have it already, you should anyway. Elsewhere is this book we have mentioned that many modern film composers seem to have been influenced by this composition. Maybe a reason for its influence is that Holst moves us through so many different moods — or effort shapes.

The string entrance is flick with a little suggestion of slash. The brass enters with a heavy dab leading to punch. A few punches, then some more dab, a little slash and wring leading to another punch, and we're back to dab and punch. More dabs leading to punch followed by press when the melody smooths out. Then it speeds up into slash and punch and holds as a little bit of a lighter wring. The main melody that comes in later in the low strings is press. This melody is (all together now!) heavy, direct, sustained, and bound. After this we go back to dab and flick till we hit punch again. You can take it from there.

Notice that more than one effort-shape can be happening at the same time. The strings can play flick and slash or wring while the brass plays a press/dab melody.

Make sure you listen to "Neptune" to hear the contrast to what you heard in "Jupiter." "Neptune" has a lot of float and some glide energy mixed with a little wring here and there.

If you want to hear a composition with some obvious slash and punch energy, listen to Stravinsky's *The Rite of Spring*.

Human moods are expressed through body language, and styles of movement are defined by effort shapes. Music is expressive of moods through its movements through time and space by way of its rhythms and melodies. The effort shapes codify movements and give us the tools to translate physical, human movement and body language into music.

When we began this chapter, we suggested that you look at your daily life as a movie. And when composing for film, it is important to observe the relationships between movement styles, cultural and socioeconomic frameworks, and the music you compose. It can be a dangerous stretch to use contemporary sounds and styles to score a film about, say, Elizabethan England.

Remember that you yourself move with a certain combination of weight, speed, directness, and so on. This combination might influence your likes and dislikes and even the style of your compositions. That's fine, but you shouldn't be bound by your own natural combination. If you want to enjoy sustained success as a music composer, you will need to learn to embrace a broader variety of movement styles (see Holst's *The Planets*). If you are lucky, you *could* become successful by virtue of your stylistic limitations — just realize that if so, it might limit how much variety you can get away with later on.

# Mods dab, rockers press

In the 1960s, during what contemporary musicologists like to call "The First British Invasion," British youth formed two cultures. These two youth cultures were known as the *rockers* and the *mods*. The rockers might enjoy the music of The Rolling Stones or The Animals, and the mods might prefer The Beatles or Herman's Hermits. The cultures clashed in their interest in music, clothing, their preferred uses of drugs and alcohol to some extent, and their general attitudes. There were occasional gang-like turf wars between the two groups, as portrayed in the classic film *Quadrophenia*. To a certain extent, a similar division existed among young people in the big cities of the United States (such as between the *Foamies* and the *Potsuckers* on the East Coast in the 1960s.).

It is interesting to note that most of the music that interested the mods can be classified as dab/glide, but the rockers seemed to prefer press/punch. Of course, there was music that crossed these lines, and other effort shapes can be observed in the music enjoyed by these two groups, but the social implications of this clear division of effort shapes between these groups suggest that certain types of people might be attracted to certain types of movement in their music. Moreover, certain types of movements in music may seem to fit with certain types of cultural frameworks.

In 1967, the Rolling Stones, in an attempt to make an album that spoke to the psychedelic influence of bands like the Beatles, recorded *Their Satanic Majesties Request*. It was deeply disliked by most of the Stones' rocker listener base, but it did cross over into the realm of tenuous acceptance by many of the mods. People expected the Stones' usual punch/press rock and roll, but got glide, dab, and float. It was the Rolling Stones' least successful album, from which they were mandated to redeem themselves with their very next release.

# Exercises

1. **Pick out five of your favorite pieces of music and determine their effort shapes.**

   Which effort shapes from Exercise 1 show up the most within your five musical selections?

2. **Search your music collection for effort shapes that are missing from your list from Exercise 1.**

3. **Compose an eight- to sixteen-measure melody using each of the missing effort shapes from Exercise 2.**

4. **If you have composed any music, determine the effort shapes you used.**

5. Pick any two effort shapes and try to write a 16-measure transition from one to the other.

6. Try to write a short musical beginning (intro) using each of the eight effort shapes.

7. Do the same thing as Exercise 6, but write endings (finales).

# Chapter 12

# Beginnings, Middles, and Endings

*T*he fact that a good composition is like a good story, with a beginning, a middle, and an end, is easy enough to tell in a song with lyrics. This is especially true in folk songs, and especially folk ballads, which are most often specifically written to tell a story. Consider Peter, Paul and Mary's "Puff the Magic Dragon," which, if taken literally, tells the listeners about the relationship between a boy and his dragon.

This narrative property of music is universal and extremely important in composition.

Even instrumental songs can — and should — tell a story, too. In an instrumental piece of music, you have a clearly defined beginning that grabs your attention and sets the overall tone of the songs, a middle that tells the story of the song, and an ending designed to wrap up the story and end in cadence. That may sound simplistic, but it really is how most music is structured, whether you're talking about a sonata, a folk ballad, or a punk anthem.

Many times, instrumental songs are fitted to a poem or a set of lyrics. In the end the words are simply removed by the composer with the intent that the overall meaning of the words should still be conveyed by the music alone. Many classical composers wrote music this way, including Johannes Brahms and Ludwig van Beethoven. Brahms actually left the lyrics in many of his compositions, only to have them performed, for the most part, as purely instrumental pieces.

# A Word About Form

While the idea of composing within a *form* may feel claustrophobic and non-creative to some musicians from the outset, it's form that ties a piece of music together and keeps it from feeling like aimless noodling. In short, form *is* beginning, middle, and end. It's a map to follow when trying to put a song together. All art is built on shape, and music is no exception.

For example, if you want to write blues music, you need to write within the constraints of the blues form. Again, here's where sitting down at an instrument and just playing around with chord progressions works wonders for creativity. Humming along with a couple of bars of I-IV-V/I is half the work of writing a solid blues song. It's similar with pop music — there's a conventional formula for that, known as the *Intro ABACBCB* form, as you can see in Chapter 13. Just playing around within the constraints of a form can give you some great basic ideas of how you want to put your song together.

When you're working with pop songs, even instrumental ones such as those performed by bands such as Tortoise and Trans Am, you work to arrange the song under some version of the pop form, such as (Intro ABACBCB) or one of the other traditional patterns of songwriting in the pop genre.

Many classical forms are actually several musical forms stuck together, such as symphonies, rondos, and sonatas. In these forms, it's almost as though you're writing several smaller pieces of music and putting them together into one big piece. In one piece of music, remember, you can even have multiple time signatures and multiple key signatures. In these kinds of classical music, having an engaging opening sequence is even more important, because the beginning and the ending are even more responsible than in other forms for tying the music together into a coherent whole.

# Beginnings

Imagine someone listening skeptically to a new CD. He puts it in the player and presses Play. Within three seconds he wrinkles his nose and skips to the next track. Five seconds later he sighs and skips to the next one.

That scenario illustrates how crucial the beginning of your music is. But even before the beginning is the title.

## The power of titling

Talk to any punk rock band — for example, we talked to the guys from Dillinger 4 for this one — and they'll tell you that "all you have to do to write a song is come up with a good title." Many, many brainstorming sessions with rock bands in general are consumed with discussions on finding the perfect title for a new song. Hundreds of titles might be thrown out during these sessions, until one wonderful title — such as "Kim Gordon's Panties" (Steve Albini), Camper Van Beethoven's "When I Win the Lottery," or, theoretically, if Maurice Ravel was a pop band and not a classical composer, "Pavanne for a Dead Princess" — carries enough weight on its own to turn into a song.

This might sound silly, but the point of coming up with a title for a song that doesn't exist is to kickstart the creative juices and get you on the path to actually writing music. Many writers do the same thing when sitting down to write a poem, short story, or even a novel — they come up with a title for a project and then sit down and try to come up with a story, poem, or novel that works under that title. Once you have the title for a song, you can sit down and start thinking of what the title means to you, how it makes you feel, and, eventually, what kind of music and/or lyrics you think would go with that title.

For example, if you hear the phrase "starry, starry night," do you think of loud, rough, fast music — or something slow and quiet and sentimental? Most people would say the latter is the case. What about the word "hoe-down"? Something sprightly, danceable, and possibly ironic would probably be the case.

Words have the amazing power of bringing up a panoply of images when spoken or read, and working with titles is a quick way to get you in the right frame of mind to compose.

## Starting a piece

The beginning of a piece of music should do one or more of the following things:

- ✔ Set the mood of the piece
- ✔ Introduce a musical idea
- ✔ Get the listener's attention

In many cases, the very first set of chords or notes is the most important part of the song. Your opening musical phrase is just like the opening phrase of a good book or story, and you should strive to instantly suck your listener into the song with a memorable opener.

Think of Claude Debussy's "Clair de Lune," Gioachino Rossini's *William Tell* Overture (as immortalized in Stanley Kubrick's *A Clockwork Orange* and in *The Lone Ranger*), or Beethoven's Symphony No. 5. These all feature openers that just about everyone in the Western world is familiar with. And although it's extremely rare for a musician or writer to put that kind of lasting punch into a composition, it's something to strive for when you write music and lyrics.

## Chord progressions

Just playing around with chord progressions (see Chapter 10) can be enough to build the basic foundation of a song and figure out how you're musically going to begin it, no matter what the genre. You can get a lot of good songs started off from just sitting down at your instrument and doing four or five bars of I-V-I chords over and over, as in C major, G major, C major or A major, E major, A major.

Try sitting down and humming along with these chord progressions for awhile and see if you can't either come up with your own song or hear some- one else's very familiar song coming out.

The greatest compositions are often surprisingly simple in structure.

# Middles

It has been said that people remember the beginning and ending of your song, but they forget all about the middle. Nevertheless, the middle is usually the biggest part of a composition and deserves attention and development.

Just as in a work of written fiction, the middle is where you develop the state- ment first presented in the beginning. If you present a problem in the lyrics, such as in Mozart's *Don Giovanni*, in which the lead character laments that he's always "running errands, never free . . . this is not the life for me" (translated from the Italian for your reading pleasure), then in the middle of the piece you would reveal or describe the character's plans to lead a completely different life — which, in the case of Don Giovanni, has disastrous consequences.

In many of Hank Williams's songs, the middle is used to lyrically describe exactly how much agony the main character of the song is in, building on the idea presented in the beginning of the song. "Your Cheatin' Heart," "Ramblin' Man," and "Cold, Cold Heart" are just three Hank Williams songs that follow this exact pattern. Here we could easily speculate that Mr. Williams came up with the catchy title, fiddled around with basic chords and got an idea for a tune to go with it, and developed the song's middle based on fleshing out the idea of a "cheatin' heart." Sounds simple, eh?

In classical music, the middle section serves as a counterbalance to the beginning. The middle is where you change keys and/or tempo, defining a clear break from the opening section of your piece. If a piece of classical music has a loud, forceful beginning section, then the middle section is often quieter and more subdued to provide stark contrast to the opening. Consider Igor Stravinsky's *Symphony of Psalms*. Conversely, if the music starts out slowly and simply, then a good way to present contrast is — can you guess? — to have a forceful, complicated middle section, as in Frederic Chopin's Étude in A Minor (op. 25, no. 11).

As in storytelling — and pretty much any kind of narrative, from fairy tales to Hollywood movies — the beginning establishes a baseline situation; the middle takes us on a journey away from that baseline, employing change and adventure; and the ending brings us back to another baseline, which is usually at least slightly different from the beginning.

# Endings

Even television jingles have a beginning, middle, and ending. The ending of anything should be a satisfying conclusion to the piece. Musically, you probably want your songs to end *in cadence*, or resolving to the I chord (as discussed in Chapter 10) just because that is an aurally satisfying way for a piece of music to end. Lyrically, you want to try to either answer some of the questions posited in your beginning, resolve the situation(s) developed in the middle, or even just have the song's narrator or main character give up and move to something else. It's just like in literature — at the end of the story, *something* has been resolved.

## Making your music "breathe"

The beginning, middle, and end of a piece of music should all be looked at as its sections, and those sections should be viewed as being composed of musical phrases.

*Phrases* are complete musical thoughts that also have a beginning, a middle, and an end to them, and this is what gives music shape. Phrases are usually short, often two to eight measures long, and generally end in a cadence. *Cadences* provide a sort of musical pause within the piece of music, giving the sense that the music is *breathing* as tension is increased and decreased between points of cadence — there's a lot more on building musical phrases in Chapter 7.

When listening to music, if you have a hard time telling where one phrase or period begins and another ends, don't despair. Music that contains only very clear phrases often sounds square, simple, and, frankly, boring. Therefore, composers are always finding ways to obscure the beginnings and endings of phrases so that one phrase blends smoothly into the next and carries the listener easily along with it. Very often, one part of the music (for example, the melody) will come to the end of the phrase while another part of the music (for example, the accompaniment) has already started the next one. That is one way to "blur" phrases. Cadences can be considered to be any method for completing a musical thought and coming to a moment of rest before moving onto another musical thought.

In general, the overall length of a piece is dependent on the ability to keep the listener's interest throughout. Compositions involving relatively simple ideas should be short in length — you can't just repeat a theme or motif over and over and over and expect your listener to stay awake. Compositions with many complex ideas should naturally be longer and more developed so that the listener is satisfied that the piece is complete.

# *Exercises*

1. **Come up with a simple statement such as** *I love you,* *Life is a mystery,* **or** *This job sucks.* **Write a melody to go along with it.**

2. **Develop your idea from Exercise 1.**

   For example: If you had written *This job sucks,* you might write something like, *The printer didn't work all week.* Give a little detail to your original statement and then a little more. Put this new idea to music.

3. **Write something that contrasts or departs slightly from your original theme, such as** *I hope we still have email.*

4. **Write an ending for the preceding two exercises. For example,** *I sent a memo to my boss saying, 'see you in Cancun'.* **Put this idea to music.**

5. **Write a short melodic phrase with no lyrics of about four measures. Leave the ending hanging. In other words, don't resolve it back to the I chord.**

6. **Write your phrase from exercise 4 again, but this time resolve the ending with a cadence.**

   If you want, you can change a few notes or the direction of melodic movement a little, but be sure it is basically the same phrase as Exercise 5.

7. **Try to write a complementary or contrasting musical phrase as a departure from Exercise 6.**

   For example, maybe move your underlying chord up a fourth.

8. **Find a way to restate your original phrase as an ending, resolving the piece back to the I chord at the end.**

9. **Analyze the form of three of your favorite pieces of music, writing the part letters (A, B, C, and so on) on a blank piece of paper as you listen.**

# Chapter 13

# Musical Forms

*W*hen we talk about *musical form*, what we're talking about, of course, is the blueprint used to create a specific type of music. For example, if you wanted to sit down and write a minuet, there is a very specific blueprint you have to follow to create a piece of music that musicians and other listeners would recognize as a *minuet*. You can write a blues piece and *call* it "Minuet in B," or "Sad Minuet" — but it wouldn't really be a minuet. It would still be the blues.

There are many different musical forms, and each one is composed of different parts that come together to define the whole.

## Combining Parts into Forms

The division of music into *parts* is convenient when your composition, like most compositions, requires repetition of various similar elements. The different parts usually share a major harmonic focus point, similar melody lines, rhythm structure, and may have other resemblances. Parts can further be linked to create identifiable musical *forms* (blues, rock, and so on).

Conventional musical theory gives alphabetic labels to the musical parts within a composition: A, B, C, and so forth. If a part is repeated in a song, its letter is repeated. For example, ABA is familiar in classical music, with an opening theme (A) that leads to a chorus or bridge (Part B) and is repeated at the end of the piece (A again).

# One-part form: A

The *one-part* form — diagrammed as just A, or AA, or AAA, depending on the length of the song — is the most primitive song structure, sometimes referred to as the *air* or *ballad* form. In a one-part form, a melody is repeated with only slight changes (if any) in each successive verse of the round to accommodate the changing rhythm of the song, such as in "Happy Birthday" or "The Hokey Pokey."

# Binary form: AB

*Binary* form consists of two contrasting sections that function as statement and counterstatement. It can be as simple as just AB, as in "My Country 'Tis of Thee." It can also be a bit more expanded — AABB — as in "Greensleeves," with the second A being a variation of the first A (as shown in Figure 13-1).

**Figure 13-1:** "Greensleeves" has an AABB binary form.

# Song form: ABA

*Song* structure is frequently based on the ABA form, also called *three-part form* or *ternary/tertiary form*. One of the simplest ways to write in song form is to simply vary and repeat the melody, as in "Twinkle, Twinkle, Little Star" (Figure 13-2).

More complicated uses of ABA appears in classical forms.

**Figure 13-2:**
"Twinkle, Twinkle, Little Star" has song (ABA) form.

See if you can find the A and B sections in Figure 13-2. Go on, we'll wait.

(If you said the first four measures were part A, the second four measures were part B, and the final four measures were part A again, you were right. If not, you should probably start this chapter over again.)

Another variation of the ABA form is the AABA form, which is used in the blues (more on this later in this chapter) and in popular songs such as "Over the Rainbow," with the B section working as the bridge linking the two stretches of A.

# Arch form: ABCBA

Music written in *arch* form is made up of parts labeled A, B, and C. In arch form, the A, B, and C are played sequentially — and then the B section is played for a second time, followed by the A to end the song. It looks like this: ABCBA.

The 20th-century Hungarian composer Béla Bartók used the arch form for many of his compositions, such as in his Piano Concerto No. 2 and Violin Concerto No. 2.

# Classical Forms

Before the Renaissance period, most Western music was composed for religious purposes or for people to dance to, and because people didn't always want to learn a new dance to go along with a new kind of music, the rhythm and ideas behind folk music stayed pretty constant and unchanging. The concept of form wasn't really recognized until the height of the classical era — from around 1700 to 1850 — when composers began actively trying to create new forms to break convention and to wow the competition and audiences alike.

Classical music is chock-full of forms. We don't have room to go into them all in detail, but here is a look at a few of them.

## The sonata

The *sonata* (also called the *sonata-allegro* form) was the most popular form used by instrumental composers from the mid 1700s all the way up until the beginning of the 20th century. The sonata is considered to be the first true break from the Church music that had earmarked Western music from the Medieval to the Baroque periods. Ludwig van Beethoven and J. S. Bach are two of the most popular composers to use this format, with Beethoven having written literally dozens of pieces of music in sonata style.

Sonatas are based on the song, or ABA, form. The first A is the *exposition*, which presents the main theme of the song, as well as two or three other minor themes. A good example of the sonata form is Beethoven's Piano Sonata No. 14 in C sharp minor, also known as the *"Moonlight"* Sonata (Figure 13-3).

**Figure 13-3:**
The beginning of Beethoven's *"Moonlight"* Sonata starts the A part.

The second part, or B part, of a sonata is called the *development*. The development often sounds like it belongs in an entirely different piece of music altogether—it is usually in a different key and may have a different time signature than the exposition (Figure 13-4).

**Figure 13-4:**
The develop-
ment of
Beethoven's
*"Moonlight
"* Sonata
begins the
B part.

Note the different key and time signature used in the B part shown in Figure 13-4, compared to the A part in Figure 13-3.

The third part of the sonata, of course, is the return to the theme or themes explored in the first A section. It is called the *recapitulation*.

Like a lot of musical forms, the sonata has its roots in language — in this case, the *sonnet*. In a sonnet, the first *quatrain* (four-line verse) consists of two sets of rhyming pairs (in music, this could be an A part), whereas the second verse consists of two completely different sets of rhyming pairs (a B section). The third verse goes back to the rhyming scheme of the A section, the fourth follows the rhyming scheme of the B section, and so on. Shakespeare, of course, was/is the reigning king of the sonnet.

## The rondo

In a rondo, the idea of linking completely different-sounding pieces of music is taken even further than in the sonata. The formula for a rondo is ABACA for five-part rondo, and ABACADA for seven-part rondo — the two main kinds of rondo. Meaning, of course, that the A section, sometimes called the *refrain*, is the only thing really tying the piece of music together, and the B, C, and D parts (sometimes called *episodes*) can be in most any key or time signature you want. Mozart was a fine example of a composer that utilized the rondo, such as in the final movement of his Sonata in A Major, the *Ronda alla Turca* section.

The rondo also has its roots in poetry. In 13th century France, the *rondeau* was an incredibly popular form of street poetry and was often set to music. In a *rondeau*, each new stanza has a completely different rhyming scheme, rhythmic structure, and even stanza length than the one that came before, with the exception that the opening rhyme scheme (A) is returned to at the beginning of each new stanza.

## Concerto

In a *concerto*, a composer explores contrasts — between having a large ensemble playing a section of music and then having a soloist or a much smaller group present the same or a very similar section of music. It's with this type of arrangement that we get our superstars of classical music, such as pianist Lang Lang and violinists Itzhak Perlman and Alban Berg. The soloists often carry as much weight as the long-dead composers themselves do.

## Symphony

A *symphony* is a melding of several different musical forms and is usually performed by an orchestra. There are traditionally four movements in a symphony:

- Sonata allegro
- Slower movement
- Minuet or scherzo
- Combination of sonata and rondo, a thematic repeat of the first movement

This is just one configuration, however. The true idea behind a symphony is that it combines several different musical forms into one piece of music harmoniously. Beethoven's Symphony No. 5 is perhaps the most universally recognized symphony ever written.

## Fugue

The *fugue* was the first musical form to fully utilize the left hand of the pianist. In this form, the treble clef and the bass clef take turns carrying the melodic line of the music. Bach, who was a southpaw himself, invented the technique of *counterpoint*, which led to the development of the fugue.

## Divertimento

A *divertimento* is a light, short form of instrumental chamber music having several very short movements. As its name implies, composers wrote pieces in this style chiefly for the entertainment value.

# Minimalism

*Minimalist* music is a modern music form marked by extreme simplification of rhythms, patterns, and harmonies, prolonged chordal or melodic repetitions, and often a trancelike effect. Minimalist music could be diagrammed as AAAAA... form, where each new A is only very slightly changed from the preceding A. Philip Glass is one of the best-known composers who use the minimalist form.

# Through-composed

*Through-composed* music is a song structure that presents new material in each new section of the composition, with no repetition of themes. Each verse of a through-composed composition has its own unique melody, which can be in a different key or even have a different time signature. Classical composers of through-composed composition include Nicholae Bretan and Schubert, whereas more modern examples can be found in Andrew Lloyd Webber operas and in the music of Tenacious D.

# Popular Forms

Discussing *form* when talking about popular music is tricky, simply because what we consider popular music has only been around for about 100 years, with more recent stylistic innovations in rock music being only about 20 years old. As a law must first be introduced as a bill, and most bills never become laws, so a form usually starts out as a *genre*. Generally, a significant amount of time has to pass for us to see whether a genre has enough lasting power or influence for a true form to emerge.

There may be some debate about whether the blues, country, and rock music are forms or genres. We will give them the benefit of the doubt and say that, for our purposes in this book, they are forms.

## The blues

The blues is one of the first original American forms of music, combining elements of field holler, gospel, and African percussion. The blues is written in song form (ternary/tertiary) and follows an AABA pattern of I, IV, and V chords in a given scale, with the B section serving as the bridge.

All blues music hinges around the I/i, the IV/iv, and the V/v chords.

### 12-bar blues

The most common type of blues is the 12-bar blues, which is often constructed like this:

| I   | I   | I | I              |
|-----|-----|---|----------------|
| IV  | IV  | I | I              |
| V   | IV  | I | V/I (turnaround) |

The *turnaround* is the part of the song where you either end the song on the I chord, or play the V chord instead and return to the beginning of the song for another verse.

If you're playing the 12-bar blues in a minor key, you could write it like so:

| i   | IV  | i | v                |
|-----|-----|---|------------------|
| IV  | IV  | i | VI               |
| ii  | v   | i | v/i (turnaround) |

Another way you could write the 12-bar blues in a minor key is as follows:

| i   | i   | i | i    |
|-----|-----|---|------|
| iv  | iv  | i | i    |
| V   | iv  | i | V/i  |

### 8-bar blues

The 8-bar blues is very similar to the 12-bar blues — it's just got shorter verses. One possible construction of the 8-bar blues is as follows:

| I   | IV  | I | VI               |
|-----|-----|---|------------------|
| ii  | V   | I | V/I (turnaround) |

### 16-bar blues

The 16-bar blues — which is, of course, four bars longer per verse than the 12-bar blues — follows the chord patterns of the 12-bar blues, with the 9th and 10th measures (bars) often repeated three times, like so:

| I   | I   | I | I                |
|-----|-----|---|------------------|
| IV  | IV  | I | I                |
| V   | IV  | V | IV               |
| V   | IV  | I | V/I (turnaround) |

### 24-bar blues

The 24-bar blues progression is very similar to the 12-bar form, except that the time each chord progression is played is doubled, like so:

| | | | |
|---|---|---|---|
| I | I | I | I |
| I | I | I | I |
| IV | IV | IV | IV |
| I | I | I | I |
| V | V | IV | IV |
| I | I | I | V/I (turnaround) |

# 32-bar blues and country

The 32-bar blues is the direct link between blues and rock and jazz music. This kind of blues has the AABA structure that was later adopted by rock bands in the 1960s (see the next section).

Although this form didn't work as well for blues as the shorter forms did, simply because it didn't work as well for the call-and-response form of lyricism that the blues was built on, it worked very well for early country music. Hank Williams used this form in songs like "Your Cheatin' Heart," and Freddy Fender used it in "Wasted Days and Wasted Nights." Later, this form was picked up and popularized by mainstream musicians and could be heard in songs like "Frosty the Snowman."

# Rock

In the 1960s, the Beach Boys used the 32-bar blues form for songs like "Good Vibrations" and "Surfer Girl" (AABA). Led Zeppelin used it for "Whole Lotta Love." The Righteous Brothers used it for "You've Lost that Loving Feeling," except that instead of using 32 bars, the turnaround happens at the 24th bar.

### Compound AABA

Other bands took the 32-bar blues form and turned it into the *compound 32-bar blues* form, or *compound AABA* form — which sounds like a wart remover, but it's not. In compound AABA form, after you play the first 32 bars, you go to a second bridge and then repeat the first 32 bars again. The Police's "Every Breath You Take" and Boston's "More Than a Feeling," for a couple examples, follow this pattern.

### Verse-chorus

Today, the most widely used form in pop music is the *verse-chorus* form. Verse-chorus pop songs are laid out like this: Intro ABACBCB.

- ✔ **Introduction:** The introduction is usually instrumental and sets the mood of the piece. It can also be a short spoken piece, as in Prince's "Let's Go Crazy."

- ✔ **A (verse):** Begins the story of the song.

- ✔ **B (chorus):** The *hook* of the song, both lyrically and musically. Should be the most memorable, anthemic part of the song. Is often the title, too.

- ✔ **A (verse):** Part two of the story.

- ✔ **B (chorus):** Reinforcing the hook by repetition. This is one reason why it becomes so memorable.

- ✔ **C (bridge):** The bridge can be instrumental or lyrical and is different-sounding than the verse or chorus sections.

- ✔ **B (end, chorus):** Repeat chorus to fade or just stop at the I chord (cadence) after one time through.

Next time you've got the radio on, see how many pop songs follow this exact formula. Perhaps the most amazing thing you'll find is not that so many songs are built exactly the same way, but how different these songs sound from each other *despite* being built the same way.

So far we have gone over most of the major forms in Western music. But besides the familiar scales and modes — beyond the world of *do, re, mi* — lies a whole other land of possibilities. Outside of the confines of key signatures and all the other conventions of tonal (traditional) music is a vast universe limited only by the constraints of time, imagination, technique, and the twelve semitones, or half steps, into which the Western octave is divided. It is a universe filled with accidentals and experimentation, sublimities and absurdities, some stuff that works — and some stuff that just doesn't.

# Jazz

The true spirit of jazz has always been improvisation, which makes calling jazz a "form" most difficult. The goal in jazz is to create a new interpretation of an established piece (called a standard) — or to build on an established piece of music by changing the melody, harmonies, or even the time signature.

The closest thing to defining jazz form is to take the basic idea behind blues vocalizations — the call-and-response vocals — and replace the voices with the various instruments that make up the jazz canon: brass, bass, percussive, and wind instruments. In Dixieland jazz, for example, musicians take turns playing the lead melody on their instruments while the others improvise countermelodies.

The one predictable element of a piece of jazz music — with the exclusion of free jazz — is the rhythm. All jazz, with the exception of free jazz, uses clear regular meter and strongly-pulsed rhythms that can be heard through the music.

# Atonal Music

To the uninitiated listener, *atonal* music can sound like chaotic, random noise. However, once you realize the amount of knowledge, skill, and technical expertise required to compose it or perform it, your tune may change, so to speak.

Actually, very little music is completely tonal in nature, and most atonal music arrives at and departs from tonality from time to time during its course. *Atonality* is a condition of music in which the constructs of the music do not live within the confines of a particular key signature or scale (other than the chromatic scale). No particular modes are employed.

When talking about atonal music, composition instructor Mike Bogle likes to jokingly refer to the "88 major modes of the chromatic scale." You would be hard pressed to label most atonal music "major" or "minor." These terms are confined to the realm of tonality.

In tonal music, one tone functions as a sort of center of gravity, and the other tones in the chromatic scale are "attracted" to it in varying degrees of strength. Not so in atonal music. There is no gravity. You are allowed to use any of the twelve tones in the chromatic scale in any way you feel like. But how do you wrap a sense of form around that amount of freedom?

## Atonality and form

In 1908, pianist Arnold Schoenberg became the first known composer to write a purely atonal composition. *"Du lehnest wider eine Silberweide"* ("You lean against a silver-willow") was the 13th song in his musical collection entitled *Das Buch der Hängenden Gärten* (*The Book of the Hanging Gardens*), op. 15. It was during this time that he first defined a 12-tone system of composition to replace tonality as an organizational tool. Atonality is one of the most important movements in 20th century music.

In this 12-tone system, Schoenberg believed that no tone should be more important than another in a musical composition. All 12 tones were to be introduced in an order chosen by the composer. Throughout the composition, these same tones must recur in the same order in notes or chords. No tone can recur until all eleven other tones in the series (or tone row) have recurred.

There were a few accepted modifications to this rule. For example, you could move all the tones up or down by a certain interval, retaining the interval relationships of the original series. You could even go in reverse (retrograde).

This was also the beginning of *serial* music, or *serialism*, a type of musical composition based on a particular sequence of pitches, rhythms, dynamics, or any other element of music that is repeated over and over again throughout the composition.

You don't have to use Schoenberg's 12-tone system to compose atonal music, and you don't have to write serial music either, but it may be useful to have some framework other than a key center to help you out.

## Atonality and instrument realities

One good idea in music composition is to write for an instrument or instruments that you have a strong technical knowledge of — it is much easier to write for a violin if you know what the violin is capable of as an instrument.

When composing tonal music, the melody and key center are anchors. Atonal music can tap into the virtuoso skills of an accomplished musician *if* you know the possibilities and limitations of his or her instrument. Certain leaps of intervals, lengths of phrases, speed of articulation, and musical range and expression are possible for one instrument but not for another. A cellist can play an extended legato phrase for endless measures without a pause; a trombonist needs to take a breath now and then. The trombonist can provide expression through power and dynamics; the cellist does that through the many variations of bowing technique.

Strange as it may seem, the *timbre* of instruments is probably more of an important consideration when writing atonal music. Atonal music doesn't provide the listener with an easy pathway through a set of comfortable expectations. Each new note can be a new statement, development, or resolution. If you want to enjoy atonal music, you will have to place your undivided attention on it. It isn't something that makes much sense as background music. You will never hear it playing in an elevator or at the grocery store.

If you are careful about what music you expect from which instruments in your composition, you could write atonally using improvisation as your compositional source. You can record your improvisations and then transcribe them later or, better yet, perform them into a sequencing program such as Logic Pro or Finale and let the program generate a score (see Chapter 2 for more). That way you can preserve some of your spontaneous sparks of intuition, but clean up the messy stuff before you print it all out. When improvising atonally, remember to be respectful of the nature of the particular instrument that you have in mind to actually perform the part later. Of course, you could audition the sounds of many different instrument choices later if you use one of these MIDI sequencing programs. What might not have worked for a guitar might end up being a great part for the clarinet.

## Atonal Music and You

You can use many of the compositional tools that you use for tonal music while working atonally. You could start with some structural tones and then add some passing tones, and so on. You could decide whether you want your melody to ascend or descend. You could make choices regarding step-wise or skip-wise melodic movement. You could fill in your notes around some rhythmic phrases. You could extract your melodic ideas from language or nature — after all, most of the sounds in the world around us are atonal.

Or how about changing a tonal melody into an atonal gem? To illustrate this idea, Figure 13-5 shows "Mary Had a Little Lamb" with a few changes to make it atonal.

**Figure 13-5:**
Mary had a crazy, disturbed little lamb.

From here, you can expand the piece by asking yourself some questions: What would the accompaniment to this sound like? Do chords exist in atonal music land? Of course they do. Remember that a chord is just a combination of notes played together.

Sometimes figuring out what to call a particular chord can be a challenge when working in the atonal realm because often a single combination of notes played together can have more than one possible chord name. For instance, there are really only three separate combinations of four pitches required to form all twelve diminished chords. The pitches in a C diminished chord are the same as the pitches in the E flat (D sharp), F sharp (G flat), and A diminished chords. They are just different inversions (Figure 13-6).

**Figure 13-6:**
Shared notes in C, E flat, F sharp, and A diminished chords — same notes, different inversions.

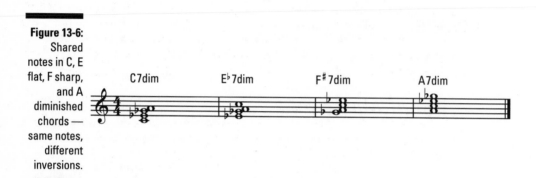

If you need to write down chord charts for atonal compositions, you should try to determine if you are in the neighborhood of some tonal movement that might suggest what to call the chord. Remember that purely atonal music is rare, and often resolves into tonality from time to time. You could also use the bass note being played at that moment (if there is one) as a root for naming your chord. Or you can determine which chord name makes the most sense in terms of movement between the chord before and the chord after the chord in question. You could also just pick what seems to be the simplest name for it. This is especially useful when writing chord charts out for guitarists, since they can rarely play all of the pitches within a complex chord anyway and usually end up playing a portion of these chords that might have a simpler name.

## Listening for atonality

Some composers can hear atonal melodies in their heads just as easily as they can hear tonal ones. This kind of musical imagination is somewhat rare, but if you have it, great! Don't be afraid to get it down somehow. Write it, record it, seal it in a jar. If you think it sounds good and you can communicate it so that others can eventually hear it, it may have a place in the world — no matter how weird it may seem to your relatives.

To hear some atonal music, we suggest listening to any of Bela Bartok's string quartets or Charles Ives's Symphony No. 4, for starters. These pieces have some tonal, some bitonal, and some atonal moments in them.

Don't be afraid to try a little atonality mixed in with your tonal compositions to add a little spice to the mix.

# Exercises

1. **Come up with a short melodic line and try writing a one-part form song. Repeat your A part three times and modify each new verse just a little bit.**

2. **Take a different melodic line you've composed from an earlier chapter and call it B. Try writing a binary-form composition (ABAB) using your A verse from the previous exercise and this new B verse.**

3. **Find one more melodic line from earlier in the book, or compose a brand new one, and call it C. Write an arch form composition with your A, B, and C verses (ABCBA).**

4. **Write a short, 8-bar blues song following the chord progression chart above. Now, expand that 8 bars into 12 bars.**

   How about 16? Give it a title and see if you can come up with some lyrics.

5. **Make something atonal.**

   See if you can write atonal variations of well-known melodies such as "Old McDonald," "Yankee Doodle," or "Silent Night."

6. **Use chords atonally.**

   Develop Exercise 1 by adding chords.

7. **Get random.**

   Try writing random notes based on a rhythmic pattern. Use accidentals.

8. **Use imagery.**

   Write random notes based on a landscape or city skyline. Use accidentals.

9. **Be comprehensive.**

   Write a melody using all twelve semitones without repeating any tones.

10. **Branch out.**

    Write a different melody with the notes in the same series that you used in exercise 9.

# Part IV
# Orchestration and Arrangement

"Does anyone else feel the flute and cello part
is a bit too appasionato?"

## In this part . . .

We discuss just a few of the techniques used by composers to liven up a piece of music, including using multiple instruments and counterpoint. We also share with you information on breaking into the world of commercial music, writing electronic and experimental music, and some tips on how to write great songs with lyrics.

# Chapter 14

# Composing for the Standard Orchestra

*W*ouldn't it be nice to have an entire live ensemble on hand, at all times, to play their bits in your compositions as you write them? Well, most likely that's not going to happen. Most, if not all, of the times when inspiration hits, you're going to be all alone, and you're just going to have to figure out on your own what parts of your composition the violins should play, or the horns, or whether you should limit your composition to only one or two instruments.

Musicians that work with synthesizers and MIDI as their primary composition tools can easily fall into the trap of believing that what they're playing on the keyboard in front of them is easily replicable on live instruments, or with a live singer's vocals. You need to take a lot into account when writing for multiple live instruments and their players — such as allotting time for horn players to take a breath between phrases, the hand-span of a bass or guitar player, the range of a singer's voice — and if you don't take these factors into account, you're going to end up with a very frustrated group of musicians.

## Concert Pitch and Transposition

There is a reason why the piano is such a well-loved composition tool. Not only do the 88 keys of the piano contain virtually all the notes you will ever need to create a solid foundation for a full orchestral piece, but the entire piano is tuned to what is called concert pitch. *Concert pitch* simply means that when you hit a C note on the piano, you are actually playing a C. If you were to hold a guitar tuner up next to the piano while you hit the key, the tuner would read C. The end. According to current standards, middle C (C4) on the piano is a tone that vibrates at 261.63 Hz. A4, the A above middle C, is pegged at 440 Hz.

However, if you were to play a C on what is called a *transposing instrument*, you would get another note entirely, and this is where it can get confusing. For example, if you were playing a B flat clarinet, and the note on sheet music was notated C, you would actually be playing a B flat. If you were to play a written C on an E flat alto sax, you would actually be playing an E flat.

The easy answer for why transposing instruments are the way they are has as much to do with the convenience of musicians as historical tradition. Most instruments are too small to contain the 88 notes of a piano, so most instruments you'll deal with as a composer have only a fraction of the piano's tones available for use. Brass and woodwind instruments are built so that by depressing or releasing sequential valves, the musician either moves up or down to the next note of the scale. This scale is read as the C scale when the musician is playing alone, even if the instrument is actually tuned to the B flat or E flat or any other scale.

All instruments in both woodwind and brass families are designed this way, and because of this, a clarinetist can theoretically pick up a saxophone for the first time and, if he can blow strong enough to make the transition work, can soon play a song he or she is familiar with on the clarinet. This same musician can pick up an oboe or a flugelhorn or any other brass or woodwind instrument and make just as easy a transition. Depending on the instrument, there may be one or two extra or fewer buttons on the instrument's body, but the main notes — A, B, C, D, E, F, and G — will be there.

Back in the day, instrument designers had two choices: Either create a series of similarly shaped and sounding instruments tuned to the same key but with different fingerings, or create the same series of instruments with different tunings but with the same arrangement of fingerings. When you consider the basic physics of the matter, you can see that there is no way for a clarinet to have the same valve pattern of an oboe and sound the same, simply because one is much smaller than the other and therefore, the smaller one naturally has a higher pitch than the other. It's the difference between the high-pitched squeal that comes from air being forced through a tiny hose and the deeper-pitched squeal that comes through a bigger hose.

When a soloist on one of these instruments performs alone, there aren't a lot of pitch conflicts to worry about. However, when you get two or more different types of horns in the same room together, the differences in the instruments' set tunings become very obvious. In order to play together, each musician has to *transpose*, or move to a different key, up or down the necessary steps so that all of the instruments in the room are playing the same C.

In the old days, back when staff paper and especially sheet music was expensive, the members of an ensemble would all work off of the same piece of sheet music, and the individual musicians had to make the necessary transpositions in his or her head. These days, however, most sheet music for ensembles is individually tailored to match the parts each musician is to play. The burden of transposition is now carried solely by the composer/arranger, who writes out individual pieces for each musician/instrument in the corresponding pitch and key.

# Pitch Ranges of Transposing Instruments

In this section we discuss some of the more commonly used transposing instruments and how we can use them in our compositions. There are many, many more obscure and personalized instruments out there that fit into this transposing category as well, but we're just going to stick to the instruments you're most likely to work with.

Many modern electronic keyboards take into consideration a natural instrument's range. As we mentioned, not all instruments can play all the notes available on your standard 88-note keyboard, or even your smaller 54-note keyboard. This wasn't taken into consideration in some of the earlier samplers and MIDI keyboards, and therefore, the synth composer was presented with the concept of having a piccolo sounding four octaves lower than possible, or timpani percussion sounding seven octaves higher than available to the actual instrument. Possibilities like that are exciting if you're planning on only composing for synthesizers, but if you're going to be using the actual instruments at any point, you have to be familiar with the physical range of the instrument.

In addition, you have to keep in mind the physical capabilities of the performers you're working with. "Fats" Waller may have been able to pound out a chord spanning an octave-and-a-half on a regular basis, but most pianists would have to use two hands to do what he could easily do with one. Maynard Ferguson may have been able to blast out those upper register notes and make it sound easy, but your average trumpet player would probably split his or her upper lip trying to replicate his technique.

Transposing instruments are the ones you're going to have to think out the parts for the most when writing music, so let's get 'em out of the way. But first, a word about our notation. The first C found on the very farthest left of the keyboard is called C1, while the middle C—found three octaves higher — is called C4. That means it's the fourth C as you go up the keyboard. The G below middle C is called G3. The highest note on the keyboard is B8. We use this notation, along with illustrations, to discuss the pitch ranges of instruments in this chapter.

## Alto flute

This is the only flute that is a transposing instrument. Although every other flute is tuned to *concert pitch*, or the key of C, the alto flute is tuned to a G natural. This means that in order to write music for the alto flute, you need to transpose the music up a fourth from concert pitch. To hear a concert C, for example, your flutist would have to see an F on his or her sheet music.

The reason people pick up an alto flute to begin with is partly because the somewhat quieter instrument can play much lower notes than the concert flute, and partly because its very cool shape is irresistible to instrument connoisseurs — alto flutes (and bass flutes) are the ones that look like the end was bent in half by Superman.

Flute tones are sweet in character and blend well with other instruments. The flute's timbre (the distinct quality of its sound), pitch, and attack (how quickly an instrument sounds after playing a key, string, or what have you) are flexible, allowing a very high degree of instantaneous expressive control. This also makes the flute a great lead "singer" in an ensemble, as it's able to follow the lead lines you write quickly and distinctively.

The range of the alto flute is C4 (the G below middle C) through C7.

| To hear | Write |
|---------|-------|
| C | F |
| C♯/D♭ | F♯/G♭ |
| D | G |
| D♯/E♭ | G♯/A♭ |
| E | A |
| F | A♯/B♭ |
| F♯/G♭ | B |
| G | C |
| G♯/A♭ | C♯/D♭ |
| A | D |
| A♯/B♭ | D♯/E♭ |
| B | E |

## B flat trumpet

When you're writing parts for a B flat trumpet, you have to transpose the music a whole step up from concert. So if the composer wants the trumpet to sound a true C in concert pitch, he has to write the part out on the trumpet player's sheet music as D. This is true for all B flat transposing instruments. Just remember to write one whole tone higher than you want to hear. But for easy reference, have a look at the following table:

| To hear | Write |
|---------|-------|
| C | D |
| C♯/D♭ | D♯/E♭ |
| D | E |
| D♯/E♭ | F |
| E | F♯/G♭ |
| F | G |
| F♯/G♭ | G♯/A♭ |
| G | A |
| G♯/A♭ | A♯/B♭ |
| A | B |
| A♯/B♭ | C |
| B | C♯/D♭ |

The practical, comfortable range for most B flat trumpet players to perform within is between the B flat below middle C and the D two octaves above middle C, as seen in Figure 14-1.

**Figure 14-1:**
The B flat trumpet range, transposed to concert pitch.

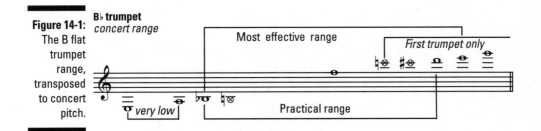

As you can see in Figure 14-1, there are certainly other notes that are available for the B flat trumpet player to use both above and below the most effective range, but unless you're very familiar with the capabilities of the performers you're going to use to play your compositions, for the majority of trumpet players out there it's best to try to stick within the effective range. The written range for B flat trumpet is F♯3 to E6.

The B flat trumpet is a loud and high-sounding instrument, best for punching out quick melody lines, which makes it a favorite for lead instrument in an ensemble. It is the "brassiest" of the brass instruments.

# B flat clarinet

The clarinet is perhaps one of the most misunderstood and misused instruments in the orchestra. Way too many people start off on the clarinet in the high school orchestra, only to ditch it as quickly as possible simply because they have no idea of the potential of the instrument. Although many other musical cultures have embraced the clarinet as the focal point of their ensemble — especially klezmer and Bulgarian folk music — most of us in the Western hemisphere think of Benny Goodman and Lawrence Welk when we think of the clarinet. Just pick up any Naftule Brandwein or, in a more recent context, Sex Mob or John Zorn record, and you'll hear how amazing this instrument can sound.

The clarinet is an extremely versatile instrument. It's got a great range, is built for speed, and is incredibly expressive. It has almost exactly the same musical range as a guitar (Figure 14-2), so it's very easy to play leads written for guitars on the clarinet, and vice versa.

The B flat clarinet is, of course, a transposing instrument tuned to B flat. To write music for it, you need to transpose the sheet music up a whole step from concert pitch. The written range for B flat clarinet is E3 to A6.

| To hear | Write |
| --- | --- |
| C | D |
| C♯/D♭ | D♯/E♭ |
| D | E |
| D♯/E♭ | F |
| E | F♯/G♭ |
| F | G |
| F♯/G♭ | G♯/A♭ |
| G | A |
| G♯/A♭ | A♯/B♭ |
| A | B |
| A♯/B♭ | C |
| B | C♯/D♭ |

**Figure 14-2:**
The B flat clarinet range, transposed to concert pitch.

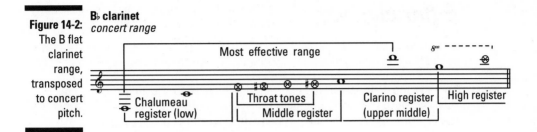

**B♭ clarinet**
*concert range*

Most effective range

Chalumeau register (low)

Throat tones
Middle register

Clarino register (upper middle)

High register

# B flat bass clarinet

The B flat bass clarinet is tuned just like the B flat clarinet, but it plays an octave lower. To write music for a bass clarinet, you need to transpose your sheet music up an octave plus a whole step. The written range is E2 to E5 (Figure 14-3).

| To hear | Write |
|---------|-------|
| C | D |
| C#/D♭ | D#/E♭ |
| D | E |
| D#/E♭ | F |
| E | F#/G♭ |
| F | G |
| F#/G♭ | G#/A♭ |
| G | A |
| G#/A♭ | A#/B♭ |
| A | B |
| A#/B♭ | C |
| B | C#/D♭ |

**Figure 14-3:**
The B flat bass clarinet range, transposed to concert pitch.

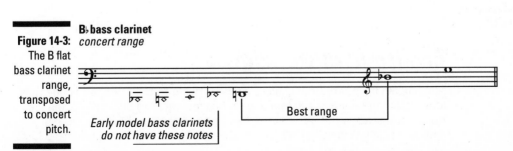

**B♭ bass clarinet**
*concert range*

Best range

*Early model bass clarinets do not have these notes*

## E flat clarinet

Sometimes called the "baby clarinet," the E flat clarinet is the highest-pitched of the clarinet family. It's the only clarinet tuned to an E flat instead of a B flat.

To write music for the E flat clarinet, you have to first transpose the music a diatonic sixth (six scale degrees) up and then down an octave — or down a minor third. Its written range is E3 to E6 (Figure 14-4).

| To hear | Write |
|---------|-------|
| C | A |
| C♯/D♭ | A♯/B♭ |
| D | B |
| D♯/E♭ | C |
| E | C♯/D♭ |
| F | D |
| F♯/G♭ | D♯/E♭ |
| G | E |
| G♯/A♭ | F |
| A | F♯/G♭ |
| A♯/B♭ | G |
| B | G♯/A♭ |

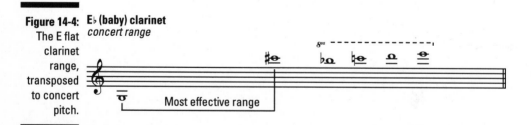

**Figure 14-4:** The E flat clarinet range, transposed to concert pitch.

E♭ (baby) clarinet
*concert range*

Most effective range

## English horn/cor anglais

The English horn, or cor anglais, is a close cousin to the oboe but is one third longer. Like the oboe, it's a double reed instrument, and because it's longer, its range extends a full fifth deeper than the oboe's. Its slightly flared bell makes for a more nasally timbre than the oboe, creating a sound that's a little like four parts oboe, one part trumpet.

The English horn is a transposing instrument built in the key of F. In order to write music for it, you need to transpose your music up a diatonic fifth (five scale degrees) from concert — to hear a concert C, the sheet music should read G. Its written range is B3 to G6 (Figure 14-5).

| *To hear* | *Write* |
|---|---|
| C | G |
| C♯/D♭ | G♯/A♭ |
| D | A |
| D♯/E♭ | A♯/B♭ |
| E | B |
| F | C |
| F♯/G♭ | C♯/D♭ |
| G | D |
| G♯/A♭ | D♯/E♭ |
| A | E |
| A♯/B♭ | F |
| B | F♯/G♭ |

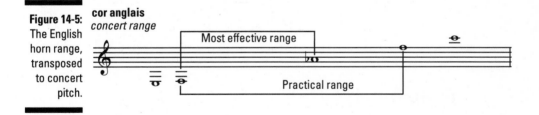

**Figure 14-5:** The English horn range, transposed to concert pitch.

# Flugelhorn

You ever see a fox hunt on the big screen or on TV? Perhaps you've partici-pated in a real live fox hunt yourself — in either case, you've heard the plain-tive call of the flugelhorn in action. The flugelhorn is built a lot like a cornet, but because the bell is a deeper funnel, the sound coming out of the flugel-horn is much richer and lower in pitch than its slightly tinny cousin. The flugelhorn is mellower and lower than the trumpet, kind of like a viola com-pared to a violin.

The flugelhorn is another B flat transposing instrument, with its easy-to-play range of F♯3 to E6 (Figure 14-6). Again, a composer would need to transpose the musical sections written for the flugelhorn up a whole step from concert.

| To hear | Write |
| --- | --- |
| C | D |
| C♯/D♭ | D♯/E♭ |
| D | E |
| D♯/E♭ | F |
| E | F♯/G♭ |
| F | G |
| F♯/G♭ | G♯/A♭ |
| G | A |
| G♯/A♭ | A♯/B♭ |
| A | B |
| A♯/B♭ | C |
| B | C♯/D♭ |

**Figure 14-6:**
The
flugelhorn
range,
transposed
to concert
pitch.

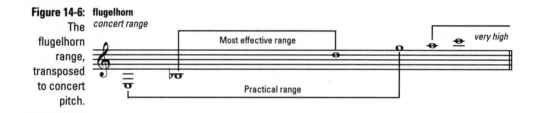

# French horn

French horns are just plain beautiful to look at, and just about everyone who writes for a horn section in a composition wants to use a French horn at sometime or another, probably because the visual idea of throwing one of those pretty instruments — which has more twists and turns than a bucket of brass spaghetti — into live arrangement is too tempting to resist.

Another nice thing about the French horn is, thanks to all those twists and turns in the piping, its ability to smoothly play music through over three octaves, whereas most brass instruments have not much more than a two-octave range.

However, although it's possible to play lots more notes on the French horn than on other horns, it's not an instrument built for speed. When writing music for the French horn, try not to use a lot of fancy ornamentation or quick parts for the player.

On the good side, the French horn is such a beautiful, pure-sounding instrument that there is nothing it doesn't blend well with. The French horn can just as easily fit in with a woodwind section as it can a brass section. The French horn is a transposing instrument set in the key of F, which means that to write music for the French horn, you have to transpose the music up a perfect fifth from concert pitch (Figure 14-7).

On paper, this is fabulously easy. Just remember that perfect fifths are located exactly two lines or two spaces on the staff above (or below) the originating note. If you're writing music for the French horn on a different instrument, such as the piano, just remember that perfect fifths are separated by seven half steps (black and white keys), or three whole steps and one half step.

| To hear | Write |
| --- | --- |
| C | G |
| C♯/D♭ | G♯/A♭ |
| D | A |
| D♯/E♭ | A♯/B♭ |
| E | B |
| F | C |
| F♯/G♭ | C♯/D♭ |
| G | D |
| G♯/A♭ | D♯/E♭ |
| A | E |
| A♯/B♭ | F |
| B | F♯/G♭ |

**Figure 14-7:**
Perfect fifths are easy to spot, being two lines or spaces apart.

The French horn's range is F♯3 to C6 (see Figure 14-8).

**Figure 14-8:**
The French
horn range,
transposed
to concert
pitch.

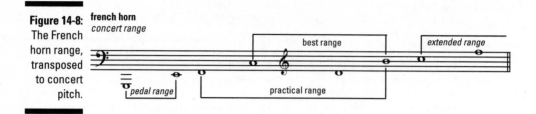

## Piccolo trumpet

The piccolo trumpet is smaller and capable of higher, brighter-sounding notes than the B flat trumpet. Thus it is used for more sprightly sounding musical sections. It's also (normally) a B flat transposing instrument, with the notes sounding a full octave higher than the B flat trumpet.

When writing music for the piccolo trumpet, you have two things to take into consideration: First, transpose the sheet music for the instrument a whole step up from concert. Second, the music is going to be played a full octave higher than middle C.

The written range for the piccolo trumpet is F♯3 to C6 (Figure 14-9).

| To hear | Write |
|---------|-------|
| C | D |
| C♯/D♭ | D♯/E♭ |
| D | E |
| D♯/E♭ | F |
| E | F♯/G♭ |
| F | G |
| F♯/G♭ | G♯/A♭ |
| G | A |
| G♯/A♭ | A♯/B♭ |
| A | B |
| A♯/B♭ | C |
| B | C♯/D♭ |

**Figure 14-9:**
Range for
the piccolo
trumpet,
transposed
to concert
pitch.

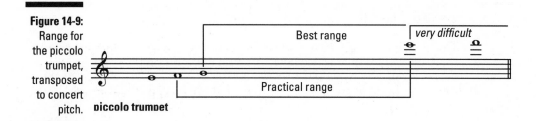

## Non-Transposing Instruments

With non-transposing instruments, what you write down on paper is the note you're going to hear. Hurray! The only thing you have to take into consideration, then, is the actual range of the instrument you're writing for — that, and the physical capabilities of the performers on the instruments.

### Concert flute

Usually reserved for solos because it is one of the quieter instruments of the orchestra, the concert flute is a high-pitched instrument with a beautiful, feminine tone that is instantly distinguishable from any other instrument. The instrument is easy for most flutists (or flautists) to play, which makes it a favorite with beginning band students who want to find an instrument with which they can quickly master the basics.

The flute's written range is C4 to C7 (Figure 14-10).

**Figure 14-10:**
Range for
the concert
flute.

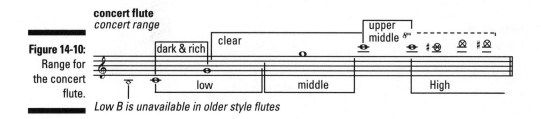

*Low B is unavailable in older style flutes*

## Bass flute

The bass flute looks almost exactly like a concert flute, except that the barrel is a little wider — just wide enough to drop the actual notes played a full octave lower. When composers write for the bass flute, they often write on the treble clef, a full octave higher that what will be played (Figure 14-11).

**Figure 14-11:**
Range for
the bass
flute.

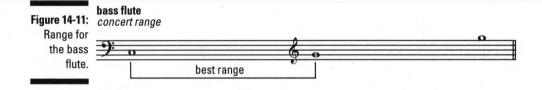

bass flute
*concert range*

best range

## Bassoon

You can just tell from the name of the instrument that the bassoon isn't some high-pitched squeaky thing. Nope, the bassoon is the beautiful fog horn of the orchestra pit.

Bassoons are notoriously tricky to play, so be kind and gentle when arranging music for your bassoonists. A great deal of wind has to be forced through the tiny metal tube that makes up the mouthpiece of the instrument, and playing the bassoon is akin to trying to blow up a great big beach ball via the tiny rubber valve.

The written range for the bassoon is B♭1 to E♭5 (Figure 14-12).

bassoon
*concert range*

**Figure 14-12:**
Range for
the bassoon.

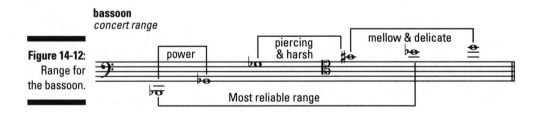

power

piercing
& harsh

mellow & delicate

Most reliable range

## Double bass/contrabass

The double bass, or contrabass, is the deepest-sounding bowed instrument of the orchestra. It may look like it belongs to the violin family of instruments (violin, viola, and cello), but it is actually considered to be the only surviving member of the *viola de gamba* family of instruments. Where members of the violin family have their strings tuned a fifth apart from one another, each string of the double bass is tuned to a fourth apart from the next.

The shape of the instrument itself is different than the violin/viola/cello — its "shoulders" are pinched in, rather than rounded out, and its body is longer and narrower overall than the other three instruments. As with the bass guitar in rock music, the double bass is the fulcrum of the orchestra, and the basic purpose of the contrabass is to hold down the bottom end of the composition.

The range of the double bass is E2 to G5 (Figure 14-13).

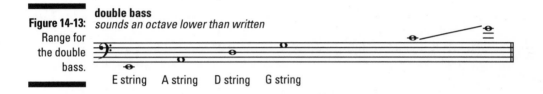

**Figure 14-13:** Range for the double bass.

**double bass**
*sounds an octave lower than written*

E string    A string    D string    G string

# Oboe

The double reed oboe family is considered to be the oldest family of woodwind instruments. Double reed instruments that looked a lot like the modern oboe were in use in Greece nearly 3,000 years ago, brought over by Egyptians who had used double reed instruments as much as a thousand years earlier than that. The direct ancestor of the oboe is credited as the *shawm*, which was probably introduced into Europe during the Crusades when the Saracen armies invaded and used this instrument in war as well as for dancing. The bore of the shawm is conical and wide, as is the double reed. The body is constructed from a single piece of wood with finger holes.

The oboe is considered a very special instrument by many composers, who relish its deep, rich, distinctive musical flavor and the way it mixes in with the rest of the woodwinds of the orchestra. The entire orchestra tunes to the A of the oboe, possibly because there isn't any practical way to tune an oboe.

Modern oboes are still made from African blackwood (grenadilla) and are made in three parts. Oboes are still handmade by expert craftsmen who are very secretive about the dimensions and the size of the apertures used in the construction. The double reed is made especially for oboes from cane which is grown on the east coast of Spain or the south of France and dried and aged for several years before being shipped to your local music store. There are, of course, synthetic reeds made for oboes today that most likely work just as well and are much cheaper, but many perfectionists still swear by the handmade ones from Europe.

The written range for the oboe is B♭3 to A6 (Figure 14-14).

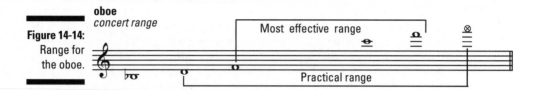

**Figure 14-14:**
Range for
the oboe.

# Orchestral harp

People have played some version of the harp for thousands of years. The pre-Hellenic (neolithic) Greeks left dozens of little marble *kouros* figures playing harps behind for future archeologists to mull over, while Egyptian artists painted florid murals depicting harpists playing in the royal court.

The notes of the harp range from C1 to G7, with each single string being a separate note. The harp is tuned to the scale of C, with each F string colored either black or blue and each C string colored either red or orange to ease navigation of the instrument.

The written range of the harp is C♭1 to G♯7 (Figure 14-15).

**Figure 14-15:**
Range for
the harp.

# Tenor slide trombone

The tenor slide trombone is another cool-looking instrument. It's the one with the long bar attached to the side of it that allows the performer to move fluidly from one note to another (or jerkily, depending on the piece or performer). The trombone is more powerful and brassy-sounding than the French horn, but its tone isn't as rich.

Because of its slide, it's possible for a trombonist to play both the whole and half steps possible on a piano, as well as the spectrum of tones in *between* those notes. However, most trombonists stay away from these *microtones* for the simple fact that most composers write their music on a standard staff, which doesn't allow for microtones.

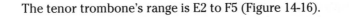

The tenor trombone's range is E2 to F5 (Figure 14-16).

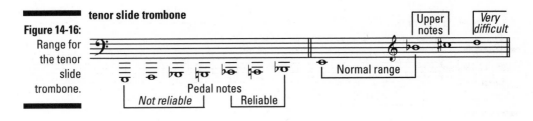

**Figure 14-16:**
Range for the tenor slide trombone.

# Viola

The viola was a favorite instrument of Johann Sebastian Bach, who appreciated the fact that its range extended lower than the violin's but higher than the cello's. All three instruments look almost exactly the same, with the main difference being, of course, size. The viola is placed on the shoulder and played with a bow, as is the violin. It is sometimes referred to as the *big fiddle*.

Prior to the 18th century, the viola was the most prominent member of the stringed instrument family. But it was supplanted by the violin when audiences began showing a preference to the brighter sound of the higher-pitched instrument.

The top string of the viola can sound a little squawky and nasally, so most composers try to stick to writing only for the lower registers when composing music for violas.

The range of the viola is C3 to A6 (Figure 14-17).

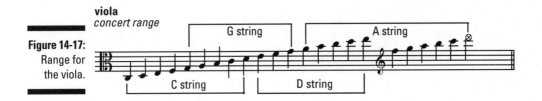

**Figure 14-17:**
Range for the viola.

# Violin

This is an instrument that needs no introduction. Due to its incredibly sweet tones and capabilities for speed and expressiveness, this stringed instrument is almost always a lead instrument in the orchestra. Violins sound wonderful whether being used for solos or performing en masse.

The violin's range is G3 to B7 (Figure 14-18).

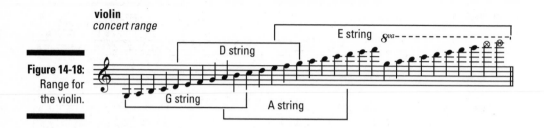

**Figure 14-18:**
Range for
the violin.

# Cello

The cello, also called the *violincello*, is the biggest and lowest-sounding member of the violin family. It's much too big and heavy to rest on the shoulder, so it's held between the performer's knees instead. (You never see a homeless person with a cello — which could mean either that cellists are some of the best-paid musicians out there, or that it's just not worth lugging the thing out into the rain for a few bucks a day.)

The cello can cover the entire range of the human voice, and consequently, a lot of "speaking" solo parts are written for it, in which the cello seems to be delivering the lyrical part of a song instead of an actual singer. As the bass voice in the string quartet, the cello is a grounding force in what might otherwise be a tinny and high-pitched ensemble.

The cello's range is C2 to E6 (Figure 14-19).

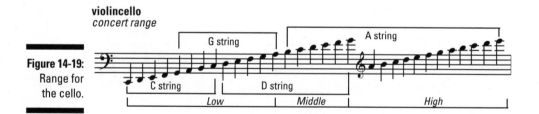

**Figure 14-19:**
Range for
the cello.

# Where they all are on the piano

Given that there's a good chance that you'll be composing your orchestral music on the piano, in Figure 14-20 we provide a handy chart to show you where these instrumental voices are laid out on the keyboard.

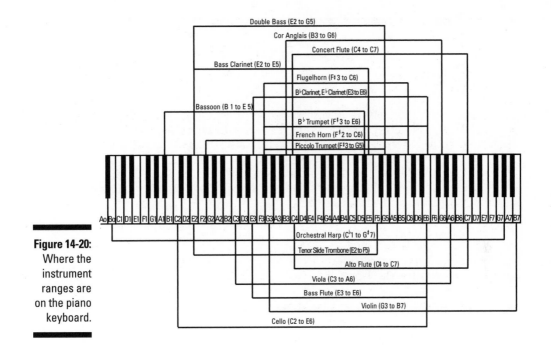

**Figure 14-20:**
Where the instrument ranges are on the piano keyboard.

# Getting the Sounds You Want

Getting the sound you want goes beyond choosing the right notes and instruments. As we have said in other places throughout this book, each instrument has a unique range of tonal colors and dynamic expressions available to it. Playing an instrument through a mouthpiece provides distinctly different possibilities and limitations, for example, than playing an instrument with a pick or a bow. Even though some symbols, such as dynamic markings and the notes themselves, are common to all instruments, each family of instruments also has its own additional symbolic language for expression.

Here we present some of these symbols and their explanations for the string instruments and the brass and woodwind instruments. Much more information can be acquired through the study of instrumental arranging. We won't go too deeply into this area for lack of space, but composition and arranging overlap each other so much that the line between them is blurry — when it can be seen at all. The melody you hear in your head played by the French horn probably already has a dynamic shape and a tonal quality before it ever gets written down. At any rate, the more specifically you can indicate what it is that you want to hear from the instruments, the more effectively you will be able to communicate your music to your audiences.

# Tips on transposing

Here are a few shortcuts to help you remember how to do the most common transpositions:

E flat instruments: Find the relative minor, make it major, then write in that key. This means that if you were writing a piece of music in the key of C, and you wanted to write a part for an E flat instrument, you would first find the relative minor of C major (A minor), then notate the music for the instrument in A major — that is, with three sharps in the key signature. All the notes in the music are then moved up a fourth, or three spaces and lines, from their original positions. Some E flat instruments include the contra-alto clarinet, the alto clarinet, the E flat clarinet, the alto saxophone, the baritone saxophone, the tenor horn, and the E flat tuba.

F instruments: Just add one sharp or subtract a flat from the key signature, and write the music in the resulting key. All notation is moved up one perfect fifth from where originally written. Some F instruments include the English horn, the basset horn, and the F alto saxophone.

B flat instruments: Move everything up one whole tone. Some B flat instruments include the B flat clarinet (soprano and bass), the soprano and tenor saxophone, the trumpet, the cornet, the flugelhorn, the euphonium, and the tenor trombone.

## *Stringed instruments*

Because the bow (or pick, in the case of the guitar) is such an important component of playing a string instrument, and because there are so many variations of expression produced by different bowing techniques, a set of symbols instructing the player as to which bowing techniques to use has been developed.

For example, a *down-bow* (pulling the bow down) can produce a more aggressive expression than an *up-bow* (when you push the bow up). This holds true for down and up picking on a guitar as well, and the guitar symbols are borrowed from the string symbols. Notice in Figure 14-21 that the down-bow looks like a picture of the heel end of the bow and the up-bow looks like the tip.

**Figure 14-21:**
Notation for bowed or picked instruments: down-bows and up-bows.

Any guitar player knows that playing several down picks in a row sounds different than picking up and down alternately (Figure 14-22).

**Figure 14-22:**
Notation for
playing the
guitar:
down-picks
and
alternate
picks.

The same thing holds true for a violin, but with a violin or other members of its family, a single stroke of the bow can produce a whole series of notes. This would be indicated by a *slur* (Figure 14-23).

**Figure 14-23:**
A violin slur
shows
which way
to bow
during the
slur.

In Figure 14-24, all four notes in the first half of the first measure are played with a single up-bow, the next two notes are down, the next two are up, and it ends on the downbeat of the following measure with a strong down-bow.

**Figure 14-24:**
Bows with
slurs on
the violin.

The slur indicates a legato style of connecting the notes. You could play the same first series of four notes on a single bow stroke, but separate them slightly. This is called *louré* (Figure 14-25).

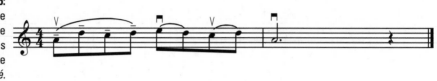

*Spiccato* is a fast, light staccato produced by bouncing the bow on the string (Figure 14-26).

Bouncing a group of notes on a single up- or down-bow is called *jetè* (Figure 14-27).

There are many more indications for string players. *Con legno* means to play with the wooden side of the bow; *Pizzicato* (sometimes shortened to *Pizz*) is an indication to pluck the strings; *Arco* means to bow normally.

For more information on stringed instrument notation, check out some of the many good books on the market.

## Brass and woodwind instruments

Grammy Award nominee and McNally-Smith College of Music instructor Mike Bogle has graciously provided simple guides to markings for brass and woodwind instruments, which we reproduce here as Figures 14-28 and 14-29.

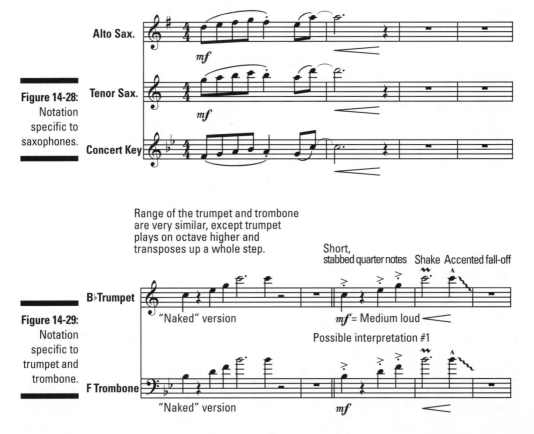

**Figure 14-28:** Notation specific to saxophones.

**Figure 14-29:** Notation specific to trumpet and trombone.

Remember that without some kind of indication of how you want a part to be played, you will probably spend a lot of time (and possibly a lot of money) figuring it out with the musicians. And nothing can shake your confidence more than the feeling that you don't have the right language to communicate your ideas to the musicians.

# Chapter 15

# Composing for the Nonstandard Orchestra

*In This Chapter*

▶ Getting to the bottom of basses

▶ Strumming along with guitars

▶ Squeezing out information on free reed instruments

*U*nless you've got great philharmonic connections, there's a really good chance that you won't be writing music for oboes and gigantic golden harps anytime soon. Even if you do have great philharmonic connections, you may still be more interested in writing pop music, or even jazz. The slower seeming, more somber-sounding instruments in an orchestra won't make many appearances in your music.

In that case, the instruments for which you'll want to know the ranges and qualities are the ones in the "nonstandard orchestra." This group includes basses (upright, acoustic, and electric), guitars (acoustic and electric), and the free reed family (accordions, concertinas, and harmonicas).

To your advantage as a composer, though, all of the following instruments used in the nonstandard orchestra are incredibly "quick" and expressive. A good solo line on a guitar can carry as much weight as a violin, while a bass guitar works as well as a bottom to your music as an upright bass or an oboe, but also has the ability to deliver complicated, quick musical lines that neither classical instrument can carry. Plus, all of the following instruments, with the exception of the harmonica and the concertina, have a huge range, so that you can play just about any piece of music written for the orchestra on just a couple of guitars and basses.

Therefore, when composing music for any of the instruments discussed in this chapter, you don't have to take nearly as much into consideration as you do with instruments in the standard orchestra. You don't have to worry about whether the line of music you're writing is too "quick" for a bass, guitar, or keyboard to pull off, because these instruments are all very fast and expressive. Range is another factor that fades into the background, as most of these instruments have as wide a range as anything else in the standard orchestra. The only thing you have to really think about is the sound of the instrument itself.

(Of course, many more instruments other than the ones we focus on in this chapter are to be found in popular ensembles, and most of them are covered in Chapter 14.)

# The Bass

The bass has a very important position in whatever ensemble it is placed in. In an orchestral setting, the *bass* — which would include cello, violincello, and double bass — is generally the lowest-sounding part of the orchestra, serving as counterweight to the higher-pitched instruments. It fills out a performance that might otherwise sound too high-pitched and tinny by giving a solid "bottom" to the musical piece.

In a jazz and pop ensemble, the bass serves as the *fulcrum*, or hinge-like supporting piece, of the band. The bass is just as much in charge of carrying the pulse or beat of the music as the percussion section is. As the instrument usually playing the tonic or fifth of whatever chord is happening, it's also in charge of carrying the key that the rest of the band is playing in. When it's time to make a chord change in a pop composition, often it's the bass line where this key change is most apparent.

## Upright bass

In the 1950s, the upright bass — also known as the *double bass* or *contrabass* — became a fixture in early rock and roll and, to this day, rockabilly music. In the 1960s, folk artists latched on to the idea of having the gigantic instrument in their ensembles, both for the visual aesthetics of the beautiful classical instrument as well as the nice, deep sound you could never get from the comparatively small body of a regular-sized acoustic or electric bass.

In pop and jazz music, the instrument's strings are plucked instead of bowed, which makes a world of difference in how the instrument sounds. It still has the same instrument range as noted in Chapter 14, but instead of sounding deep and sonorous, you get a lively vibrato that shakes you to your toes.

When you play it really fast, such as in rockabilly and bluegrass music, it can sound a lot like you're snapping loud, musical rubber bands (especially in the hands of an amateur). Put an upright bass in the hands of a really capable musician, such as, for example, Reid Anderson of The Bad Plus, and you have a sound that combines both the deep, resonating tones of the classical contrabass and the speed and tonal flexibility of a bass guitar.

# Electric bass guitar

The modern electric bass guitar is the smaller, handier offshoot of the family of big orchestral basses. In 1951, inspired by the success of the electric guitar, Leo Fender built the first commercially available electric bass guitar.

As it was designed to be electronically amplified, there was no longer any need to have a gigantic hollow body to amplify the sound, which meant that a guitar-sized solid body could be just as deep and loud as a contrabass. Further modifications to electronic pickups — coil, passive, active, hybrid, and humbucker — have led to the possibility of creating tones that range from the grittiest, dirtiest rock and pop to completely pure, clean notes, all on one instrument.

Generally, the four strings of the bass (electric, acoustic, and upright) are tuned E-A-D-G, one octave below the lowest four strings of the 6-stringed guitar. It has a range of E2 to G5 (the second E on the piano keyboard up to the fifth G). Five- and six-stringed basses have identical tunings to four-string basses, but they extend the instrument's range on the low end with a B string and/or increase its solo capabilities on the high end with a high C string.

However, because it is a stringed instrument, the possibilities of creating higher and lower tones by using alternate tunings, à la Richard Thompson or Nick Drake, are considerable.

# Acoustic bass

The acoustic bass is the mellow cousin of the electric bass, and, being born in the 1970s, is the youngest member of the bass family. The famous Ernie Ball — famous to people who buy guitar and bass strings and accessories, that is — invented it in California after hearing the *guitarrón* used in mariachi bands.

Nowhere is the difference between an electric and acoustic instrument as apparent as it is when you compare the electronic and acoustic basses. The acoustic bass lacks the driving power necessary for pushing a band along simply because the lowest notes of the instrument are not loud enough to adequately thump out the pulse of a song over the other instruments. It also lacks the wicked snap of the electric bass that characterizes so much funk and rock music. Even with an electric pickup in place to amplify the sound, an acoustic bass fails miserably as a punchy pop instrument.

What it is really good for, though, is accompanying a lead line of a song. In this setting, the rich sound of an acoustic bass serves to beautifully bottom out the high notes in an acoustic ensemble. Paired with an electric guitar, an amplified acoustic bass helps fill out the tinny-ness of a classic Danelectro or Rickenbacker. In an acoustic setting, the acoustic bass adds a feeling of weight and volume to an ensemble.

# The Guitar

With almost all instruments in the guitar family — except the ones with alternate, customized tunings — the strings are tuned to E, A, D, G, B, and E (with the low E tuned to the second E below middle C, and E4 being the E above middle C on the piano keyboard).

Guitar-like instruments have existed since ancient times, with one precursor to the modern design being a two-stringed version used by the Hittites in Syria around 1500 B.C. The first "real" guitars appeared around the 14th century in Spain. They had seven strings instead of six, with the first six tuned in pairs (each of the three pairs of strings was tuned to the same note) and the seventh its own note. (There was no standardized tuning in those halcyon days before rigid guitar theory, so musicians were actually free to tune their strings any way they wanted to.)

Over the next three centuries, strings were added, removed, and doubled as the guitar began to take its modern form. By the end of the 18th century, the double courses of strings were turned into single strings, and six differently tuned strings became the standard for the instrument. Guitar makers in the 19th century broadened the body, increased the curve of the waist, thinned the belly, and changed the internal bracing, while the wooden tuning pegs were replaced by longer-lasting modern machine heads.

As an instrument of classical music, the guitar came to prominence largely through the efforts of the Spanish composer Francisco Tarrega and the Spanish guitar virtuoso Andrés Segovia.

Using conventional tuning, with the strings tuned to EADGBE, the range of a guitar is E3 to E6, though the guitar sounds one octave lower than written. That means the guitarist reads the notes you write, but the sound that comes out is actually an octave lower.

Because the guitar does have such a wide playable range and is quick enough to render complicated melodic phrases on, it's often used as a lead instrument in an ensemble, especially in pop or rock music.

# Acoustic guitar

Because an acoustic guitar is not electrically amplified, one of its most important features is the wood it was made from. The soundboard of an acoustic guitar especially needs to be made of high-quality wood to get the best sound across.

This isn't to say that your average cheap plywood guitar is no good, but it's not concert quality. Laminated and plywood soundboards give a guitar great durability and might work just fine as practice instruments or in bar bands, but they don't have the natural vibrato or amplification that a fine wood soundboard gives a guitar. For example, a spruce soundboard gives a guitar a crisp, high-end sound and a loud bottom end, with the overall sound much bigger, fuller, and louder than any other type of soundboard. A cedar or redwood soundboard gives an acoustic guitar a beautiful ringing tone, and a mahogany soundboard produces a sweet, thick, mellow sound. Koa-based soundboards have a really strong mid-range, with thick, warm-sounding high and low tones.

Of course, once you stick an electric pickup on an acoustic or a microphone in front of it, its natural sound will be altered according to the quality of the amplifying device. Look for pickups and microphones that amplify the acoustic with the least amount of interference.

# Electric guitar

Although there were certainly inventive bluesmen who experimented with electrifying their git-boxes — such as Blind Willie Johnson and One String Sam — Adolph Rickenbacker is credited with inventing the first solid-body electric guitar in the 1930s. Les Paul tinkered with the design in the 1940s, and the electric guitar we know and love today was born.

The electric guitar was initially built for volume, so that it could both be heard over other instruments and crowds of noisy people. As the body of an electric guitar is completely solid and usually made of resin, there's no empty wood chamber for the sound of the strings to be amplified in. Therefore, when it is unplugged, the best sound you're going to get from it is about as noisy as a beehive. Plug that sucker in, though, and you've got an instrument that plays even faster and easier than an acoustic, due to the lower action (closer proximity of the strings to the guitar neck).

A large variety of types of music can be played on guitar, due to pickups and amplifiers that can either distort the guitar's natural sound to the crackly hiss of a surf guitar or reproduce it so clearly that it sounds like an amplified acoustic — all from the same guitar.

## Twelve-string guitar

A twelve-string guitar is much like a six-string guitar with one obvious exception — it has twelve strings instead of six. When you're tuning a twelve-stringed guitar, the best way to do so is to think of it as having six pairs of strings, instead of twelve individual strings.

The first (highest) two strings are *unisons*, tuned to an E; the second set are also unisons, tuned to the same B. The third pair of strings, G, are either unisons or an octave apart, depending on preference. For the three bass courses, D, A, and E, each pair is tuned an octave apart.

The effect of this tuning gives the twelve-string guitar a nice, full, bright-sounding ring, while the doubled treble strings sound fuller and richer than on a six-string. This is because the unisons are not exactly unisons, and the octaves not precisely octaves, which gives the instrument a natural chorus effect — the fuller sound coming from the slight interference between similar but not exactly identical tones.

## Steel guitar

Plenty of guitars have lots of shiny metal on them, either for structural reinforcement, amplification, or decoration, but the real qualifier of what makes a steel guitar a *steel guitar* is that steel guitars are played by sliding a metal bar along the neck while picking. The effect of this is that the notes sound like they're being bent from one pitch to the next, very smoothly and twangy, like the stuff Hawaiian crooner Don Ho was famous for.

There are many types of steel guitars, but the most popular ones are the *lap steel* (or Hawaiian) guitar, the *Dobro*, and the *pedal steel*.

The lap steel is held on your lap — just like the name implies — with one hand moving the *steel*, a kind of sliding mechanism, up and down the neck, and the other hand plucking out the tune, either with a pick or with fingers.

A Dobro looks a lot like a regular guitar, except that the neck is much thicker and stronger, and a much thicker gauge of string is used on the guitar to further amplify this already fairly loud instrument.

A pedal steel guitar is set on a stand and looks like one or two guitar necks, minus the body, mounted on a box. Pedal steels also can have as many as ten strings per neck.

Steel guitars are not tuned like conventional guitars, either, and each kind of steel guitar has its own specific tuning, which can also vary from performer to performer. Chords are formed with a solid steel slide instead of your hand, so steel guitars are usually tuned to an open chord, so that only bar chords have to be formed, such as an open G (D, G, D, G, D, lowest string to highest), an open A (E, C#, E, A, C#, E), a high G (G, B, D, G, B, D), a high A (A, C#, E, A, C#, E), a C6 (C, E, G, E, C, A), and so on.

Mucking around with higher tunings like those can really screw up the neck of a regular guitar (and snap a few strings), hence the additional reinforcement of the neck and the higher gauge of guitar string used on steel guitars.

# Free Reed Instruments

The *free reed* family consists of accordions, concertinas, and harmonicas. According to Chinese legend, the first known free reed instrument, the *cheng*, was created around 3000 B.C. when a scholar named Ling Lun disappeared into the mountains of China in search of the phoenix. When he returned, he had not captured the phoenix itself, but *had* captured its song for mankind.

The cheng, which is still in very limited use today in traditional Chinese ensembles, is shaped to resemble the phoenix and has between 13 and 24 bamboo pipes, a small gourd which acts as a resonator box and wind chamber, and a mouthpiece. It's the first instrument known to demonstrate the free reed principle, which basically means that wind moves over a set of reeds in either direction to create a specific pitch.

Free reed instruments are different from woodwind and certain brass instruments, which also have reeds and use pressurized air to produce noise but only produce a pure sound when the air is blown through the mouthpiece. You don't suck in through a clarinet's mouthpiece to play music, but you can suck air through a harmonica or accordion bellows to produce notes that sound just as good as when you blow the air out. (Over the centuries, the cheng evolved into the small, box-like *sheng*, or Chinese mouth organ, which was the direct inspiration for the European mouth organ, or harmonica.)

## The harmonica

There are two types of harmonicas, one which belongs in the family of free reed instruments, and one that doesn't. The one that doesn't is the one that first bore the name *harmonica*. None other than Benjamin Franklin invented the *glass harmonica*, which was a much more complicated version of the graduated glass bowls and champagne glasses that one would rub a wet finger along the rim of to produce a clear, ringing tone. Franklin's harmonica was a series of shallow glass basins of different sizes fixed onto a spindle that would continuously rotate. To produce music, one would simply wet one's finger and touch the basin that matched the pitch you wanted to hear.

The harmonica that we all know and love today is not this bulky and possibly dangerous instrument. The free reed harmonica was originally invented in Germany and England almost simultaneously in the 1820s. Successively higher tones of the scale are produced by alternately blowing or sucking air through the mouthpiece.

A harmonica's range is limited according to its size (from little tiny 6-note instruments to orchestral harmonicas, which can be made to the musician's specification), simply because the instrument is very small. Generally, though, most harmonicas are designed to play 19 consecutive scale notes, with each kind of harmonica tuned to a specific scale.

# The accordion

The first version of the accordion was an 1820 model called the Handäoline, invented in Germany. Nine years later, the first real accordion, with ten melody buttons and two bass buttons, was patented by Cyril Demian in Vienna. Later versions added more buttons, enabling players to produce a wider range of notes and chords. The *piano accordion*, called so because it has a piano keyboard along one side, and a series of buttons on the other, was developed in the 1850s.

The piano accordion is almost universally acknowledged to have one of the best education systems on any instrument. The *stradella bass system* (the buttons), when combined with the piano keyboard, requires players to develop a knowledge of both the chromatic sequence of pitch as on the piano keyboard and also the chord relationships and chord types as arranged in fifths on the buttons. This makes it unique among all musical instruments, having both single notes and preformed chords available at one time.

The instrument is played, of course, by drawing (stretching) and pushing (compressing) the *bellows*, causing air to pass over the metal reeds. This airflow makes the reeds vibrate, which produces different pitches.

# The concertina

The concertina was officially developed in 1830 by Sir Charles Wheatstone after several years of building prototypes, a few of which still exist, such as the *symphonium*. Its fully chromatic range was suited to, and for a while extremely popular for, classical pieces, with its fast action lending it nicely to "party pieces" such as "The Flight of the Bumble Bee." Nowadays there are two main kinds of concertina: the English and the Anglo.

A typical English concertina has 48 buttons, with each button assigned the same pitch no matter which direction the bellows are moved. The English concertina is preferred for pieces with vocal accompaniment.

The anglo concertina comes mainly in 20-button and 30-button varieties, and like the harmonica each button can produce two notes, depending on whether the air is blowing or sucking. The 20-button anglo is more or less confined to playing in two keys only, typically C and G. The 30-button model adds incidentals, enabling the player to venture into other keys, such as D and F. The anglo is popular in folk music, especially Irish traditional music.

Accordion and concertina ranges depend on both the size of the instrument, the key it's set in, and how many buttons are present. A full piano accordion, such as a classical Wurlitzer, has a range of around six octaves.

# Chapter 16

# Composing for Multiple Voices

* * * * * * * * * * * * * * * * * * * * * * * * * * * * * * * * * * * * * * * * * * * *

*In This Chapter*

▶ Telling stories through music

▶ Writing parallel harmony parts

▶ Dealing with independent voices

▶ Dissecting the elements of musical tones

▶ Going over some do's and don'ts

▶ Exercising your multiple voice composition

* * * * * * * * * * * * * * * * * * * * * * * * * * * * * * * * * * * * * * * * * * * *

*I*t's not always enough to just write a good melody and have some chords playing behind it as accompaniment. Sometimes you can create more interest in a piece of music by having more than one sound moving in a melodic fashion at one time.

What we mean by this is that along with that flute melody and the harp arpeggios behind it, you may feel inclined to add a melodic accompaniment from some other instrument. Maybe it's another flute, or it could be a vocal, a clarinet, or whatever works for you. This idea of multiple melodic voices opens up a lot of creative territory and presents new challenges of its own.

## Story Lines and Instrumentation

One of the creative territories that you open up when considering more than one melodic voice in your composition is the ability to use instrumental choices as characterizations in your music. In his well-known orchestral composition, *Peter and the Wolf*, Sergei Prokofiev uses instruments to directly represent specific characters in his story. For example, the duck is an oboe, the bird is a flute, the cat is a clarinet, and the wolf is three ominous-sounding French horns.

This use of specific instruments playing certain motifs to indicate certain ideas and characters is fairly common. Another example of specific characterizations (sometimes called *leitmotifs*) is to be found in the song "Tubby the

Tuba" by Paul Tripp and George Keinsinger. In this composition, several instruments take on personalities as the Tuba seeks something more melodically expressive than the usual oom-pah, oom-pah.

You don't have to be as direct and literal as Prokofiev or Tripp-Keisinger with your characterizations, but you can definitely choose specific instruments to convey moods, have dialogs, create contrast, and generally tell an emotional story. The story doesn't need to have specific characters attached to definite instruments.

When writing for multiple voices, whether you are telling a specific story or being totally abstract, you are always establishing and developing relationships within your music. Just as in a conversation, multiple melodic voices in a musical composition can represent different forces in your music. For example, you could assign each of the following things to different instruments:

- ✔ Agreement
- ✔ Discourse
- ✔ Argument
- ✔ Playfulness
- ✔ Conflict
- ✔ Confusion
- ✔ Chaos

A storyline can form in the imagination of each listener. You don't have to provide anything but the music.

# Writing Multiple Harmony Lines

One way to get two or more voices to work together is to keep them harmonically and rhythmically aligned. This technique is called *parallel harmony*, but that term can be deceptive. There are times when voices harmonized in parallel do not exactly move together in perfectly synchronized motion. The idea, rather, is to stay within the *tonality* of the piece and observe the same rhythmic phrasing without the parts running across each other, away from each other, or towards each other.

Notice how the last three notes in the second part of Figure 16-1 don't move parallel to the first part. If they did, we would lose the tonal relationship between the two parts.

**Figure 16-1:**

**Figure 16-1:**
Parallel
harmony
lines don't
have to be
always
perfectly
parallel.

Another idea might be for one voice to move and the other to stay a little more stationary. This is known as *block harmony*. In Figure 16-2, we are still using the same rhythmic phrases for both voices. (We will break free from this later.)

**Figure 16-2:**
In block
harmony,
one voice
moves
around
among the
notes more
than the
other.

You could also choose to harmonize the second voice by moving it obliquely, or in a contrary direction (Figure 16-3).

**Figure 16-3:**
Two
harmonic
lines can
also move
in totally
different
directions.

Ideas such as these can work well if your intention is to convey rhythmic and tonal *inter*dependence between the two voices. In these examples, the voices are basically married by the rhythmic phrases they share. Even when they move in opposite directions they still feel closely connected.

When writing parts like this, the tonal blend of the instruments you choose is critical. If the instruments have too strong of an independent tonal quality, their combination can spoil the marriage presented by the musical composition, unless they play in unison, in octaves, or in larger instrumental sections.

# Independent Voices

Sometimes the feeling you want to convey in your music is one of two tonally related, but rhythmically independent melodic ideas. In a case like that you might be weaving two entirely different melodies together — or the same melody at different times. You can use instruments with contrasting tonalities or ones that blend well for this sort of thing.

One way to create this sense of independence is to have both voices play variations of the same melody, but stagger the starting points. This creates an interlaced, tapestry-like effect, as seen in Figure 16-4.

**Figure 16-4:**
Same melodic lines, different starting points.

One of the challenges of this "staggered" type of approach is the danger of becoming too hopeful that your entire melody will hold up to harmonic scrutiny when it overlaps itself. You may find that there are some dissonances to be resolved by altering a few notes in one or the other melody line from time to time.

By the way, the example in Figure 16-6 has a few tonality "don'ts," which we get into later in this chapter.

The example shown in Figure 16-5 is based on this idea of overlapping melodies, but voice 2 has been rewritten to retain the same feel and shape as voice 1, without committing so many harmonic and compositional blunders. You will notice, if you play this piece, that the harmonic choices have a few different, unexpected turns in them. Some accidents are fortuitous.

**Figure 16-5:**
Overlapping melodies are cleaned up this time for tonality's sake.

 The idea is to not settle for poor harmonic choices just because they are easy. A fancy, dissonant moment can be a charming curiosity that you want to defend *because* it is a little different. But don't be afraid of applying a little thought to these moments before you decide on keeping them.

You could also use the same or similar melody for the second voice, but change it rhythmically. Maybe slow it down and stretch it across more measures than the first voice's melody. All of the tools and techniques found in the chapters on melodic composition are available to you to use on any or all of your multiple melodic voices. You just have to be aware of the harmonic and rhythmic relationships that exist between parts.

If you can figure out what your structural underlying harmony and melody are, you should be able to resolve the moments where your melodies uncomfortably collide. Learn to apply enough elbow grease to turn unwanted chaos and dissonance into something that makes sense. You may have to think about it a bit and try a few ideas out — but hey, that's music composition.

On the other hand, sometimes the accidental surprises generated by overlapping melody lines provide unique opportunities for harmonic development. Dissonance isn't always a bad thing. Don't just throw things out without considering them. Remember that surprises and departures from the expected can become fulcrums in your composition that can lead you into new key modulations and new melodic interactions. Sometimes the hardest thing to do is to find somewhere for your composition to "go." There are few more effective and natural sounding transitions than those that evolve from your melodies' interactions with themselves.

# Counterpoint

Strictly speaking, we have already been working with counterpoint in the last few examples. *Counterpoint* is when two or more melodies with different rhythmic phrases occur at the same time. If and when they bump into each other, they share tonality. Fugues are good examples of counterpoint. J. S. Bach's two-part and three-part inventions are well worth listening to in this regard. Prior to Bach, most music of the 15th and 16th century was contrapuntal and counter-melodic. Tonal music didn't really take hold until a little later.

When working with counterpoint, you don't have to restrict yourself to a single motif being worked at different times and places in several voices. You can introduce entirely different melodies for each voice. Later, you can switch them or develop them in any way you like.

One musical school of thought works on the premise that in music there *are only melodies*. What we call chords are just groups of melody notes that happen to be played together. This can be a good compositional approach. You can just write several melodies that work together. At places where several melody notes sound together, your music will arrive at some tonal definition that could be called a chord, but you don't have to think in terms of chords, necessarily.

Figure 16-6 shows an example of two different melodies working together to create a very definite sense of tonality. You can hear the underlying chord progression, even though there are never more than two notes sounding together at the same time.

Back in the 17th century, the English composer Henry Purcell wrote several pieces of music called *catches*, which were basically extended "rounds." Most of these catches were drinking songs whose lyrics were usually about sex, drinking, and/or music ("sex, drugs, and rock and roll" has been around longer than you may think). The catches would start with a voice singing a melody. After eight or sixteen measures, another voice would start at the beginning, as the first voice continued along. Another eight or sixteen measures later, a third voice would start. The actual melody would keep changing over the entire piece, and the tonality of the piece would remain intact even when the melody overlapped itself.

**Figure 16-6:**
Two different, independent melodies can define tonality with only two notes playing at a time.

Another way to express this idea is to just write chords and derive your melodies from them as we did in Chapter 8 with non-chord tones. There is no reason why you couldn't extract a melody from the upper chord tone, another from a middle chord tone, and so on. They don't have to have the same rhythmic phraseology.

When combining voices, it's important to really consider the way each tone combines with every other tone. So let's take a little stroll through musical tones themselves.

# The Five Elements of a Musical Tone

No matter what sound you are using in your composition, there are five ingredients that give it its identity. It doesn't matter if you are using synthesizers, orchestral or folk instruments, or found sounds — the five ingredients are always there.

Knowing these ingredients may help you to decide what sounds you want to write for, or it might help you to find or create the appropriate synthesizer sounds for your piece. The five elements of a musical tone are as follows:

- ✔ Pitch
- ✔ Duration
- ✔ Intensity
- ✔ Timbre
- ✔ Sonance

# Pitch

*Pitch* refers to the particular note that is being sounded. Differences in pitch are caused by differences in *frequency*, or how many times a second a string vibrates back and forth, for example. In the U.S., 440 *hertz* (vibrations per second) equals the note we call A. There are other A's as well, of course. The A that is an octave lower is 220 hertz, an octave higher is 880 hertz, two octaves higher is 1760 hertz, and so on. Pitches are indicated by the notes' position on the staff.

# Duration

*Duration* is the length of the note, or how long its sound lasts. A half note has a longer duration than a quarter note. The duration of a note can be affected by the acoustics of a room. If the room has a lot of reverberation, it will increase the duration of the notes. They will hang in the air awhile after the musician has stopped playing them.

# Intensity

Changes in *intensity* are indicated in music with dynamic markings such as *pp*, *mf*, *f*, and so on. Intensity is not always the same as loudness or volume. Something can be sung or played with intensity and not necessarily be loud, though the two concepts are connected.

# Timbre

Pronounced "tamber," *timbre* is the harmonic content, or tone color, of the musical tone. It is caused by the combinations of *overtones* that naturally sound along with the *fundamental* pitch that was written for the instrumentalist to play. These combinations of overtones — also known as *harmonics* or *partials* — provide the "fingerprint" of each different instrument. The reason a flute sounds different from an oboe, even though both are playing the same pitch, is because each of these instruments has a different mixture of overtones, or harmonic content, inherent in its sound.

Really, the difference between an "Ah" vowel sound and an "Ooh" vowel sound is nothing more than a difference in harmonic content or timbre (all else being equal, of course). Most instruments have a *timbral palette* that includes many shades of tone color. Part of the study of playing an instrument is learning to control and draw from this palette. The voice has the most intuitively controlled variety of all the instruments in the timbre department.

## Sonance

We are used to thinking of *resonance* (re-sonance) as something that continues to sound (re-sound), so we can think of *sonance* as a sound that is there and then gone, sounding only once. These brief sounds are also called *transients*. An example of sonance could be the noise that a guitar pick makes as it starts a string in motion, or the little spitting sound at the beginning of a trumpet note. The hammers of a piano, the scratching of a viola bow, the consonants and breathing noises of a singer are more examples of sonance. Without these noises, the instruments would sound very different indeed. Though sonance carries no pitch content, it is easy to see how important it is as a component of music.

When writing for multiple voices, always have these elements in the back of your mind. These five elements are all we have to work with in the universe of music. If you can control these elements in your compositions, you will find a vast creative playground to explore. You will be better able to choose which instruments you want to be playing which parts, and you will also have a better idea of how to substitute synthesizer sounds for real ones.

If you design your synthesizer sounds to replace the timbre, sonance, intensity, duration, and pitch characteristics of an orchestral instrument, instead of trying to imitate it directly, you will come up with some very interesting sounds.

# Some Do's and Don'ts

As you may have noticed, we like to encourage you to break rules from time to time, but you can save yourself a lot of aggravation and avoid sounding amateurish if you at least learn to observe a couple of rules for writing for multiple voices.

## Don't write more than three independent melodies at one time

If your intention is to create a sense of chaos and leave your listeners confused, then have at it — but it is almost impossible for a listener to follow four completely independent melody lines. Even in string quartets it is common for some instruments to provide parallel or block harmony while the others move independently. Often one instrument will *tacet* (rest through a number of measures) while the others carry on their complicated conversation.

## Don't cross melody lines over each other

This is almost never a good idea, especially when you are writing multiple voices for the same instrument, such as for two or more singers. This rule introduces the concept of *voice leading*. Good voice leading ensures that your melodies, chord voicings, and harmonic movements maintain a logical relationship. Introducing unmanageable elements to the tonality of your piece can completely upset your compositional blend and balance. If you want to learn more about voice leading, pick up any good book about arranging.

## Do be deliberate in the use of octaves and unisons

Often when you are writing for multiple voices, you will find that you have given the same note to two voices quite accidentally in the middle of some harmony. Momentarily stepping on the same pitch can weaken the harmonic movement that you were developing before that point. On the other hand, unisons and octaves have strengths of their own. Be observant and be intentional. This is a common area where young composers make mistakes.

## Do consider tessitura

*Tessitura* is a term used to describe the average range of a musical part or piece. It is also used to describe the range of an instrument. If a part is written in a *high* tessitura for a vocal or a wind instrument, the part will take on a higher energy level. Writing in a *lower* tessitura generates a more relaxed attitude, with less dynamic range. When writing for multiple voices, dynamic ranges will actually vary quite a bit if the instruments' parts aren't placed properly within the instruments' tessitura.

# Exercises

For the following exercises, and just in general, it might be a good idea to have a small, easy-to-use, convenient recording device. The quality isn't so important. A cassette recorder or direct-to-CD recorder would be fine. Recording one melody and playing or singing a second melody along with it as you listen back can be very helpful. If you have a computer music recording program, you can make your melody loop as you try different things out.

1. **Write a short melody of four to sixteen measures using only I, IV, and V chords.**

   Now add a parallel harmony that stays within the tonality of the piece. Notice the places where the harmony has to move (or not move) differently from the melody in order to keep peace with the tonality of the music.

2. **Write a two-part block harmony for a familiar song, or for the melody you wrote for Exercise 1.**

   Try to write parts with the least amount of movement possible. Move them only when harmony notes are doubling the melody (unisons are not permitted in this exercise).

3. **Come up with a simple chord progression and see if you can write two distinct melodies that work with the chords. Try to fit them together.**

4. **Take a single melodic motif and see how many ways you can weave it around itself.**

   Change registers, keys, and rhythmic phrasing as much as is required to make a good fit. You might want to try this one with a friend. One of you could sing or play the motif one way, while the other experiments with the possibilities.

5. **Try to write a harmony to one of your favorite melodies that moves in different directions and at different times than the melody.**

6. **Pick your favorite exercise from this chapter and write a third melodic part using any technique that you have learned.**

# Chapter 17

# Composing Commercial Music and Songs

*L*et's face it: Everybody's got to make a living.

Sure, in a perfect world, every talented musician would be able to survive comfortably off of writing pretty love songs and waltzes. But we all know for a fact that that is rarely the case.

Most musicians who make a living off of their music don't do it through just writing songs. The music world is full of incredibly talented studio bassists, guitarists, and drummers with little name recognition outside of the studio. There are oodles of technically gifted DJs and electronic musicians who make their real income composing jingles for car commercials.

In the case of the band Stereolab, for example, they made more money from having one of their songs used in a Volkswagen commercial than they did for all the albums they had released for nearly a decade prior to the commercial.

# Composing for Film

Probably the most lucrative career that a music composer can pursue is composing for the silver screen. This endeavor is complex, challenging, and fraught with competition. The film composer must have an understanding of synchronization and editing; must be able to musically conjure a wide variety of colors and moods; must be able to work with a wide variety of deadlines, timetables, attitudes, and personalities; and must be adept at switching back and forth from the computer to the orchestra, from the scene to the score, and back again.

Fortunately, over the past five years or so, opportunities have grown for different approaches to composition for film. It wasn't that long ago that almost everyone writing music for film was trying to create sensationalistic scores. Think of *Star Wars* and *Jurassic Park*, for examples. Almost every film score sounded like Gustav Holst's *The Planets*. It was pretty hard to find a film score that didn't rely on sheer bombast and magnitude.

But since then we have had very successful movies with much more underplayed music tracks. Think of *The Life Aquatic* or *Napoleon Dynamite*. These examples show that a simple score can not only be effective, but can also take on a life of its own. You can expect this trend toward variety to continue as audiences become bored with the repetition of one or two styles. And with greater exposure to foreign films, the influences increase — listen to the music in *Water*, *Frieda*, or *Kung Fu Hustle*.

When composing for film, there is rarely an instance when you can use a piece of music you previously composed to fit a scene. Almost all music for film has to be written specifically for the scene. Because film scores often rely on and return to one or two main themes, you may find a phrase or a motif in your "saved bits" folder that would be appropriate — but you will have to make your composition fit perfectly into the exact amount of time required by the individual scene. You can't just awkwardly cut from one musical idea to another without regard to the musicality of the cut itself.

There is an old saying in this business: "You can teach someone to edit music, but you can't teach someone to edit musically." So when the film you are working on cuts from a tender love scene to an intense car chase scene, the music has to tell the director's story without being clumsy or drawing too much attention to itself.

If an independent film is being produced in your area, you might be able to put together a demo of your work to present to producers, directors, and filmmakers for consideration. However, you will probably have to do a lot of work for free at first. Be sure that you retain ownership of all of your copyrights and publishing if you are not being paid handsomely for your work (see the nearby sidebar on copyrighting for more information on how to do this).

## Copyrighting your work

We've all heard of the "poor man's copyright," which is when you fold a print copy of your composition into thirds and mail it to yourself so that the post office's dated cancellation mark is printed directly on the back of the paper. Well, the "poor man's copyright" is not actually valid in U.S. courts. It was overturned in a 1976 copyright revision.

Whenever intellectual property is put in a tangible medium, meaning it's written down or recorded, it's automatically copyrighted as of that moment. The author now has the six basic rights that copyright gives: 1. the right to reproduce, 2. the right to make derivative works, 3. the right to distribute, 4. the right to perform, 5. the right to display publicly, and 6. the right to perform via digital transmission.

One good thing to do with your material is to register it with the U.S. Copyright Office. This sounds imposingly legal and possibly very expensive, but really, it's neither. It's a very simple process that could possibly save you from a lot of future hassles in court.

To register your musical work with the U.S. Copyright Office, you first need to download "Form PA" from the Copyright Office's site at www.copyright.gov. After filling out this form, put it, along with a non-returnable audio recording of your work to be copyrighted or a lead sheet or sheet music of the material, and a check for $45 into a package. Copies should be legible, and both words and music on the recording should be clear and audible. The title of the composition should be clearly written on the recording and/or sheet music.

Send the package to:

Library of Congress
Copyright Office
101 Independence Avenue, S.E.
Washington, D.C. 20559-6000

This Copyright Office process serves as a date/depository for intellectual property; however, just because it's filed with the Library of Congress does not mean you're not infringing on anyone else's copyright either. Basically, they all go to a storage warehouse and wait for authors to file copyright-infringement lawsuits. Then they go dig it up for the courts and look at the time stamps of the submitted original.

# *Working with time code*

Film and video, as you know, are made up of a series of individual frames that flash by so quickly that we don't notice the individual frames at all, but see motion instead. Nonetheless, all of us have paused our DVD players and seen what an individual frame looks like. It just looks like a still photograph.

Imagine a sudden cut in a movie from a tender love scene to a car chase. There is what is known as a *time code address* for the exact frame where the cut takes place. It might look something like: 1:04:28.13. This means one hour, four minutes, twenty-eight seconds, and thirteen frames. A time code address is also referred to as the *SMPTE time* (Society of Motion Picture and Television Engineers).

Knowing this, you would have a couple of choices in deciding what to do with the music for that cut. You could

- ✔ Cut the music from the love scene and jump in with chase music.
- ✔ Use the same music for both scenes.
- ✔ Fade the love scene music out while fading the chase scene music in (crossfade).
- ✔ Decide not to use music at all for one of the scenes.
- ✔ Compose a piece of music that makes a musical transition from one mood to another at exactly 1:04:28.13.

There are probably other choices, but these are the most obvious ones to us.

If you switch music at the scene change, you will have to be careful in order for the transition to sound natural and musical. This means that you will have to choose a tempo and a starting *time code address* for the first piece that will land you on the scene change at a musical point — like the first beat of the 17th measure, or some other musical accent point. This is where computers come in mighty handy. If you know the exact length in hours, minutes, seconds, and frames of each scene to be scored, and you have a general idea of your tempo, you can slightly alter the tempo so that you come out at a good musical transition point at the exact frame you want.

## *Working with proxy movies*

You will be watching the movie and "shuttling" it back and forth — continuously stopping and rewinding the film, or fast-forwarding it in order to get a feel for the overall film or just a single section you want to score — as you come up with your musical ideas. The movie is loaded into your computer software along with your music. You don't really need to work with a high-resolution copy of the film, so it is a good idea to request a proxy movie.

A *proxy movie* is a copy of the movie made at lower resolution. Lower resolution means lower quality, but high-resolution movies require a lot of processing power from your computer, and you want to save the processing power for your musical compositions. Later, after you export your work onto the proxy movie, your music can be transferred over to the high-res version of the movie. Proxy movies have all the same content as the high-res version as far as scenes and SMPTE addresses are concerned, they just have smaller file sizes so you can work faster.

# Composing for Video Games

Composing music for video games is another exciting way to go as a composer. The music from the *Legend of Zelda* series may be some of the most recognizable instrumental music of the decade. Currently music composition for video games relies heavily on MIDI. There have been a few notable exceptions, but in general video game developers put music fairly low on the list of things to allocate game memory for. Gaming is about the game play. On the other hand, the wrong music can really hurt a game's popularity, so game developers do care about it. The music gives the game an important part of its character.

Whether you are or aren't a gamer, you should study the way music is used in games if you want to be successful at this field of composition. Usually, there are at least four or five pieces of music that are connected with certain areas of game play. There might be music for wandering around, for doing battle, for equipping your character, for being first in a race, and so on.

Sometimes a gamer will hear the same piece of music over and over again for quite long periods of time. The music has to either be good enough to stand the test of extended game play, or be invisible enough to provide a mood without demanding too much of the gamer's attention.

Music for video games can be composed from old, unfinished compositions you may have lying around, or you can come up with brand new music. You can live anywhere once you have a game or two under your belt, but it is hard to get a start in this field. We suggest you do some surfing on the Internet to find out who the game developers in your area are, if any, and contact them. Put together a demo reel of short examples of your musical compositions. Just give them ten or twelve seconds worth of eight or nine contrasting musical ideas. Try to edit them together so that the whole collection has a flow to it and doesn't sound too disjointed.

Along with MIDI, there are other technical considerations when composing for video games, so you will have to be technically inclined, but at first you should concentrate on the musical side. If you are technically inclined, the rest will come in time.

# Composing for TV and Radio

Composing music for television shows is kind of a cross between composing for film and composing for video games. You will usually need to come up with several themes that get used frequently, but you have to continue to write custom music for certain types of TV shows. Sometimes the theme song for a TV show and the incidental music are composed by different people. There is a lot more prestige and consequently more money involved in theme songs, but often these are commissioned works written by high-profile artists.

This field is also very difficult to break into, and you will need to pound the pavement with a good, well-edited, short demo that contains as much variety as you can pack into it. One good idea is to find local television productions that require custom music. A couple of those under your belt can help your quest. There may be a public access station in your area, and you may find some enthusiastic novice television producers who would love some musical contributions. And look for people making documentaries. You will probably work for free for awhile.

Writing music for advertising can be a very lucrative career if you can break into the big-time national market. Local merchants often use selections from the many libraries of stock music tracks for their ads, but if a merchant wants their name in the jingle, someone will have to compose the piece for them, and it could be you. If you find this kind of job, you will be working mostly with 30-second spots with a few 60-second radio and 15-second spots every now and then. The 30-second jingles actually have to be 29 seconds long. There is no room for running short or long in this arena, so you have to develop a feel for composing a complete piece of music with a beginning, middle, and end that runs exactly 29 seconds.

An advantage to the young composer writing music for advertising is that you almost always get to work with the top musicians in your area. You will meet people who are comfortable working with a click track (metronome), can read charts, and are familiar with the working environment of the recording studio.

Don't go into this field believing that you are going to be able to make much of a creative statement in your music. You will receive direction from producers, agency representatives, musicians, and even corporate executives or their representatives. Sometimes their direction will make sense to you, but often you will find yourself losing control of your work. Be ready to let it go. Consider yourself somewhat successful if you are being paid for your work.

In the jingle scene, the simpler the music is, the better. The idea is to compose something that will stick in the listeners' heads without going over those same heads. A challenging or provocative piece of music will slow everything down, invite criticism and skepticism, and probably someone higher up the food chain will have his or her way with the piece until you yourself are sorry for the infraction you committed against the *less is more* rule governing the jingle music business.

In this field you are expected to work very quickly. If you need time to come up with ideas or make changes to your writing, jingles might not be the right direction for you to go in. You might get a little scrap of lyrics and a sense of the musical style desired on a Monday afternoon — and be expected to record your piece that Wednesday morning. On the other hand, having tight deadlines can motivate you. Steve Horelick, composer of the music for *Reading Rainbow*, once said, "The best motivation for me to complete a composition is someone holding a gun to my head and saying, 'I need it tomorrow.'"

You will probably do a lot of jingle demos for free before you actually sell one to a client or a music house. You should feel fortunate if the studio time is being paid for on behalf of your work in the meantime. Again, a compilation demo of your work is very important (see the final section in this chapter for more on demos). People in the professional creative world will not give you very much time to demonstrate your talent, so you have to squash it all down into a short tour of your past successes.

Look on the Internet or in the local yellow pages for music production houses and advertising agencies. These days many music houses are one-person operations, so you may meet with some dead ends. Not all ad agencies handle radio and TV, but be persistent and businesslike and try to get your demo into as many hands and ears as possible.

It is also a good idea to study the jingles that are currently airing. You will often be asked to copy their style, so you will be expected to know what is going on in the field.

# Composing for the Orchestra

The personal and emotional rewards for composing commercial music for a concert orchestra to perform are hard to beat. The creative freedom of not having to answer to the demands of a movie scene or an advertising executive is intoxicating. Even a high school band or choir performing your compositions can have you oozing pride and a sense of accomplishment. And there is always a chance that a more respected orchestra could decide to play one of your compositions in concert. You may even have your piece recorded and released on CD. Most of us dream of the immortality that a successful composition can bring.

These emotions are often not enough to drive a young composer to get a composition ready for a good orchestra. Money for new compositions is very hard to come by. It can be extremely difficult to find an orchestra willing to take on the task of rehearsing and preparing to perform works by unknown composers. Motivation can run out before anyone has even looked at your score. Set some self-imposed deadlines for getting your piece done. Hold a gun to your own head and say, "I need it tomorrow."

You can apply for grants if your work qualifies. Find someone who knows how to write grants or go on the Internet and do some research. A demo of your composition done in MIDI can be helpful — but if it is poorly executed it can actually be hurtful. Talk to high schools and colleges in your area. Some schools take pride in performing works by local or regional composers. There might be some semi- or non-professional performance ensembles in your area that could be open to experimentation. It is easier to get a string quartet played than it is to get a symphony played simply because of the number of musicians involved.

Good orchestral musicians are in the habit of being paid for their services, so if you have the money you could produce your own performance event. This is an expensive proposition, so it would be a good idea to have it profession-ally recorded while it is being performed. The extra cost will be less than trying to make a recording happen at another time (although you can do this too, if you like).

# Composing for Yourself

Similarly to composing for an orchestra, this is perhaps the toughest road towards making a living with your music — but the most rewarding road in terms of feeding your muse and drawing from your untrammeled creativity. There aren't any limits or restrictions on what instruments or sounds you use; you don't have to stay in a particular key signature; you are not limited to portraying a particular vision other than your own; you can work with whomever you please.

This is a perfect path for you if you are independently wealthy, infinitely patient, indomitably persistent, or any combination of these things. Or maybe you just want to hear your musical ideas played back on a CD and couldn't care less about monetary success or fame. There are some very tal-ented musical minds at work out there who can't get anyone to listen to their work. And there are a lot of wannabe composers out there who don't really have all that much talent. One might argue that there are a few who have hit the big time somehow without a lot of talent to back up their success.

There are many ways to the top of the mountain, and there are many different mountains to climb in the music world. You have to define what success means to you. Don't let someone else define it for you.

The Internet is probably the best marketplace for your work if you are com-posing for yourself. There are many ways to market yourself on the Internet. You could create your own Web site and/or start a page on MySpace or Facebook. You can get an account with download services such as iTunes or distribute your product through services such as CDBaby.com. No matter which of these directions you take (maybe all of them), you still have to get people to go to your music somehow. For that, you might enlist the help of someone who can optimize your Web presence to give you and your music greater exposure.

## Mark Mothersbaugh, founder of Mutato Muzika

I got involved in scoring films because a friend of mine, Paul Reubens, asked me if I would score a TV show for him. And that's kind of where it started, with *Pee-Wee's Playhouse*. Since then, I've done music supervision, I've done scoring, and I also write songs for films, too. Sometimes I just come in for a couple of days and write a song, depending on what the movie is, or what the company needs. For some of my projects, like *Rugrats*, for instance, I wrote eight or nine songs that ended up being part of the characters' dialog — music that ended up being integral to the movie, as opposed to writing songs that were added onto the storyline.

When people come to me for film scores, it's usually because they heard something I did that made them interested. A while ago, I scored a movie called *Welcome to Collinwood* that was a very, very small film. It was kind of Oscar Peterson/Django Reinhardt, very fast bebop jazz, and immediately afterwards, people are calling me up about that because they were looking for someone who could do that type of retro music.

There are people who have heard things I did in Devo or like the projects I've done with Wes Anderson, and they're looking for that kind of sound. I rarely get called to do horror films. I've done television projects that were horror projects, but feature films — you know, people tend to get categorized, and so they end up going to a Marco Beltrami or a Chris Young for horror soundtracks, since they've both done so many of those types of scores. And then those guys, too, they have the same dilemma where they don't want to be typecast horror-movie guys, so they actively seek out projects where they can break out of the genre.

The one rule we would suggest for you to follow in order to carve a place for yourself in the music world is not to follow any rules (except maybe this one). If you are composing for yourself, you have only yourself to please. If your music sounds like everyone else's, you won't leave much of an impression. Nearly every composer who has earned the honor of being remembered did something new when they were composing. We don't remember the copies, only the originals. If no one is commissioning your work, you have nothing to lose by being genuinely original. On the other hand, remember that there is really nothing new under the sun. You are working with the same twelve tones that everyone else has had to work with. But that doesn't mean you can't put things together in new ways.

# Composing Teams

One good, tried-and-true way to get work in film, television, or video game scoring is to apply to work with a composing team. Composing teams are companies that are contacted directly by production companies to write and perform scores for their films, shows, and games. Many professional musicians have worked in composing teams, such as Devo's Mark Mothersbaugh, who founded the West Hollywood music production company Mutato Muzika, and Camper Van Beethoven's Jonathan Segel, who worked at Danetracks.

Composing teams have been very popular in the world of animation, since pretty much right from the beginning. What would Bugs Bunny have done without Carl Stalling — or Donald Duck without Spike Jones to provide accompaniment to his pratfalls? Animation features and shorts almost always have a musical segment included, and because there is such a need for music in this field, there's a much better chance of breaking in as a beginner.

Check the credits of your favorite animated television show (or your kids' favorite shows) to see who's providing the music. If it's a company name, and not an individual's, this is a place you can send your resume. Requirements for becoming part of a composing team include existing talent and ability in writing the type/style of music that the team works with, great people skills (to get along with and work with other team members), and living in an area where these teams exist.

As of yet, long-distance teams that collaborate via the Internet or some other method are not common, but Web companies such as Rocket Network are working hard to create extensive online collaboration networks that may soon change the way composing teams are formed and operated.

You can also try and find out if composing teams exist in the city/town you live in and make yourself known to the people in charge of the teams. Get your demo to them and emphasize your willingness to work on the team with the other composers. Once hired, make sure that you're at least getting cue sheet credit for ASCAP (American Society of Composers, Authors & Publishers), BMI (Broadcast Music Incorporated), and/or SESAC (Society of European Stage Authors and Composers) royalties for the music you write — even if you're not getting screen credit. Without cue sheet credit, you're only *ghostwriting*, which has its own set of challenges, one of which is a flimsy-looking résumé.

# Helpful Organizations and Web Sites

There is nothing more important when working in the film industry than being persistent. Talented musicians are born every day, but truly persistent ones are made, not born.

If you aren't spending most of your time between musical jobs sending out a stack of résumés and demos and researching possible job opportunities every single day, then you probably are not going to make it.

However, if you are up to the challenge, here are a few really good Web sites to check out to get you on your way to becoming a working film composer.

## Film Connection

www.film-connection.com

The Film Connection Web site has everything from job openings in the film music industry to firsthand success stories sent in by people who have long and religiously visited the site for job information. You'll find hundreds of links to composing teams, individual musicians working in the industry, film companies of all sizes and genres, and help wanted listings.

## American Composer's Forum

www.composersforum.org

For the past 30 years, the American Composer's Forum aim has been to join communities with composers and performers, with the goal of encouraging the creation of new music. The site includes lots of news for musicians and composers alike, as well as job opportunities and links to other members of the prestigious organization.

## American Composer's Forum, Los Angeles Chapter

www.composers.la

This offshoot of the original ACF was created specifically to discuss music in the L.A. area, much of which, naturally, has to do with the film and television industry. Like the original site, this site has lots of news about music opportunities and companies in the L.A. area, including a hefty help wanted section.

## Film Music Network

www.filmmusic.net

This site is a great place to regularly check on job listings — which are posted right on the home page, so you don't have to dig around for them. You'll also find breaking news about production companies and composing teams around the world.

# Working with Agents

Unless you are working full-time for a company, you're going to be considered a freelance musician by most people you deal with — which can be both good and bad for your working relationships. On the bad side, if the company can find someone cheaper than you who is just as good, or merely adequate, they'll probably go with that composer. Another bad aspect of being a freelancer is that a disreputable company might decide not to pay you for work completed, or cut the project off just short of completion and steal your composition. Unless you've got a great lawyer on your side and a lot of time on your hands, these cases are almost always hopeless for the freelance composer.

On the good side, as a freelancer you get to choose your own work hours and most often work from home. You have to own your own equipment, of course, but that also means you get to work on the equipment that you're most comfortable with. Also, if you get a hinky feeling about a company that you're working with, and you can afford to withdraw from the project, you have the choice of dropping them and approaching a different company for work instead.

When you hire an agent, a lot of the bad aspects of freelancing change. For one thing, a good agent will find work for you and, having a stake in whatever money you make, will only approach companies that have a good reputation. So, no more getting ripped off. Secondly, many bigger production companies, such as Disney, absolutely will not work with anyone or any company not represented by an agency. Most television stations also only work with an artist or company through an agent.

There are, of course, horror stories about musicians' agents, but most of them have to do with choosing an agent without checking his or her reputation first. The best way to find an agent is to find out what agencies represent some of the musicians or composers you admire — easily found by a quick search on the Internet. Start with those agents first and see where that gets you. Many times, even if these agents turn you down, they'll refer you to a another agent that might suit your needs better.

# Songwriting

Just about everyone has written at least one song in their life, whether it was as a three-year-old making up new lyrics to "Twinkle Twinkle Little Star" or, later, playing around with chord progressions and making up lyrics on the spot to accompany the resulting instrumental. The fact of the matter is that writing songs isn't very difficult. However, writing good songs, or at least songs that other people outside of your immediate family can truly enjoy, can be very hard.

Good songwriters use form to give their songs the emotional impact needed to make them memorable. Just like the easiest poems to remember and even — on a much less sophisticated level — rally cheers and anthems have some sort of rhyming or rhythmic structure to them. The songs that are easiest for audiences to truly connect with are the ones built according to form. The way songs are put together is not arbitrary, and forms weren't invented just to create formula songs without depth or originality. These forms exist and persist because songwriters, and audiences, have found that they help listeners to understand and remember the message at the heart of a song. Chapter 13 talks a lot more about form.

Even when your songs come spontaneously, there will come a point when you have to decide what form you want to use (we go into form in more detail later in this section). Sometimes you may come up with a single verse or a chorus idea first. After that first flash of inspiration and an exploration of what you want the song to say, you need to have an idea of the type of form you want to use to help you get your idea, or the story behind your song, across most effectively. You may do that unconsciously, as a natural result of having listened to and studied music all your life.

But sometimes — especially if you've only listened to bubblegum pop, or rap music, or math rock — you may not be able to write anything that doesn't sound like a blatant imitation of a song you're already familiar with. You have to remember that what you already know or feel about form could be limiting.

## Deciding on lyrics and tempo

If you're starting from a lyric, the mood and subject matter will probably dictate the tempo of the music. If it's a happy song that demands an up-tempo sort of rhythm to it, you might want to use a form with just a few sections, such as AAA or ABA. If it's a slow or mid-tempo ballad — for example, a good country ballad like Hank Williams' "I'm So Lonesome I Could Cry" — you can use either the longer or shorter forms.

If you're writing your lyrics first, then you're going to have to choose a beat that works with those lyrics. If your lyrics use a lot of multisyllabic words, or if you have a lot of short words that fit together in long phrases, then you're probably going to need to choose a fast beat that matches the rhythm of your dialog. Listen to anything by a fast-singing punk rock band, such as early Suicidal Tendencies or Husker Dü to see what we mean.

On the folk music front, compare the lyrical tempo of one of Bob Dylan's especially wordy songs, such as "Leopard-Skin Pill-Box Hat," to "Just Like a Woman." There's no way that you could take the lyrics of "Leopard-Skin" and set it to the beat of "Just Like A Woman" — the words wouldn't fit rhythmically against the music, and you would end up with a lot of words left over at the end of the song.

The tempo you choose for your song will be also at least partially determined by how easy it is to sing your lyrics. If your song is rhythmically clumsy, a fast tempo may tie knots in your tongue trying to get them all in. Think of Shakespeare and his constant use of iambic pentameter. Not only do his words sound nice to the ear, but they've been easy for performers to repeat without fear to being tongue-tied for more than 400 years. If you want a rapid-fire, one-syllable-per-eighth or sixteenth note lyric, you have to be extra careful that the words are easy to pronounce and sing together. It's a good idea to experiment with a metronome by singing or speaking the lyric against various tempo settings.

Fewer words to a song generally pose fewer problems, but the challenge is to phrase them in an interesting way against the rhythm. You can stretch short spoken phrases against slow musical phrases easily drawing short words out as Hank Williams and Patsy Cline did in their music, or by using long pauses between phrases like Leonard Cohen sometimes does. In songs with few words, the way you deliver your lines — or the way your singer delivers your lines — is just as important as the words used.

## Building rhythm

We discuss how you can build rhythm around a lyrical phrase in Chapter 4. Now it's time to explore that a little more. Take a phrase from Henry Purcell's *Dido and Aeneas*:

> Thy hand, Belinda! Darkness shades me,

If you were to break it up simply by spoken rhythmic accents, it would look like Figure 17-1.

**Figure 17-1:**
Adding accent marks to Henry Purcell's lyrics to indicate rhythm.

Thy     hand,     Be- lin -da!  Dark -ness   shades   me,
 ∧        ∧        —    ∧  —      ∧    —        ∧       —

Note this basic rule when matching lyrics to beats in music: Weak (unaccented) syllables are usually placed at weak metric points — those that are weaker than those where the surrounding accented syllables occur. An accented syllable may occur at any place, but an unaccented syllable before or after an accented syllable must fall on a rhythmic point weaker or equal in strength, meaning that weak syllables should occur on upbeats when next to a strong syllable. Of course, eventually, rules are meant to be broken, and many outstanding, musically rebellious songwriters — such as psychedelia's poster child, Donovan — made a lasting career of fitting lyrical accents against musical downbeats.

If we wanted to use this naturally occurring rhythm in a piece of music, we could write it as shown in Figures 17-2 through 17-4.

**Figure 17-2:**
Creating one possible Purcell rhythmic example.

**Figure 17-3:**
A second Purcell rhythmic possibility.

**Figure 17-4:**
A third possibility for a Purcell rhythmic example.

Any one of those rhythmic patterns could, and does, work for the Purcell phrase. As does (naturally) the one he actually used (Figure 17-5).

**Figure 17-5:**
**Purcell's**
**own choice**
**for *Dido and***
***Aeneas.***

As you can see in Figure 17-5, Purcell managed to stick to the convention of matching weak and strong accents in his lyrics with the weak and strong beats of each measure, yet still managed to present his lyrics in a completely different rhythmic pattern than the more obvious patterns that were available to him.

## Choosing your form

Once you've set the tempo and decided on the delivery of your lyrics, you've begun to lock yourself into your form. If it takes one minute to get through a verse and chorus, and you're looking for a three-minute song, your options have already shrunk further.

You should also consider how much space you're going to need to tell your story. Though it's always a good idea to condense, the AAA... form, or the one-part song form, gives you the most room to stretch lyrically. But it leaves no room for a chorus or a catchy hook. A lot of folk music is written in this form, and it's a good medium for telling a musical story.

*Ternary* forms (ABA, AABA, compound AABA, and so on — see Chapter 13 for more on song forms) can give you plenty of lyric space as well as room to develop a strong musical foundation, particularly if you use pre-choruses to present new lyric information each time. One-section and two-section (ABABAB) forms at fast tempos are easy to write long, complicated lyrical stories to — however, they can be melodically boring because the melodies repeat so often.

On the other hand, if you stick to writing spare, condensed lyrics, you have many musical options available to you. You can either set your lyrics to a fast tempo — for example, a rock song — or set them against a slow ballad. Either way will leave plenty of room to accommodate the individual phrasing styles of different singers. Spare lyrics presented in a slower tempo have more of an obligation to be interesting, which means bring in a good vocalist to deliver them, or have a good voice yourself. You're making the listener wait for that lyric to unfold, and it had better be worth the wait! The same is true, of course, of the music.

Eventually, like anything else, once you work with these forms, they become second nature to you. You'll also find that you will get yourself into problematic situations for which you will have to find creative solutions. A substantial amount of innovation in music is initiated by a need to find a graceful way out of a jam. If you already have a repertoire of solutions, you're ahead of the game.

## In the beginning

Sometimes the first five seconds of a song are the hardest to come up with. You may know you want to write something, but you may only have a vague idea or a feeling about what it is you want to express. Or you may even know exactly what you want to say, but have little or no idea how you would get your idea across to another person.

There is a lot of pressure put on songwriters to make that first five seconds the most interesting for the listener, too. How many times have you flipped around on the radio, listening to a second here, a second there, before settling on the one song that grabs your attention?

 The first couple of seconds of your song are also the most important because if you start well, you'll have a lot less trouble down the line. Once you get past the beginning, many times, the music and lyrics dictate where it's going to go on its own, and you just have to grab hold and try to keep it on track.

Many times songwriters begin writing a song by grabbing an existing song that they like and writing completely new lyrics for it. From there, they modify the music to match the mood and then work on the lyrics some more to match the new music, and continue editing and rewriting the music and lyrics until they either come up with something they're happy with or toss the song into their "scrap file" to be worked on or used for something else later. This technique works especially well when you've got a group of people together to work with (your band, for example), where everyone can add their input on where the original song should change and the identifying traits of the new song should begin.

Another way to begin a song is to just play around with chord progressions. Most pop songs use the same chord progressions — jazz musicians often make fun of pop musicians for playing only three-chord songs — so, if the basic chord progressions you come up with sound too familiar to you, don't sweat it.

Chord progressions can't be copyrighted; only lyrics and melodies can be copyrighted.

Still one more way to start a song is to think of a title for it first. A good title can lead to specific images and ideas you want in your song. For example, you could decide to call your song "Nice Shoes." From that title, you could start writing phrases about watching a person walking, what you think of when you see that person's shoes or where they're going, and so forth. Musically, the title and words could lend themselves to the rhythm of a person's gait — sauntering, pacing nervously, jogging, or what have you. From there, the music could decide whether it was a menacing or sad song with lots of minor chords or a happy, carefree song using mostly major chord progressions.

Action words, short phrases, or specific images work well as inspiring titles.

## Making your song moody

The mood of the song determines the music you put to your lyrics — or, if you are a songwriter who's more comfortable writing music first and then working on lyrics, the mood of the music you write will determine how your lyrics are interpreted by your audience. If you present happy lyrics set in a dark-sounding minor key, or if you put a very depressing set of lyrics to a happy-sounding upbeat tune (such as Morrissey of The Smiths used to do), your audience will think you're being ironic or sarcastic — and if that's the feeling you want to get across, then you'll have succeeded. However, if that's not what you were intending, then you probably want to head back to the old drawing board.

A good rule of thumb is to remember that all music is a form of communication, and a song with lyrics is perhaps the most blatant form of musical communication. Not only are you talking to your audience through your words, but you are talking to them through your music as well. If a lyrical phrase in your song asks a question, then the music can go up at the end of the musical phrase right along with the words. If the lyrics are quiet and somber in a section of an otherwise loud and boisterous song, there's no reason why the music can't get as quiet and spare as the vocalist singing the lyrics in that part of the song. Ideally, even if the vocals were removed, the emotional message should still be clearly carried by the music.

## The hook

"Don't bore us, take us to the chorus."

This is a dictum among song publishers. What it means is that your song needs to have a hook, and the listener shouldn't have to wait around too long for it. A *hook* is a phrase or group of phrases that sums up the idea of the song, sticks in your head like peanut butter to the roof of your mouth, and repeats throughout your song at critical points. It is the part of the song that will be remembered (sometimes begrudgingly) when the rest of the song is long forgotten.

Usually the hook is the chorus, but not always. Sometimes an instrumental interlude between verses can be a hook (think of the guitar part to "Satisfaction" by the Rolling Stones). What we can say about hooks is that if your song doesn't have one, you will have a hard time finding anyone to publish or perform it.

So where do hooks come from?

Many places. They can come from common expressions in daily use. Every generation has its jargon. For example, how often do you hear someone say, "It's all good"? How about "24/7"? Many expressions go into and out of popularity over the years; any of them can be a good starting point for coming up with a memorable hook. Listen to conversations and try to observe which simple phrases get used a lot. They don't even have to have a lot of depth. You will be able to provide depth when you begin to flesh them out.

Sometimes a hook comes from putting a new spin on a common idea. It can even come from putting a new spin on a common musical idea. Originally, rock and roll utilized snare accents on beat 2, the *and* of beat 2, and beat 4. At some point the *and* of 2 was dropped and accents were put only on 2 and 4. Then someone tried accenting all four beats with the snare. These were small changes in the drums, but they provided a large change in feel and provided musical hooks. Christopher Cross used a major ninth chord in "Sailing." Hendrix introduced us to the 7 sharp 9 chord. If you use the same hook a lot, it can become your little identifying trademark. If you use the same hook too much, it can make you a one-hit-wonder.

One common songwriting technique is to start with a strong musical or lyrical phrase — it doesn't matter which. This phrase will likely become the hook, but it probably won't be the very first thing that we hear in the finished song. You are going to build up to it with your music and/or lyrics. Think of other lyrical or musical ideas that support this phrase. Toss the phrase around in your head for a couple of weeks until it magnetically starts to gather more words, more music, more storyline ideas, and generally develops into a hook. Now you can write verses that lead to the climax that your hook should provide.

Your hook will probably end up being the song title, but not the first lyrics the listener hears. Not many songs actually start right out with the title in the lyrics. So try writing your hooks first. That way you will at least be sure your songs have them. Even if the phrase you work with doesn't become a hook, it is often a good idea to write songs from the inside out and not necessarily force yourself to start writing your song from the beginning.

## Selling yourself

Composing music is an art. If you want to make any money at it, however, it's also a business. Unfortunately, most creative types are not necessarily very good at selling themselves in a persistent and organized way. For some reason, the idea of sales and marketing seems to strike fear and loathing in the hearts of many. The fact is that the only people in the world who can claim to have only one job are salespeople. Everyone else has to be a bit of a salesperson from time to time along with whatever else they think of as their career.

When you consider it, you are selling every time you try to persuade anyone to do anything. Everything from convincing your kids that they should eat their greens to suggesting a good book to a friend involves the very skills that you

need to promote your music. One reason that it seems harder to sell a song to a publisher than it is to sell beans to your 4-year-old is because it is hard to draw the line between enthusiasm and boastfulness. It always seems more appropriate for someone else to say great things about you than to say them yourself.

Along with this, you might not be so confident that your work is really any good to start with. In fact, if you like your own work too much you run the risk of getting stuck at your current level, because you aren't seeing the areas that need improvement. Because of this, it is often a good idea to find an agent or manager to help get your stuff out there. Still there are a lot of things you can do for yourself, and some composers are very good at promoting themselves.

# Making a Great Demo

You are going to need to put together a demonstration recording of your work. There are still a few places where sheet music scores may be enough to get you in the door, but the music world has gotten used to the idea that your calling card should be in an easily-accessible audio format. If you are a songwriter, your demo should include a few songs in their entirety, but to get into the custom music composition world, you are going to have to do some cutting and pasting (or have it done for you) to create a short recording compiling excerpts of a variety of your works.

## Keep it short

Most people in the music business in the position to hire you or pay for your music aren't going to give you much time to make an impression. If you are fortunate enough to arrange an interview or submit a demo, you will be expected to deliver a brief but complete musical picture of yourself in about ten minutes. Maybe three of these will be taken up by listening to your demo.

Because most compositions follow structural forms such as AABA and so on, it is not uncommon for people to just listen to your music through the first B section and then skip ahead to the next piece. Don't be offended by this. In fact, what you should do is cut out only the choicest moments from as diverse a variety of your works as possible, and paste them together in a musical — or at least interesting — way. Try to edit these snippets into logical musical phrases. Sometimes you can cut out a nice phrase that includes a complete lyrical thought. Other times you will want to use four-, eight-, twelve-, or sixteen-measure cuts, as these lengths are often the natural length of a musical phrase.

## Only include the best stuff

Find the most exciting moments of your music. You need to be able to listen with a certain amount of pride if you end up sitting there while your demo is getting played. Nothing is worse than a flash of embarrassment or feeling the need to apologize for some awkward moment playing on your demo.

## Organize it

The order of selections on your demo is also important. Start with your best work, and follow it with something that contrasts with it. Be careful not to have pieces in the same key or with the same groove or attitude back to back. You can fade one out as the next one fades in. You can butt them right up against each other so that the last beat of one is also the first beat of another. You can put a little space between them if you want the listener to reflect on the mood of a certain piece, or if the key change between the two pieces is a little too challenging to the ear. Break up the landscape and present as diverse a musical palette as possible. Be creative. That's what they want to hear.

In short, you need to treat the creation of your demo CD as a composition itself. It is a medley of your greatest hits (even if they are future hits).

## Have more ready to go

You should also have available the full-length versions of your recorded works. If someone likes your demo they may be willing to give you their ears for a lot longer. They will then want to hear how you develop your ideas from beginning to end. They will want to get a feel for your sense of music. But they won't give you much time at first. We have listened to many excellent demos that tell a very complete story about the artist's work in 90 seconds. A minute and a half is the perfect length if you are good with editing.

Don't make your demo longer than three minutes.

## Identify yourself

Make sure that anything you leave with anyone — be it a CD, resume, cover letter, or whatever — includes your contact information. Your name, phone number(s), email, and address need to be on every item. If your resume is more than a page long, put your contact info on all pages. Put it on the CD label and on the jewel case. Often pages get separated, and CDs get left out of the case. You don't want to make people search for your information if they want to contact you.

## Invest in quality

All this information assumes that you *have* recordings of your work, of course, or can have some recordings made. The usefulness of demo recordings cannot be overstressed, but a poor recording or a poor performance can often do you more harm than good. If you are going to invest your own money in your dreams of becoming a recognized music composer, the best investment is to somehow procure professional quality recordings of good performances of your work. If you can do it yourself, great. But most often, the wise choice is to concentrate on the music and let a professional help you with the technical side. At the end you will at least get to hear your completed work, and that is really the main point of writing it in the first place, isn't it?

## Copyright it

One last thing: Be sure to register a PA (performing arts) copyright form with the Library of Congress before sending your stuff around (see earlier sidebar on this). Most professionals in this business aren't interested in stealing your material, but in the age of the Internet, publishers are wary of works that have not been copyright protected. The fear is that you may have put your music out on the Internet, and someone else could have easily filed a copyright using a download of your music. Publishers and record companies don't want to risk being sued for copyright infringement, so show them that you have been careful; copyright your compositions.

# Chapter 18

# Composing Electronic Music

Y our average electronic home-recording musician has to know almost as much about computers as he or she does about music itself. The amount of necessary (and unnecessary) pieces of music hardware and software is constantly growing and evolving, so much so that many musicians long for the days when a four-track tape recorder was the height of home-recording technology.

That said, electronic music is here and likely to stay. This chapter introduces you to many of its advantages and limitations.

## Software and Hardware for Composition

If you're the type of musician who likes to spend as much time experimenting with technology as writing and recording music, then learning how to use new technology isn't much of a problem. There is a fascinating array of new instruments and programs to work with, from ultra-sensitive microphones that can record insects' voices and the steady slurping of deciduous trees, to keyboards with three playable sides to each key that can produce microtones and previously impossible chord constructions.

However, if you're the type of musician who has to be dragged kicking and screaming to the 21st century of home recording, then the playback capabilities of a MIDI theremin probably don't interest you. And that's okay. If this is the case, there are really just a few software — or combined software and hardware — packages that come in handy.

## Sequencers and digital audio workstations

For composers who are more comfortable composing music on an instrument than sitting down and writing down notes, a good sequencing program such as any generation of Cubase, Sonar, ProTools, or LogicPro is a great place to start. Although early sequencers required a composer to sit down at a computer and plug notes into a staff by use of a mouse — or, worse yet, a computer keyboard — most modern sequencing programs come with input hardware that fits right into an input jack in your computer. This way, if you want to compose your music on any MIDI-capable instrument, such as a guitar, a keyboard, or a microphone, you can play the music right into the computer. There, the music is saved for future editing. Generally, when MIDI hardware accompanies a sequencing software package, the combination of the two is called a *digital audio workstation*.

Many sequencing programs have the capability to record as many as 70 tracks. Some claim to be able to record an infinite number of tracks. This means that you can play a melody line on an instrument, record it, play an accompaniment to the melody line for the second track, lay down a rhythm track on top of that, throw another instrument into the mix for the next track, and so on.

Sequencers are great to work with if you want to cut sections of music or specific instrument tracks *out* of existing compositions. They're also fantastic for creating your own *loops*, which can be used directly after composition to throw into your full-length compositions (more on looping later in this chapter).

The downside of many music sequencers is that they have only limited music-notation capabilities and are only able to follow and notate a simple melody line being played. The latest sophisticated hardware/software sequencer packages, such as LogicPro and CakeWalk, are able to notate much more complicated pieces of music.

## Music notation software: scorewriters

For the composer who wants to write sheet music for other musicians to follow, or even create original pieces of music for publication purposes, music notation software called a *scorewriter* is important to know how to use.

Although older, less-sophisticated scorewriters insist that a composer plug the notes into a staff directly by use of a mouse or keyboard, newer versions of Finale, Encore, and Capella allow a user to plug a keyboard or other MIDI instrument directly into a piece of accompanying hardware and play the music directly into the computer, just like a sequencer. Then the software interprets what you played and produces the written music notation for it.

## What is MIDI?

MIDI stands for Musical Instrument Digital Interface. It's basically a process that digitizes the timbre and quality of sound coming out of an instrument, meaning the attack, vibrato, modulation, sustain, and so forth — the things that make up the "feel" of an instrument's specific sound. Then, because the sound is now digital, notes on the keyboard can be assigned to the sounds. When you play a MIDI synthesizer, and the MIDI file being used is "bowed violin," for example, every note you play will have the timbre and quality of an individual violin string being bowed. MIDI is not a straight audio recording of an instrument — it's simply the encoded characteristics of an instrument.

Scorewriters make it very easy for a composer to write different sections of the same piece of music for a variety of instruments, such as brass and woodwind instruments. The program automatically does the transpositions necessary for instruments set in specific keys, which is very handy when you are playing the music to be notated on a keyboard or guitar.

There are also a few scorewriters available with *optical character recognition* (OCR) capabilities. This means that you can scan a piece of music directly into your computer — via a scanner, of course — and then either edit that piece of music through the scorewriter program or play it through the program's MIDI output to see what it sounds like. Programs with this feature include SmartScore and Sibelius.

## *Repetition and the computer*

As we have seen from previous chapters, *repetition* plays a large role in music composition. *Binary* and *ternary* compositional forms include repeating motifs and the storytelling concepts of *statement*, *development*, *departure*, and *resolution* or *recapitulation*. The central concept is this: If something is worth listening to once, it's probably worth listening to twice (or more).

Computer-aided composition benefits from the computer's editing prowess and greatly speeds up composition. You can structure an eight-measure phrase and, instead of having to write it all again, you can simply copy and paste it into the next eight measures. Once copied, you can make changes to it as you see fit. You can add and delete material and experiment with any aspect of the phrase or motif you like. You can paste it in again as many times and in as many places as necessary. You can then compose another eight measures — say, for a bridge or a chorus — and perform the same copy, cut, and paste operations with it. Modern computer programs make this all very easy.

## Sound libraries

With many computer programs, such as Apple's Logic Pro, a variety of sounds (called *sound libraries*) are included in the program that allow you to audition your parts played with simulations or samples of actual orchestral and non-orchestral instruments. You can try out dozens of ideas with these sounds and get a general preview of how they will sound when a score is printed and parts are performed on real instruments.

One potential drawback of having all of these different instrument sounds at your disposal is that if you're writing music that will eventually be played by real instruments, there is the danger of writing a part that seems easy on your keyboard or guitar but that your average tuba player or saxophonist can't easily, or even possibly, play. The keyboard and guitar are both very quick instruments on which it's not a big deal to rapidly play up and down a wide range of notes for long periods of time. However, when you hand it over to a saxophonist or a tuba player, you may be greeted with a very angry glare and a declaration of surrender, simply because you didn't take into account that these musicians need to occasionally take a breath.

When composing on a computer, the sounds provided by the program are limited in their verisimilitude, owing to the fact that they are not subject to the physical realities of performance on actual instruments. There are no real bows bowing, no real breaths taken, no limits of range, and so forth. You can only get a rough idea at best of what will happen when you get real musicians to play the parts, unless you compose with these limitations in mind.

On the other hand, perhaps you don't *want* real instruments to ever play your composition. With a computer, you have an entire orchestra at your fingertips that likes and respects you and doesn't get huffy when handed impossible parts. Thanks to our friend technology, you can invest in massive third-party libraries of excellent orchestral sound recordings. Some even have elements such as "bowing" for strings that can be manipulated through MIDI control and that sound just like the real thing.

These libraries are quite expressive and expensive, but they take up a lot of hard drive space and require powerful computers to access all their attributes for a lengthy composition. Many film composers, such as Cliff Martinez (*Solaris, Narc, Traffic*) and John Murphy (*28 Days Later)*, exclusively use computers to compose and record music and prefer to do so simply because they can work on their own schedules and creative whims and don't have to deal with any other musicians' foibles or creative interference. If you know what you are doing with sound libraries in conjunction with a good music program, you can avoid the real orchestra altogether.

# Composing on Computers

It's often a good idea to start your computer composition with the rhythm. Setting a metronome going and establishing a time signature at the beginning will make editing easier later on, because you will be able to use measures and beats as timing references for cutting and pasting once your computer knows where to put the measure lines. Good computer programs allow you to make changes to tempo and meter later if your composition requires them. Even if you are starting with just a melody in your head, taking time to set the correct tempo can be an aid for the creative and technical processes involved.

If you are writing a song or something else that has a strong groove, it is often a good idea to come up with a little MIDI drum track for two or four measures, copy it into the whole length of the tune, and use *it* instead of the boring click of a metronome. Later you can replace it by re-recording the drums with more variety — or even re-record it with a real percussionist playing to your original groove track.

## Thinking in sections

The next thing you can do is to think in two-, four-, or eight-measure phrases as you add other rhythm section parts (bass, keys, guitar) to your composition. You don't have to follow this or any other rule, but most Western music runs in sections composed of multiples of two or four measures. Thinking in these terms also makes cutting and pasting easier.

You can work up all your parts for each section separately. Then you can cut and paste the entire sections into their proper places within your composition. You can have a verse, chorus, and bridge, all with multiple instrument parts in them. The individual parts can be moved around — or you can move the entire sections. Then you can make changes within each occurrence of these parts or sections so that there is some development of your musical ideas throughout your piece.

## Linear composition

Of course, you don't have to compose by writing sections and copying and pasting them in. You can always write in a *linear* fashion. You can play melodies or even entire performances across the composition in real time. If you are using MIDI recording instead of recording *audio* tracks (exception: *audio loops*), you can slow the tempo down temporarily just enough so that you can perform a difficult part that may be beyond your technique as a musician at the correct tempo. Then you can set the tempo back to the correct setting for playback. The nice thing about linear performances with MIDI is that you can preserve the spontaneity and freshness of a *first take*, editing out just the bad notes later.

You can also write the notes into a staff one at a time with mouse clicks or key commands just as you might do with pencil and paper. You have the advantage of being able to hear your work back instantly (if not always with the exact sound you intended).

When working with MIDI, whether or not you plan on printing out a score and parts, you can always make changes on a note-by-note level, so you never have to be stuck with a part you don't like.

## Loop composing

There is a growing trend these days to construct compositions using ready-made phrases of music of varying lengths, styles, and instrumental content. These phrases are known as *loops*. Two of the most popular types of loops are *Apple Loops* and *REX* files.

Loop composition is not new. What is relatively new is the ability to take recorded audio materials and change the tempo and/or key independently. For many years now it has been fairly easy to do this with MIDI, but if you receive a MIDI loop from another musician you still have to attach a sound to it. MIDI sounds still haven't quite hit the same nerve that real recordings of musicians playing real instruments such as a piano or guitar seem to hit.

The problem with audio materials of real instruments is that when you play them back at a faster or slower tempo, the pitch rises or drops. It sounds unnatural due to the fact that along with the pitch changing, the other formants of the instrument, such as sound duration, vibrato, attack, and so on, are being changed as well. This gives the recording an unnaturally eerie or comical quality when all you wanted was to change the tempo. To create an audio loop with the ability to change pitch or tempo independently, the audio file has to be chopped up into small pieces and accordioned out or in, depending on whether you want the tempo slower or faster, or whether you want the pitch to shift down or up. Fortunately, that is now pretty easy to do.

You can record a piano phrase of several measures, run it through the Apple Loops utility to make it into a loop, and then can send it to another person to use in their next compositional construction. That person can change the tempo or the key — or both — and paste it in between other complementary loops. Strictly speaking, this would be more in the nature of assembly than composition, because you would be using someone else's musical ideas. Of course, if you are making the loops yourself, you are back to the realm of composition again.

There is a demand for such loops, and it could become profitable if you can get hooked up with the right business connections.

Loops are generally two, four, or eight measures long to make them easier to use, as most music is constructed in multiples of four measures. You can use the same loop over and over again throughout your construction, or you can break up the scenery a little and insert a different loop every so often. You can also use a different loop every measure if you like. And of course, you can have piano loops playing on one track while drum loops are playing on another and a guitar loop is repeating over and over again on another.

Loops are a bit like a collage of pre-recorded sounds. But keep in mind that any commercially available loop is going to be available to everyone who bought the same disc of loops. If you are comfortable with the idea that your music is an assembly of phrases that are not uniquely your creations, then loops may be for you. Keep in mind that they can certainly act as an inspiration for your own creativity if you think of them strictly in that way and are willing to get rid of them after they have performed their inspirational duties.

## Music concrête

*Music concrête* is a type of music that sprang directly out of the evolution of music technology. In the 1930s, French composer Pierre Schaeffer began experimenting with splicing bits of analog tape together to create music completely different than the source material. As a throwback to classical music being inspired by poetic forms, music concrête has its roots in the 1920s Surrealist literary practice of cut-up and fold-in composition. In *cut-up*, writers would take existing pieces of literature and rearrange the order of the phrases and words by cutting up the source material and physically rearranging it, whereas in *fold-in* compositions, a group of writers would write random phrases, one at a time, on a piece of paper, folding the paper over after each turn so that the next writer couldn't see what the previous writer had written.

Music concrête basically means that you are making music out of existing sounds. This can range from human voices (as in Steve Reich's "It's Gonna Rain" and "Come Out"), spinning around on a radio dial (Ben Azarm's "Neoapplictana"), static (Apollon and Muslimgauze's "Year Zero"), or a combination of power tools and bird songs (such as in the music of Japanese noise rocker Rhizome). A list of significant pioneers of the music concrête movement must include Swiss musician Christian Marclay, whose most notorious composition, 1988's "Footsteps," was created by having thousands of people walking across many copies of the same slab of vinyl and then taking the damaged records and playing them on a turntable, recording the best bits for an album under the same title.

Throughout the 1980s, rap artists used the ideas behind music concrête to completely change the way contemporary pop musicians would create music. Through their use of *samples* and loops of existing music and dialog, artists such as Del Tha Funky Homo Sapien and Ice T brought music concrête from art galleries and other experimental music forums into the forefront of popular music.

When using loops for your music, you will find yourself confronted with almost limitless choices of which loops to use and where to use them. Loops are often arranged in categorical file hierarchies. These categories may include instrument, genre, key, meter, tempo, style, length in measures, and so on.

It is best to try to find a loop that comes close to the key, meter, and tempo that you have chosen for your composition. Even though you can change all these things as you see fit, there are limits to how far you can stretch an audio file and still have it sound decent. On the other hand, experimentation is often a catalyst for creativity, so if you get lost or bored, try a loop that *doesn't* fit categorically at all with your compositional ideas.

## Computer as recorder: musical scrapbooking

Another use of the computer in composition is the simple ability of the computer to make basic recordings of your ideas. You don't always have to think of the big picture when you are composing. Large compositions start from small beginnings, and the computer can be there to archive your musical imagination.

Keep a folder on your hard drive for your little, inspired noodling sessions. When you feel like putting your hands on an instrument but have no particular chords or melody in your head, click Record and just play what comes to your fingers. Later, if you don't like any of it, you can delete it, but often you will land on a good moment or two that you can develop out later. It is useful to play into the computer using a decent MIDI keyboard, but you can re-record any ideas that you develop later on the real piano, if you prefer that sound. Go back to the saved bits in your file folder when you are looking for ideas to develop.

Create a simple setup for yourself to record so you aren't bothered with technical concerns during moments of musical inspiration. Make it easy for you to just flip a switch or two and begin recording. Don't let yourself get too fancy during these noodling sessions. Technology can be a creativity killer, although it can be a creative process as well under the right circumstances.

## The bad news

Well, it's not exactly bad news, but a warning is warranted here: The computer can never replace your ears or your imagination. Quite often when using the computer for music you will find yourself getting hooked on the visual aspect and the quick responsiveness of computers.

## Andrew Broder, electronic music composer

I don't know if I'm a great lover of new technologies. I mean, they're there, and I'll use whatever's at my disposal that I happen to think sounds good. There are some computer programs that are just like, well, learning quantum physics. They're mind-blowingly difficult to learn. But so is learning how to really immerse yourself in learning how to play the piano. It's just as complicated, and it's just as much of its own world, and requires the same kind of facilities in a person, the same kind of dedication, the same kind of curiosity. But there's a danger that your music can become too reliant on new technology, and the music sometimes can feel

empty when it just becomes a matter of keeping up with what the latest products are. That said, though, it's really cool to be able to make a whole album on your home computer.

Everything was new technology at some point. Reel-to-reel recording was new technology at one point, same with the electric guitar and the synthesizer. Those all came along, and people went through those same kind of debates with them as to whether or not it was kind of cheating or somehow more artificial to use than an acoustic instrument. So, as far as I'm concerned, what matters is the end result.

The fact that computers have provided us with visual tools for musical editing is wonderful. It lets us look at larger chunks of our work at once. We can see (not just hear) where our writing has come from and where it is going. And it provides us with a level of control of even the smallest things beyond the wildest aspirations of pencil and paper. But the ears on your head (and inside your head) ought to be the final arbiters of quality when it comes to music. A piece of music is no shorter or longer than the entire amount of time it takes to listen to it. Its emotional effect is cumulative. You can't really judge it without listening to it from start to finish. Computers can sometimes trick us into working on bits and pieces and forgetting about the flow of the entire composition. Be careful!

## Saving and backing up

All who have worked extensively with computers have experienced the hollow feeling in the pits of their stomachs that comes from the realization that much valuable, hard work has been lost due to computer crashes, forgotten saves, and the tendency to not back up often enough. A lot of good music has evaporated in these ways even as computers advance and our storage methods and software applications advance. Remember floppy disks? Cassettes? It is important to remember that the information stored on a computer drive, CD, or DVD is not actually the thing that it represents. Those bits are not your composition.

It is critical that you save your work frequently, and back it up by making copies onto external hard drives and/or hard media such as CDs and DVDs. In addition, we highly recommend that you make hard copies of everything. Print out your scores and parts and make recordings of all your work. Through the course of their careers, many musicians have had to transfer work from analog tape to VHS Hi-Fi, to DAT, and finally to MP3 audio files and CDs. No one knows what the next 30 years will bring or how relevant your musical ideas may be by then, but you need to make it a habit to keep archives of your work that can be accessed by modern methods.

# Chapter 19

# Composing for Other Musicians

• • • • • • • • • • • • • • • • • • • • • • • • • • • • • • • • • • • • • • • • • • • • • • • • •

• • • • • • • • • • • • • • • • • • • • • • • • • • • • • • • • • • • • • • • • • • • • • • • • •

*T*here comes a time in almost every composer's life when he or she is going to have to work with other musicians. And while it's fine to sit and jam with a couple of guys (or gals), shout chord changes to one another, record the session, and call the end result a song — it's entirely another thing to sit down and write a piece of music that any musicians with some basic music theory knowledge can read for themselves, without your being there to explain verbally what you want to hear from them.

The best way to communicate your compositions to others is to write them down. There are many ways to write music down, and in this chapter we cover the ones you're most likely to run into.

## Composing with Lead Sheets

The simplest, most basic type of sheet music is called a *lead sheet*. Lead sheets are mainly used by pop and jazz musicians — types of music that allow for individual interpretation of how an instrument's musical accompaniment should go.

A lead sheet is composed of a single staff with the notes of the melody written out on it, and the accompanying chords written above the staff, as seen in Figure 19-1.

**Figure 19-1:**
This lead
sheet is
for the
traditional
song, "Little
Brown Jug."

Most guitar-centric or popular music magazines publish at least one or two lead sheets per issue, ones that are usually based on contemporary songs. There are also stacks and stacks of books that compile many lead sheets, called *fakebooks*. The best-known fakebook is called, perhaps confusingly, *The Real Book* (Hal Leonard Corporation, currently in its 6th edition). In a fakebook, you're provided with a melody line, chord name, a guitar chord chart showing the proper fingering for each chord to be played, and the lyrics of the song.

For many cover bands, making their way through a fakebook of modern rock tunes is about as deep into music theory as they ever get. Or need to get. Being able to work off a lead sheet or fakebook as a musician can be immensely satisfying, as they give a musician the room to make up his or her own version of the song.

Many times, a very basic lead sheet is all a good jazz or pop ensemble needs to get rolling. A good rule of thumb is that the bass player of the band is the one with the most detailed sheet music, because, as the fulcrum of the band, the bass player needs to know exactly when a chord or tempo change is to be expected. So if you wanted to only write one part for a whole ensemble to work off of, you would write out a specific bass line, showing the note values and tempo needed as well as the notes to be played for the bass part.

By writing the chord symbols above the staff on that same lead sheet, you then provide enough information for the pianist and the guitarist to work from. Then, because the bass player is playing something very specific and is already defining the basic rhythm of the piece, the percussionist would be able to use this same chart to figure out when to play. Instead of needing an individual rhythm chart, a drummer can look at a bass player's melodic phrasing and see where the accents are. Knowing how to put together a good lead sheet that everyone in the band can use can save you a lot of time.

Listen to any old jazz or funk record — especially from the catalog of Stax Records, which represented such performers as Otis Redding and Booker T. & the MGs during their heyday — and you can hear this musical process unfold for yourself. They almost all start off with the drums and a bass riff.

# Composing with Guitar Tablature

A distinct type of lead sheet, designed specifically for guitar and bass, is called *tablature*, or just *tab*. Instead of using standard musical notation symbols, tab uses ordinary ASCII numbers and letters, making it ideal for reproducing music for the Internet and online newsgroups where anybody with any computer can link up, copy a tab file, and read it.

Tablature notation has existed for more than 800 years, with the first known examples appearing in Asia. Up until the 1600s, the majority of musicians used tablature to write music for just about every instrument you can think of, from stringed instruments and horns to early keyboard instruments. However, tablature had some serious limitations, a major one being that each piece of it was so instrument-specific that there was no possible way for a lute player to reproduce a piece of music on a harpsichord, or any other instrument, by reading his lute tablature. The system began to fall out of common use when the five-lined staff and modern music notation was standardized in the 16th century.

Basically, tab sheets tell you what notes to play. However, there is no way to tell a musician reading tab exactly how long or short a note needs to be — the way quarter notes and half notes and so on do — so it may be necessary for musicians to hear how a piece is to be played before they can successfully read any tab you've written. There are some cases where note flags are written above tab characters, but this is not a standard practice and is mostly confined to tablature written for more archaic instruments like the lute and the contrabass.

Tab is very easy to read, though, and many beginning musicians, or musicians without any real music theory background, prefer to have their music written for them this way. The basic idea of tab for guitar is that you start out by drawing six parallel horizontal lines (four for bass), which correspond to the strings of the instrument. The top line is the highest-pitched string, and the bottom line is the lowest-pitched. An example is shown in Figure 19-2.

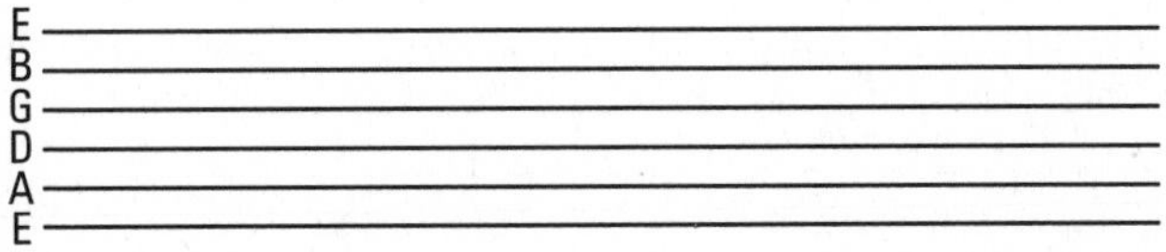

**Figure 19-2:**
A blank tablature for guitar basically represents the guitar's strings.

If you're writing a piece for a bass, you would write out something like Figure 19-3.

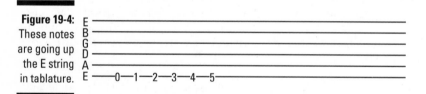

**Figure 19-3:**
A blank bass tablature shows four "strings" instead of six.

Next, you write numbers on the lines to show you where to *fret* the string — meaning upon which fret to apply pressure (in case there's any confusion). If a zero appears, this means play the open string (no fretting).

The tab shown in Figure 19-4 means play the sequence of notes: E(0), F(1), F#(2), G(3), G#(4), and A(5) on the bottom E string by moving up a fret at a time, starting with the open string.

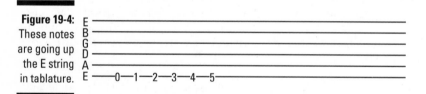

**Figure 19-4:**
These notes are going up the E string in tablature.

If two or more notes are to be played together, they are written on top of one another, such as in the example of a G barre chord shown in Figure 19-5.

In Figure 19-5 you would play all these notes together at once, as a chord.

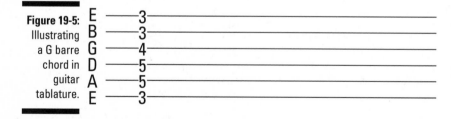

**Figure 19-5:**
Illustrating a G barre chord in guitar tablature.

You might see the same chord written out something like Figure 19-6.

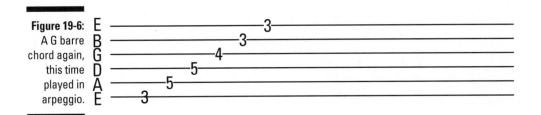

Figure 19-6:
A G barre
chord again,
this time
played in
arpeggio.

Writing tab like Figure 19-6 would mean you want your guitarist to strum the chord, but more slowly, with each individual string plucked, starting at the bottom string and ending at the top.

Most modern tablature doesn't show note values, but as a general rule the horizontal spacing of the numbers on the tab should tell you which notes are the long ones, and which are the short and fast ones. As an example, Figure 19-7 shows the first few notes of "The Star-Spangled Banner" in tab. As you can see, the different spacings correspond to the different note lengths.

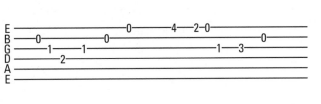

Figure 19-7:
The spacing
in "The Star-
Spangled
Banner" tab
indicates
roughly how
long to play
each note.

To show technical markings in tab, the standard practice is to write extra letters or symbols between notes to indicate how to play them, such as the example in Figure 19-8, which indicates a hammer-on (playing the note by simply bringing the finger down on the fret, without plucking the note). In that example you would play the open E twice, then hit the A string at the fifth fret and hammer on to the seventh fret.

**Figure 19-8:**
Writing
"h" is the
convention
to tell a
guitar player
to hammer
a note on.

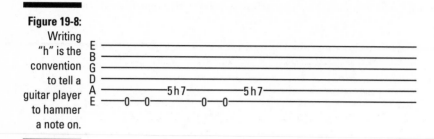

Following is a list of the extra letters and symbols most often used in guitar tablature:

| *What to write* | *What it means* |
| --- | --- |
| H | Hammer-on |
| P | Pull-off |
| B | Bend string up |
| R | Release bend |
| / | Slide up |
| — | Slide down |
| v | Vibrato (sometimes written as ~) |
| T | Right hand tap |

# The Score

A piece of music that includes all the notation — precise melodic lines and harmonic accompaniment — the composer intended for the instrumentalist to play is called a *score*. A score can be as simple as the melodic and harmonic accompaniment of a child's song for the piano, as in Figure 19-9.

In Figure 19-9, you can see that all the notes the composer intended to be played by the musician are right there on the paper. There are no chord charts listed over the staff to suggest improvisation, and there is no mystery as to how long each note is supposed to be held. Although improvisation might still be possible, and even welcomed by your audience, there's no need for it.

A more advanced score is shown in Figure 19-10.

**Figure 19-9:**
This score shows the opening of "When the Swallows Homeward Fly" by Franz Abt.

**Figure 19-10:**
This is the score for Beethoven's Symphony No. 7, second movement.

As you can see, this is a multi-instrumental score, meant for a large ensemble to play. Generally, the only people who would see this particular score would be the composer and the conductor of the orchestra. The other members of the orchestra would only receive the sheet music for the parts they were meant to play. Therefore, if you were the second violinist, for this particular section of music, you would only receive a fragment of the score to read from.

This separation of parts in written scores is why it's so important for concert musicians in an orchestral pit to pay attention to the music in front of them, the music being played around them, *and* the conductor in front of them. The performers don't have the entire instrumental score in front of them, so if they miss their cue, they might as well pack up their instruments and leave.

## Writing for Ensembles

Take a look at the orchestral score in Figure 19-10 again. If you were to play each instrument's section straight out on the piano, you might think that many of the instruments on here are playing completely different notes from each other. If you got a lot of pianos together and had everyone play the part of a different instrument from this sheet, you'd end up with a real mess. This is because many of the instruments used in your standard orchestra are *transposing instruments*, meaning that they're tuned to different keys. (Take a look at Chapter 14, on writing for the standard orchestra, for much more about the specific tunings for these instruments.)

Most composition software automatically helps with the transposition for you when you're writing a full score like this one — which makes your Average Joe Composer's job a lot easier than it was even 20 years ago. Many software programs, such as Finale, even ask how many instruments are going to be used in your composition before you even begin writing, and present you with as many staffs as needed, as shown in Figure 19-11.

Many such programs are also equipped with MIDI capabilities, making it possible to hear all the parts of your composition played out — in *tutti*, that is, with all the instruments playing together — before giving it to a live ensemble.

## Working with Foreign Scores and Ensembles

Many times, especially when working with older scores or with traveling ensembles, you'll have a score come across your desk that's not written in English — you'll still be dealing with quarter notes, half notes, and so forth on the staff itself, but the chords and major and minor keys all have different names. Because the majority of classical music has been written in non-English-speaking countries, there's a good chance this will happen a lot.

This can especially be the case with a multi-instrumental score that changes key mid-score, where writing one "Sol (G)" in the blank space between staffs in the middle of the page, right where the key change happens, is quicker than changing every key signature for every single instrument on every single staff (such as in many of Tchaikovsky's orchestral scores). It's also handy when reading older folk music scores or working with European folk music ensembles that use different symbols for their lead sheets.

**Figure 19-11:** Finale presents the proper blank sheet music for multiple-voice composition.

Table 19-1 shows a simple chart of note names to help you cross the language barrier more easily.

| Table 19-1 | Note Names in Different Languages | | |
|---|---|---|---|
| *English* | *Italian* | *German/Dutch* | *French* |
| C | do | C | ut |
| C sharp | do diesis | Cis | ut dièse |
| D flat | re bemolle | Des | re bémol |
| D | re | D | re |
| D sharp | re diesis | Dis | re dièse |
| E flat | mi bemolle | Es | mi bémol |
| E | mi | E | mi |
| E sharp | mi diesis | Eis | mi dièse |
| F flat | fa bemolle | Fes | fa bémol |
| F | fa | F | fa |
| F sharp | fa diesis | Fis | fa dièse |
| G flat | sol bemolle | Ges | sol bémol |
| G | sol | G | sol |
| G sharp | sol diesis | Gis | sol dièse |
| A flat | la bemolle | As | la bémol |
| A | la | A | la |
| A sharp | la diesis | Ais | la dièse |
| B flat | si bemolle | B | si bémol |
| B | si | H | si |
| B sharp | si diesis | His | si dièse |
| C flat | do bemolle | Ces | ut bémol |
| natural | bequadro | auflösungszeichen | bécarre/naturel |
| major | maggiore | dur | majeur |
| minor | minore | moll | mineur |

As you can see, the French and the Italian note names follow the solfege tradition of the 11th century Roman Catholic Church. Solfege was a system of note reading invented by Father Guido D'Arezzo for teaching Gregorian chants, forever immortalized by Julie Andrews in *The Sound of Music*: "*Do re mi fa sol la ti do.*"

# Part V
# The Part of Tens

The 5th Wave          By Rich Tennant

"Hey George, give it a rest. Let's have lunch. I picked up some bluefish. Man, I love bluefish. Do you love bluefish, George?"

# In this part . . .

We share some of our favorite composers, books, and musical periods with you. We also talk about some of the career opportunities open to composers, including how to get your foot in the door. Finally, we provide a comprehensive reference to modes and show chord triads for every note on the scale — and we finish up with a glossary to help you quickly look up word definitions.

# Chapter 20

# Ten Composers You Should Know About

## In This Chapter

▶ Surveying some of the more extraordinary composers

▶ Spanning centuries and genres

▶ Expanding your exposure to giants of music

• • • • • • • • • • • • • • • • • • • • • • • • • • • • • • • • • • • • • • • • • • •

*L*et's face it: There's just no way to pick the ten best composers, or ten most important composers, or even the ten handsomest composers of all time. Everybody's got an opinion on what makes a composer great, and if you go to the library or bookstore looking for books about composers, you'll be faced with a daunting wall of personal opinion on this matter.

Taking this into consideration, what we've tried to do here is pick ten extraordinary composers who challenged musical conventions and public perception of what music is supposed to be — just ten out of dozens of pioneers in the world of music.

## Claudio Monteverdi, 1567–1643

If you had to name one person who was the "missing link" between the music of the Renaissance and the Baroque periods, it would be Claudio Monteverdi. Monteverdi brought an unparalleled level of sophistication and respect to vocal music, turning it from something only peasants and priests could enjoy into full-blown opera performances designed to entertain the ruling and intellectual elite.

Even as a child, Monteverdi was musically precocious. His first publication of sheet music was issued by a prominent Venetian publishing house when he was only 15, and by the time he was 20 a variety of his works had gone to print. His first book of five-voice madrigals succeeded in establishing his reputation outside of his provincial hometown and helped him find work in the court of the Duke Gonzaga of Mantua.

Monteverdi became known as a leading advocate of the then radical approach to harmony and text expression. In 1613, Monteverdi was appointed *maestro di cappella* at St. Mark's, Venice. There, Monteverdi was active in reorganizing and improving vocal music, specifically *a capella,* as well as writing music for it. He was also in huge demand outside of the Church for his operas and made a decent living from opera commissions.

Monteverdi can be justly considered one of the most influential figures in the evolution of modern music. His opera, *Orfeo,* was the first to reveal the potential of the genre, while his follow-up, *Arianna,* may be responsible for the survival of opera into the 18th century and beyond. Monteverdi's final opera, *L_incoronazione di Poppea,* is his greatest masterpiece and arguably the finest opera of the 17th century. Monteverdi was also one of the first composers to utilize the techniques of tremolo and pizzicato on stringed instruments.

In his collections of sacred music, Monteverdi displayed his knowledge and mastery of other musical genres as well. His masses are a monument to the old style, whereas his motets, written for virtuoso singers, are the most thoroughgoing exhibition of the modern style and the *seconda prattica.* His most important contribution to secular and vocal music, however, is that he introduced a more intensely expressive and dramatic element into music than had previously been felt. Today he is regarded less as a revolutionary than as one of the outstanding composers of his time, who combined the old with the new to forge a style of music with a dramatic range, emotional expression, and sensuous lyricism that had never been heard before.

# Charles Ives, 1874–1954

American composer Charles Ives was an experimental and boldly original pioneer in musical expression. Without him, the brilliance of the American experimental music scene in the 1930s would have been delayed by years, or perhaps never even happened. Recognition of his forceful, often eccentric genius came late in his life and much more fully after his death.

In a way, Charles Ives really lived two lives: an outward, tradition-bound public life as a very successful executive at Mutual Life Insurance, and an inward reflective life full of paradoxical and revolutionary musical ideas. By being gainfully employed in insurance — and he bordered on being a millionaire due to his brilliant ideas regarding estate planning — Ives found he didn't need to rely on his music to bring in any money and could therefore write and record his music according to how *he* wanted, and not how any perceived audience wanted.

The musical environment in late 19th-century America, when Ives began composing, was conservative, cold, and retrogressive and was still attached to the nearly exhausted European Romantic tradition. Though he sometimes wrote traditional pieces, Ives mostly experimented with new musical procedures.

By the 1920s, Ives had experimented with practically every important musical innovation that would still be considered new music 50 years later, including atonality, bitonality, polymetric patterns, polyharmonic and polytonal particulars, quarter tones, microtones, tone clusters, and tone rows. Realizing that his music was too unconventional for most people to enjoy, he composed primarily for his own pleasure and, except for works for organ and church choirs, most of his compositions remained unperformed for years.

During most of his life, Ives was treated simply as a musical eccentric. Fortunately, he lived just long enough to see his work begin to be accepted. His Symphony No. 3 (*The Camp Meeting*) won the Pulitzer Prize in 1947. In all, Ives wrote a staggeringly large amount of music: four symphonies, numerous large and small orchestral and chamber works, two finger-breaking, sprawling piano sonatas, four violin sonatas, many choral pieces, short solo piano, and organ works, and nearly 200 songs.

# Béla Bartók, 1881–1945

Béla Bartók was another very important figure in 20th-century music. The Hungarian-born composer and pianist's most lasting contribution to music is his incorporation of Hungarian folk music into his compositions. Not only is he considered one of the greatest composers of the 20th century, but he was also one of the founders of the field of *ethnomusicology*, or the study and ethnography of folk music. As a composer, Bartók was an influential modernist, who used such revolutionary techniques as atonality, bitonality, polymodal chromaticism, octonal scales, diatonic and heptatonic second and seven-note scales, whole-tone scales, and many other principles outside the realm of what was then considered musically acceptable.

The defining event of Bartók's musical life occurred in 1905, when he and fellow Hungarian composer Zoltan Kodály journeyed into remote rural areas of Hungary to collect the peasant songs of the Magyar, an ancient semi-nomadic people that had lived in the region for possibly thousands of years. The melodies and rhythms of Magyarok folk music incorporated scale and rhythmic patterns that lay completely outside the traditions of 19th century Western music. Ironically, these scales and rhythms were a lot like the ones being "invented" and explored by early 20th-century modernists such as French composers Clause Debussy and Maurice Ravel.

Before Bartók and Kodály's examination of the Magyars' music, most people had considered Magyarok folk music to be Gypsy music. In actuality, the old Magyarok folk melodies discovered by Bartók and Kodály were almost all based on pentatonic scales similar to those found in various Oriental folk traditions, notably those of Central Asia and Siberia.

From 1905 on, Bartók considered the documentation of rural folk music his true calling in life. He recorded thousands of examples from Bulgaria, Hungary, Romania, Turkey, and other areas. Eventually he wrote down a vast amount of this material in musical notation, organized it systematically, and analyzed and wrote about it. This contribution to the developing discipline of ethnomusicology ranks among Bartók's most important achievements.

For Bartók the composer, the discovery of peasant music had a liberating influence. Bartók based some of his compositions directly on the music he collected, as in the *Improvisations on Hungarian Peasant Songs* for solo piano. But more commonly, he composed his own material in a style that reflected his absorption of the melodic and rhythmic aspects of the folk music he studied, but still retained many of the classical elements of mainstream classical music.

Among Bartók's important works are his *Mikrokosmos* (1926, 1932–1939), which consists of 153 piano pieces in six books of increasing difficulty. Ranging from basic five-finger exercises to the virtuosity of "Six Dances in Bulgarian Rhythm," *Mikrokosmos* is both a unique 20th-century teaching method for piano and a thorough introduction to Bartók's compositional style. Other major works include six string quartets, the one-act opera *Bluebeard's Castle*, *Music for Strings, Percussion, and Celesta*, and *Sonata for Two Pianos and Percussion*.

# Igor Stravinsky, 1882–1971

Igor Fyodorovich Stravinsky was a Russian-born composer who spent most of his musical career challenging established musical conventions. His compositions were technically challenging enough that no critics could dare fault him for writing "easy" music, yet engaging enough thematically that they couldn't just dismiss him as obsessed with technique and random experimentation.

His most famous composition, 1913's *Rite of Spring*, was so radical in its overt sexuality both musically and choreographically that the Parisian audience rioted violently in the theater during its opening performance, with some attendees even taking the mayhem into the streets outside. The protests were so loud, in fact, that the dancers on stage had trouble hearing the orchestra playing. It wasn't very long before the composition was heralded as genius, and subsequent performances were both well attended and well received.

Stravinsky's initially disturbing yet wildly popular compositions, which included *The Rite of Spring*, *Fireworks*, and *Firebird*, all drew heavily from the Russian folk music of the "common" people — music that before had been considered inferior for concert performances. Another defining feature of Stravinsky's larger pieces is that he made no attempt to link the movements of his compositions in a harmonious way. Instead, he made a clean break from one movement to the next, almost as though he was presenting an entirely different song. These lurches from one symphonic movement to the next were incredibly disorienting to 19th-century audiences, who were used to being gently and harmoniously led through a composition from the beginning to the end.

The binding energy of his orchestral compositions is much more rhythmic than harmonic, and the driving pulsations of *The Rite of Spring* marked a crucial change in the nature of Western music. Stravinsky, however, left it to others to use that change, for after completing his Chinese opera *The Nightingale*, he turned aside from writing large orchestral pieces to concentrate on small chamber orchestra music and piano compositions.

# Aaron Copland, 1900–1990

If ever a classical composer could be said to have defined the sound of "American" music, Aaron Copland has to be at the top of the list. His music was the aural equivalent of the movie western: big, bold, short on subtlety and long on orchestral exclamation points. He was a true pioneer of American music and showed the world how to write classical music in an American way. He was an American composer in a time when Americans were rarely recognized as composers in the music world.

Although his earliest work was heavily influenced by the French impressionists, he soon began to develop a personalized style. After experimenting with jazz rhythms in such works as *Music for the Theater* (1925) and the Piano Concerto (1927), Copland turned to more austere and dissonant compositions. Concert pieces such as the Piano Variations (1930) and *Statements* (1933-1935) rely on nervous, irregular rhythms, angular melodies, and highly dissonant harmonies.

Copland's immense output of Americana-inspired classical music, such as *Fanfare for the Common Man, Rodeo, Billy the Kid, Appalachian Spring, The Twelve Poems of Emily Dickinson*, and *El Salon Mexico* showed other American composers that they didn't have to pretend to be European to be taken seriously. Like many composers of his time, he drew heavily on the folk music of his country, bringing the sound of the Old West into the classical arena. Many of his compositions, especially *Billy the Kid, Fanfare for the Common Man*, and *Appalachian Spring*, have been used in many movie westerns and, most recently, parodies of movie westerns. You might think you don't know Copland, but you'd have to have been living under a rock for the past 40 years to have completely missed his music.

Copland's work had (and still has) a universal appeal that seemed to fit into anything American. His compositions *Hoe-Down* and *Fanfare for the Common Man* were reworked in the 1970s by Emerson, Lake & Palmer. In the 1990s, the

National Cattlemen's Beef Association used *Hoe-Down* as the background music to their marketing campaign, "Beef … it's what's for dinner." This piece was also used during the 78th Academy Awards. *Hoe-Down* resurfaced once again in Spike Lee's film *He Got Game*, where it played in the background of a neighborhood basketball game. It's difficult to overestimate the influence Copland has had on film music. Virtually every composer who scored for western movies, particularly between 1940 and 1960, was shaped by the style Copland developed.

# Raymond Scott, 1909–1994

If you've ever watched a Looney Tunes cartoon, or really any cartoon in the Warner Bros. catalog, you've heard the music of Raymond Scott, a.k.a. Harry Warnow. Ironically, Scott never consciously wrote any music for cartoons, and, according to his wife, never even watched cartoons. Scott simply sold the rights to a huge chunk of his music to Warner Brothers in the 1940s, and the rest is animation history. Carl Stalling, music director for Warner's *Looney Tunes* and *Merrie Melodies*, was allowed to adapt anything in the Warner music catalog, and he immediately began making liberal use of Scott's scores. Scott's music scored more than 120 Bugs Bunny and Daffy Duck animated shorts, while today *The Simpsons, Ren and Stimpy, Animaniacs, The Oblongs, Batfink,* and *Duckman* are just a few of the cartoon series that regularly use Scott's music. His best-known composition, "Powerhouse," was used ten times in 2003's full-length feature movie, *Looney Tunes: Back in Action*.

To the casual observer, it might seem like Scott had given the best work of his life away, but Scott was involved in so many other music projects it probably felt like getting a lot of money for nothing. Almost immediately after graduating from Julliard in 1931, Scott had been working as a professional musician, with the support of his older brother, Mark Warnow, who was the musical director for the very popular radio show *Your Hit Parade*. While still in his early 20s, Scott became the pianist for the CBS Radio house band, where he met the members of his first band, the Raymond Scott Quintette. Coming from a classical background, Scott disliked the popular jazz tradition of improvisation, but also disliked the concept of sheet music, believing that good music would just stick in the heads of the musicians involved without need to write it down. He wrote nothing down on paper, insisting that the other members of his group follow lead lines often hummed at them from behind the piano.

The Quintette existed from 1937 to 1939 and sold millions of records, despite being labeled a novelty jazz band. When Scott was appointed music director of CBS radio in 1942, he made history by breaking the color barrier by organizing the first racially integrated radio band, which included saxophonist Ben Webster and trumpeter Charlie Shavers.

Far from being simply a musician and bandleader, however, Scott was also heavily involved in music technology. As far back as the 1940s, Raymond Scott had a home recording studio, where he would cut and splice reels of his band's rehearsal sessions to find the best parts of the music. In 1946, Scott started his own company, Manhattan Research, Inc., which he announced would "design and manufacture electronic music devices and systems." Dr. Robert Moog worked for Scott for a short time before starting his own company up and claimed he was a huge influence on his own direction in music. At Manhattan Research, Inc., Scott invented the the Electronium, which was one of the first synthesizers ever created; the Karloff, an early sampler capable of recreating sounds ranging from sizzling steaks to jungle drums; and the Videola, which fused together a keyboard and a TV screen to aid in composing music for films and other moving images.

Raymond Scott continued to write and record music during this period, releasing records of electronic ambient music well before Philip Glass and Terry Riley, and in 1971, he was hired as director of Motown's electronic music and research department — and was kept there for many years just in case the future of music really was "electronic." He continued to compose and invent electronic instruments until his death in 1994.

# Leonard Bernstein, 1918–1990

Leonard Bernstein was an American composer, conductor, and pianist who wrote music that can only be described as exuberant. Just about every single piece of music he wrote was incredibly uplifting, irresistibly happy, and full of energy — much as Bernstein himself physically appeared when taking the reins as conductor, both at the New York Philharmonic and elsewhere. His success as a composer for both Broadway and the orchestra helped forge a new relationship between classical and popular music. His guiding principle was that music could and should play a vital role in the lives of all people, not just academics. In 1967, he wrote, "Life without music is unthinkable, music without life is academic. That is why my contact with music is a total embrace."

Bernstein's limitless energy and virtuosity were legend in New York in the 1940s, where he seemed to be everywhere at once. In 1944, he collaborated with his friend, the dancer and choreographer Jerome Robbins, on a new ballet entitled *Fancy Free*. The acclaim that greeted *Fancy Free* convinced Robbins and Bernstein that the ballet contained the seeds of a full-fledged Broadway musical. With their friends Betty Comden and Adolph Green, they quickly created *On the Town* (1944), which became their first Broadway hit. At the same time, he began building a conventional conducting career, with the advice and counsel of such mentors as Koussevitzky, Artur Rodzinski, and Dimitri Mitropoulos, virtually reinventing the role of the serious American composer, freely moving between Broadway and the concert hall. With Comden and Green and their friend Judy Holliday, he performed in night-clubs as part of The Revuers. The night before his impromptu New York Philharmonic debut, mezzo-soprano Jennie Tourel, at her Town Hall debut recital, gave the first performance in New York of Bernstein's "I Hate Music."

Bernstein seemed comfortable writing in any form he chose. His composition included three symphonies, including a tribute to his Jewish heritage, Symphony No. 1: *Jeremiah,* to the musicals *On the Town*, *Wonderful Town*, and *West Side Story*. He also composed the operetta *Candide*; the operas *Trouble in Tahiti* and *A Quiet Place*; *Chichester Psalms* for chorus and orchestra; the ballets *Fancy Free* and *The Dybbuk Variations*; *Mass*, for "singers, dancers, and players"; and the song cycle *Arias and Barcarolles* (1989).

# Arvo Pärt, 1935–present

Arvo Pärt is one of those composers lumped under the term *minimalism* that doesn't really belong there. There has to be a better way to describe his music, however, because instead of simply condensing a piece of music to its bare tonal center, Pärt is just somehow able to find the very best couple of notes for his compositions. His composition process is legendary, with reports of him sitting at the piano for hours and hours on end, hitting the same key over and over, trying to find the perfect way to sound that one note.

Far from resulting in tedious, mechanical-sounding music, Pärt's music is so pure and perfect that many have dubbed his work *sacred minimalism*. Pärt, who received his musical training almost equally within the Catholic Church and in music school, draws heavily on the tradition of Gregorian chant in his vocal works, applying the same principal of using only the absolute best notes for both the instruments and the voices used in his compositions.

Throughout Pärt's career, he has demonstrated a voracious musical curiosity and daring experimental spirit that has allowed him to become not only Estonia's premiere composer, but one of the best-known choral and sacred music composers of the 21st century. Thirty years of musical experimentation with influences as wide ranging as Russian neoclassicism, Western modernism, Schoenbergian dodecaphony, minimalism, polytonality, Gregorian chant, and collage have led him to a style of music he calls "tintinnabulation," also called "sacred minimalism" by colleague Steve Reich. This method, which takes its name from the Latin word for bells, places unusual emphasis on individual notes and makes extensive use of silence.

# Steve Reich, 1936–present

Steve Reich could easily be considered the father of all industrial music, and his influence can be felt in the music of bands as wide ranging as Einstürzende Neubauten to Nine Inch Nails. Way back in the 1960s, Reich was using tape loops of people speaking as rhythmic devices in his compositions, created at the San Francisco Tape Music Center. These tape pieces, such as "It's Gonna Rain" (1965) and "Come Out" (1966), are the earliest examples of *phasing*, one of Reich's most used and most well known techniques. In phasing, two tape loops are set into motion at two slightly different speeds, so that the tapes begin in unison and slowly shift out of phase, creating a new set of harmonies and rhythms. It's like music concrète, or "found" music, but taken one step further, creating controlled and fully realized compositions out of random chaos.

This process was later incorporated into several pieces for traditional acoustic instruments (or instruments and tape), such as in "Piano Phase" and "Violin Phase." In addition to the initial process of phasing, Reich also introduces into "Violin Phase" the notion of "found" or "resulting" patterns (new melodic figures created from the overlapping voices of the original "theme"). In 1970, Reich set out on an intensive study of Ghanaian drumming, which is the tribal drumming of the indigenous peoples of Bali in which a single "song" can last all day long. His highly influential percussive recording, "Drumming," came directly out of this experience. This piece is an enormous, hour-long elaboration of a single rhythmic cell, developed and re-orchestrated through four distinct sections.

Reich's 1988 piece, the Grammy award-winning "Different Trains," marked a new compositional method in which speech recordings were used as the percussive instrument and accompanied by a live string quartet. In this piece, Reich compared and contrasted his childhood memories of his train journeys between New York and California in 1939-1941 with the very different trains being used to transport contemporaneous European children to their deaths under Nazi rule.

# Eric Whitacre, 1970–present

While many of the composers on this list have made their mark because they wrote music that broke through the musical conventions of the day, Eric Whitacre had been making waves by digging deep into the history of Western music and revitalizing the relatively ancient genres of a capella music and polyphonic chant. His compositions draw their lyrical inspiration

## Steve Reich, composer

*Minimalism* is a term used by journalists and music historians, and it's fine for them, but use a word like that for one of my compositions, to me, and I'll tell you to go to the bathroom and wash out your mouth. What would happen if you or I went to Paris and dug up Claude Debussy, and said, 'Excuse me, Monsieur, are you an Impressionist?' He would said, 'No!' and go right back to sleep. Because these are terms taken from painting and sculpture, and applied by journalists and historians to musicians. To musicians, these terms mean absolutely nothing. It's just a short-hand way of lumping types of musicians together into a movement or scene that doesn't exist.

from many of the most important poets of the past century, such as Octavio Paz, e. e. cummings, Edmund Waller, and Emily Dickinson, and imbued those words with the spiritual beauty of *a capella* Gregorian chant.

Many of Whitacre's works have entered the standard choral and symphonic repertoires and have become the subject of several recent scholarly works and doctoral dissertations. His works *Water Night, Cloudburst, Sleep, Lux Aurumque,* and *A Boy and a Girl* are among the most popular choral works of the last decade. One major aspect of Whitacre's compositions is that he builds complex chords using the human voice. The challenge of playing his music is that everything has to be sung perfectly in tune, without vibrato or any vocal affectation, or the sophisticated chords won't work.

Whitacre has received composition awards from the Barlow International Composition Competition, the American Choral Directors Association, and the American Composers Forum. In 2001, he became the youngest recipient ever awarded the coveted Raymond C. Brock commission by the American Choral Directors Association. Whitacre's chorale music has even inspired the creation of a number of national and international music festivals specifically for chorale and wind instruments. Australia now hosts an annual Eric Whitacre Wind Symphony Festival, while in Italy, both Venice and Florence hold a Venice Whitacre Festival.

# Chapter 21

# Nine Career Opportunities for Composers

*Y*ou don't need a book to tell you that making a living as a composer is hard. And it's not because the money isn't out there waiting for you to come along. It's simply because that for every legitimate composing job out there, there are dozens — or even *hundreds* — of budding, starry-eyed composers out there, waiting in line for their big chance.

Does that mean you should give up? No, it means that what's going to set you apart from every other composer out there — besides your massive talent — is your ability to persevere against what might seem like tremendous odds. That, and the ability to seek out work on your own and not sit around and wait for want ads in the paper or the music journals to pop up.

The following careers are just a few of the opportunities open to composers that may not have crossed your — or your competition's — mind.

## School Bands and Choirs

Every year, high schools and colleges across the country put on musical performances for both parent and community audiences. Sometimes, the music used for these performances comes from well-known sources, such as

*Oklahoma!* or *Grease*. Sometimes, though, the school in question wants to use completely original music, preferably written by a local composer. It's an extra bonus if that composer once attended that school.

The best way to get your foot in the door as a composer at your local high school or college is to approach the music department head in person with a selection of your own original music. Call up the school in question, set up an appointment, and then come prepared. You'll want to bring a portfolio of your original written music to present at the appointment, plus a recording of it for the music director to listen to at his or her leisure.

Granted, most high schools and universities don't have a huge budget for paying composers for original work, but having this credit under your belt may open doors you can't currently imagine. Your name will be on the printed program of the performance, and every single person attending the performance will receive a copy of this program. If the performance is a success, there's a chance that schools outside of your community will want to use your music.

The trick to writing music for either a high school/college choir or musical is that you have to take into consideration that you're writing for kids. Talented kids, probably, but still kids. Therefore, you want to keep the instrumentation and vocals just easy enough for them to handle, but challenging enough for them to feel like they've accomplished something. Think somewhere between Andrew Lloyd Weber's *Phantom of the Opera* and the music from *The Muppet Show*.

Make sure you copyright any work that is accepted for use in a performance. A "poor man's copyright" should do for this purpose — simply fold your score into thirds, staple it closed (don't put it in an envelope), then mail it to yourself. If you do put it in an envelope, send it Certified Mail, Return Receipt Requested. The post office's dated postal mark on an unopened copy of the score, or your signature for delivery, will hold up in most preliminary court settings in case of copyright infringement. (For information on making a more secure copyright, see the sidebar "Copyrighting your work" in Chapter 17.)

# Incidental Television Music

Spend any amount of time in front of a television set, and you'll be amazed at how much incidental filler music is used on any given program. There's music to accompany car chases, love scenes, deep or funny or confusing or dangerous or poignant moments, and so on. Even your local news programs probably use little musical segments at the beginning and end of the shows.

For major network shows, you're going to need a good, persistent agent and a whole lot of experience behind you to get your music in those action/love/flashback scenes. However, the world of cable TV is a whole lot more approachable to the beginning or mid-level composer. Your locally produced cable or public-access stations are good places to start. Their budget is likely to be small or nonexistent, so you're probably going to have to do a lot of free work right off the bat — but people do watch these shows, and this is a credit you can put on your résumé.

Scout out programs that you personally think are interesting or show great promise and then call up the station and find out when those shows are taped. You can then either show up in person on the day of the taping and try to hand your demo CD to the hosts or actors of the show in person, or leave a phone message and a copy of the CD in the program's station mailbox. Make sure you call back to confirm that they received the CD and to see if you can set up an appointment with the people in charge of the program's music. Don't be a pest, but be persistent. If you don't hear anything back within a reasonable frame of time, brush the dust off your jeans and go knock on another door.

Local news programs are another place to try and place your music. Call ahead of time and try to get an appointment with the music director. If an in-person interview isn't possible, try mailing a copy of your CD and a résumé to the director. Always include your contact info (address, phone number, email address) and follow up with a phone call about a week after sending the demo.

# Musical Theater

Musical theater is another area where your mastery of music composition can be utilized. Generally, the composer writes the music, and a lyricist writes the words, although it's not unusual for one person to act as both composer and lyricist. In most cases, composers leave the dances or underscoring to the orchestrator and dance arranger. Only a very few people have succeeded as both composer and lyricist as successfully as Noel Coward, Robert Meredith Wilson, or Jonathan Larson. If you can find a good lyricist to partner up with early in the game, you can save yourself a lot of hassle.

Most show tunes are written on an AABA structure, with a verse and a chorus/refrain. The verse (A) sets up the premise of a song and helps move the story of the musical along, and the chorus (B) states the main idea. For example, consider the title song to *Oklahoma!*, where the verse begins "They couldn't pick a better time to start in life," and says how happy the leads will be living in a "brand new state." The chorus starts with a joyous shout of "Ooooo-klahoma," and then sings the praises of that territory.

Broken down very simply, there are three basic types of show tunes used in musicals:

- ✔ "I Am" songs
- ✔ "I Want" songs
- ✔ "New" songs

"I Am" songs explain a character, a group of characters, or a situation. "I Want" songs tell us what characters desire — what motivates them. Most love songs fit into this category. "New" songs include any songs that don't fit the other two categories, such as instrumentals. "New" songs are there because they serve special dramatic needs, such as the dialog-free big fight scene in *West Side Story*, set to "the rumble" ballet.

The chances that you're going to have your music performed on Broadway right out of the gate are slim to none. So once again, this is a good time for you to check out the musical theater offerings in your own neck of the woods and see if you can get hired writing music for local productions. Dinner theaters that feature live musical entertainment sometimes hire one or two composers or musical directors to work with all of their productions.

When you do land yourself a gig, any gig, put in your own fair share in getting the word out about the production. Send press releases to newspapers and local critics. If any good reviews of the production go to print, especially if they mention you by name or your music, photocopy them many, many times and include a copy of the positive review with any future résumés you send out.

# Concert Composition and Performances

Any pop musician will tell you that the big money in music is in playing concerts. This is why some bands and artists are always on the road. It applies to classical performers as well. Sure, some people will buy a major label classical recording to listen to in the car, but the real cash comes from ticket sales at concert halls.

Your best bet for booking a performance at a club is to talk to the club's booking agent. Or hire a tour manager to set up performances for you on a national or international basis. If you're just planning on playing small, independently run venues on the local level or on tour, you probably don't need a manager, and a little bit of Internet and phone book research can give you the names of hundreds of clubs that would love to have you stop by and play for free, or for popcorn and beer, or for a percentage of ticket sales. You also usually get a table to sell your CDs (and T-shirts) before and after the performance. A good tour manger also has the connections necessary to book you at larger venues where money up front, a guaranteed rate, or a substantial percentage of ticket sales are part of the deal.

If you're not comfortable performing in front of people, but you have lots of music that is performance-ready, you can get that music performed by selling or even lending out your performances on a profit-sharing basis to a local classical ensemble to perform at events. Unless you're composing for an ensemble as big as the Kronos Quartet, you're not going to make a whole lot of money this way, but you can get your name out for people to see, and it's one more credit to put on the ol' résumé.

# *Producer/Arranger*

Just about every rap star and electronic music performer has had a "producer" credit at one time or another. Ask them what they did as "producer" on the record, however, and they may give you a blank look. "Why, I *produced*! What kind of question is that?"

The truth is, being a producer can range from singing backing vocals on a of couple tracks to really giving a record a complete overhaul with a patient and guiding hand. If you're very famous, then the first example is probably the extent of your production work. You're attaching your very famous name to a lesser-known person's name, and hopefully attracting your fans to this person's record (and vice versa).

Real producers are people like Genya Raven and Steve Albini (who prefers to call himself a *studio engineer* instead of *producer*). They go into the studio with the band and help tweak their sound and make it more marketable, or just better. A good producer can call up other musicians in the trade, like horn or steel pedal or xylophone players, to fill in what they think are missing parts of the existing music.

As a composer and overall expert in music, you can make a huge difference in the evolution of a band by working in the producer capacity. Start with small, local bands first, and if it seems like this is something you are very good at, the word of mouth and studio association will start bringing the clients in. There are lots more bands out there than there are producers (especially good producers). A good producer is never short on steady employment.

Don't be afraid to start at the bottom. Many producers need assistants, and this is a good way to gain experience and get your foot in the door if a producing position opens up.

Knowing how to write arrangements is another side of being a good producer — it's also a good career in itself. An arranger can take a piece of music written for one instrument, or multiple instruments, and make it better suited for another instrument or another set of instruments entirely. A familiarity with instruments' physical and tonal capabilities and excellent, second-nature transposition abilities are essential to being an arranger.

# Industrial Music and Advertising

*Industrial music* — not the dance music, but the music of the working world — is any music that is used for a specific, usually commercial, purpose. Advertising music (jingles), convention music, and music written for music libraries all fall under this category.

The best way to break into advertising as a new composer is to actively go out and seek local businesses and find out if they need music for any television or radio campaigns. Local bars are a great place to start, because they almost always use music in their advertising — an extra bonus for them (and you) would be for you or your band to perform at the bar in question. Local clothing and shoe stores are also good places to try, as they also use music in their advertising and are always trying to find a new way to sound "fresh" and "cutting-edge."

## Business conventions

If there's going to be a big business convention in your town, find out if any local businesses are going to have a booth at the event. Many times, the most stodgy-seeming company, such as medical suppliers or stationery stores, will hire a musician or a small band to play music at their booth in order to attract attention away from their competitors. As with any potential job, call ahead to set up an appointment — or at the least, try to find out who is in charge of setting up the convention booth for the company. Mail a copy of your demo disc to that person and follow up after the appropriate length of time (one week is usually good).

## Music libraries

Music libraries, or *song banks*, can range from a single CD with one composer's interpretation of *public domain* scores (musical copyright expires 70 years from the composer's death and becomes "public domain") to Web sites that sell thousands of sound effects to full-length compositions from any number of musicians and composers. Many of the Web-based music libraries, such as Audiosparx (www.audiosparx.com), are always open to working with more musicians, and will pay you 50 percent of whatever they earn from people downloading your sound effects or music. Plenty of musicians make a small but steady income working with music libraries, which then sell music and sounds to video game companies, independent film companies, and even phone companies (for ringtones).

# Film Scoring

One of the most lucrative careers that a music composer can pursue is writing scores for films. It's a very difficult arena to get into, though, and if you're not able to stomach competition or rejection, it's probably not for you. If you do get your moment in the sun, however, just remember that your score has to fit the film, it has to be evocative emotionally, and you absolutely have to be able to stick to all deadlines and timetables thrown at you, no matter how impossible they seem. See Chapter 17 on more about being a film composer.

# Video Game Scoring

Video game scoring is another very lucrative career for composers, and also one of the most challenging. You have to have an intimate knowledge of every game you're scoring for, including the sounds needed for every possible scenario in the game. Most video games are wall-to-wall sounds, all the way through, and therefore require a composer to write a lot of music. An intimate knowledge of how rhythm and changing tempos affects mood is necessary, as is the ability to compose both highly unpleasant, discordant music and triumphant-sounding music to fit scenes on a very tight deadline. There is more about video game scoring in Chapter 17.

# Songwriting

Another good career for composers is that of a songwriter. Many big-name pop stars depend on songwriters to come up with lyrics for them, and if you can get your foot in the door in this highly competitive field, you'll have no trouble finding money to fund your own pet projects.

A good place to start finding leads is the book *Songwriter's Market* (Ian Bessler, Writer's Digest Books). *Songwriter's Market* lists hundreds of agencies, record labels, publishing companies, and production companies looking for songwriters to work with, as well as pay rates and basic contract information.

# Chapter 22

# Ten Recommended Books for Composers

*W*alk into any bookstore and check out the Music Books section, and you'll find yourself before a wall of daunting choices. Stop by any given online bookstore and search for *music*, and you'll be faced with even more. It seems there are nearly as many books written about music composition, the music business, and music appreciation as there are albums or compact discs containing music.

Here are just a few of the good ones.

## Songwriter's Market

by Ian Bessler, Writer's Digest Books

*Songwriter's Market* is one of the most respected of the market guides and worth picking up every year when a new edition comes out (the 2008 edition is the latest as of this writing). For more than 30 years, the guide has provided up-to-date contact information on music-publishing houses, record companies, managers, booking agents, and record producers. It also explains what sorts of musicians and composers these organizations want to work with for the coming year. Besides that, the book lists how much money you can expect to be paid for projects from each record label and music publisher mentioned. There's also lots of information on composing and songwriting contests, as well as information on networking groups and unions that are beneficial for composers and musicians.

Plus the book has a huge, easy-to-understand section on the business side of being a composer or songwriter, including how to read contracts or even write your own basic contract, what sorts of fees are acceptable when signing with a manager or agent, and advice on copyrighting your material. There are also about a dozen interviews in each edition with professional composers and songwriters on how they found success in their given field.

# The Shaping of Musical Elements, Vol. II

by Armand Russell and Allen Trubitt, Schirmer Books/Macmillan, Inc.

If you've taken a beginning theory class in college, you may have read or heard of this series. Where the first volume introduced many of the basic principals of music theory, form, and analysis, *Vol. II* concerns itself with the historical development of music since the 17th century. Baroque, Classical, and Romantic era music is analyzed and dissected to its minutest parts, with good and detailed explanations of what each composer was either trying to do with his music or what his music inspired the next generation of composers to do. The book progresses into the 20th century, with analytical stops at every point in musical history.

It's a really ambitious (and pricey) book — we feel particularly sorry for any student expected to cover all this heady material in one year at music school, even with the benefit of a professor close at hand. You could spend years familiarizing yourself with the concepts and techniques discussed in this book and have a lot of fun doing it, too.

# The Norton Scores, Vols. 1 and 2, 10th Edition

edited by Kristine Forney, W. W. Norton & Company, Inc.

These books are an absolute must for anyone interested in seriously dissecting classical music. *Vol. 1* contains full orchestral scores from the early secular period to Renaissance, Baroque, and Classic periods of music, including works of Beethoven, Bach, Scarlatti, Haydn, and more than a dozen other composers. *Vol. 2* features scores from the 19th century on and includes scores from Schoenberg, Bartók, Copland, and others.

The best way to use these books is to own or check out a recording of the score being studied so that you can follow along with the written material. For the novice score reader, this is an exciting new way to study music; for the more advanced score reader, these books provide the opportunity to really study a composer's technique in a whole new way. Both books are written for the expert and the novice alike, with significant sections of the scores highlighted to make following the piece easier without dumbing down any of the material.

Another great thing about these books is that you have all this truly amazing sheet music at your fingertips. When you're feeling particularly uninspired to write your own music, sit down and analyze and play a section of Mozart's *Don Giovanni* or Bach's *Brandenburg Concerto* — it might be just the thing you need to get inspired to write something entirely new!

# How to Grow as a Musician

by Sheila E. Anderson, Allworth Press

This is a really fun and informative book to read, one that is aimed specifically at the touring and recording musician. There is a lot of information here about booking a tour, mentally preparing yourself for live performances in both familiar and unfamiliar settings, marketing yourself, and even figuring out how much to charge for different types of performances. Contracts and royalties are discussed in great detail, as are all the hidden fees that can pop up even after a contract is signed.

Anderson's background as a jazz radio journalist makes this a great book to just sit down and read even if you're not planning on going on tour or even into the studio; the book contains tons of great stories about the ups and downs of being a professional musician, including anecdotes from jazz greats like Ruth Brown and Michael Wolff. It also contains advice provided by attorneys working within the music business.

# Analysis of Tonal Music: A Schenkerian Approach

by Alan Cadwallader and David Gagné, Oxford University Press

*Schenkerian analysis* is a method of musical analysis based on the theories of Heinrich Schenker, a music theorist of the early 20th century. In Schenkerian analysis, the basic goal is to reveal the tonal structure of a piece of music by reducing the music using a specialized, symbolic form of musical notation devised by Schenker. The analysis reveals the inner musical workings of the music, dividing it into what is called the foreground and the fundamental structure. The *foreground* is the part of the music that immediately attracts a listener's attention, such as the rhythm or the repeated chord changes; the *fundamental structure* is composed of the arrhythmic pitch events that help keep the music from sounding mechanical.

The beauty of Schenkerian analysis is that it is completely subjective, and there is no right or wrong answer to how each individual dissects a piece of music. Each analysis reflects the musical intuitions of the analyst, and shows what he or she thinks is the underlying structure or most important parts of a given piece of music. It's a more philosophical way of studying music than most theoretical approaches, and one more way to learn how to really sit and listen to a piece of music, instead of allowing it to disappear into background noises at a cocktail party.

# The Virgin Directory of World Music

by Philip Sweeney, Owl Books/Henry Holt & Company

This is an extremely well-organized summary of traditional music from around the world. The book is divided into specific regions of the world: Africa (North, West, Central, South, and East), Europe (North, South, and East), the Middle East and India, and so on. Each division is then broken down into the states and countries of those regions, with detailed descriptions of the types of traditional music coming from those regions. There's even detailed mention of notable performers who recorded and released albums of the music of their region, from Ladysmith Black Mambazo to Jamaica's Jolly Boys.

# The Rough Guide to Classical Music, 4th Edition

edited by Joe Staines and Duncan Clark, published by Rough Guides, distributed by Penguin

The Rough Guides are arguably the best music-critique book series out there, with titles ranging from *The Rough Guide to Reggae* to *The Rough Guide to Opera*. This book works for people who are just taking their first steps into the world of classical music appreciation — and for those who are massive classical music fans already but want to see if they've overlooked any essential composers or recordings. Each composer's entry is divided into the types of music the composer delved into, where his or her influence is most felt in later composers' works, and even the political pressures that made them write the types of music they did.

Overall, the guidebook contains the biographies of more than 160 classical composers, spanning from as far back as the 14th century to the present, and offers print reviews of some of the most relevant recordings of each composer's work. The main performers on these recordings are also discussed in brief, with an explanation of why the album being mentioned is the absolute best one for you to pick up.

Fun to either read straight through or to jump around in as a reference book, it's an indispensable guide to anyone who wants to learn more about classical music without getting bogged down by the snobbery that can accompany the genre.

## American Mavericks

edited by Susan Key and Larry Roethe, University of California Press

This book is gorgeous enough to be a coffee table book, and, if you're as obsessed with music as we are *and* you have a coffee table, you really should pick up a copy. It's loaded with fantastic photographs of unique American composers and their equally unique choices of instruments. It features in-depth profiles of composers as varied and dissimilar as John Cage, Aaron Copland, Steve Mackey, and Carl Ruggles. The book also comes with a CD containing 18 tracks of music — one for every composer and several from albums that are just about impossible to find in your local record store.

## RE/Search #14 & #15: Incredibly Strange Music, Vols. 1 and 11

RE/Search Publications

Anyone familiar with the RE/Search books already knows they're in for a treat when they pick up either one of these books. For those not familiar with the RE/Search series — well, you should be. They're a lot of fun to read.

*RE/Search #14 and #15* are both filled with interviews with fringe performers and radio personalities all about their personal record collections. In *#14, Vol. 1*, Ivy and Lux from The Cramps talk about their collection of easy-listening records, Eartha Kitt talks about her own records and the scandal caused by her performance at President Johnson's White House, Gershon Kingsley reminisces about his first recordings on a Moog synthesizer, and Martin Denny talks about the world of exotica. *Vol. 2* features Jello Biafra on Les Baxter, Robert Moog on the theremin, Juan Esquivel on the Latin music of the 1950s, and Yma Sumac on her own mythical life. Both volumes contain many, many more interviews and articles than what we've just mentioned here, but these are just a few examples of why these books belong in every music-lover's collection.

# Chapter 23

# Ten Periods of Music History to Explore

**In This Chapter**

▶ Exploring the variety of classical music

▶ Getting hip to jazz

▶ Expanding your exposure to different kinds of rock

▶ Using the Internet to find the fresh and now

*I*t's one thing to sit and read piles of sheet music and composition books and learn how notes scientifically fit against one another, but it's another thing to truly try to "get" music. To do so, you've got to listen to it, lots and lots and lots of it, and to as many different types as you can. And boy, is there a lot of music out there to explore.

The most interesting periods of music are usually those at the turning point from one accepted style to the next, such as the break from baroque music to classical music, guitar rock to Krautrock and later to math rock and so on. These turning points are generally not recognized at all by general audiences from that period and are, in fact, often dismissed as passing fads; with hindsight, it's much easier to tell which composers and what period of music ended up making the greatest impact on the course of Western music.

Because this book is mostly concerned with the Western musical tradition of composition, we've confined our choices here to the Western canon. However, there is more than half a globe not even mentioned here that is worth writing extra volumes about.

## Classical Music

The term *classical music* has become sort of a catch-all phrase for any sort of "highbrow" music that uses orchestral instruments and arrangements — violins, solo piano, flutes, oboes, and so forth — therefore lumping about

1,500 years' worth of music into one neat little category. A purist, however, would say that true classical music has to be music composed approximately between the years 1750 and 1820 in Europe, with lots of copycats coming afterwards in America.

We're not purists, in case you couldn't tell by now, so we're sticking with the broad, lumping term *classical* to describe the types of music discussed in this section, which are some of the most significant milestones to happen to Western classical music along the way.

## Medieval period: the monophonic phase (590–1200)

In the 7th century A.D., Pope Gregory, later canonized as the patron saint of musicians, declared that the human voice was the only instrument appropriate for glorifying God. All instruments were therefore banned from worship services, to be replaced by more and more complex vocal choirs.

Although some may look at this decree as being a step backwards in the evolution of human music, it was actually the first step forwards in truly exploring the capabilities of the human voice. The Gregorian chants — named after Gregory, but not directly invented by him — were the apex of a capella, *monophonic* (as in, everyone sang the same notes together) singing of the time, expanding on the storytelling plainchant singing that had come to Rome through the indigenous peoples of Europe who had been conquered and assimilated by the Romans.

As only the human voice was allowed within the structure of Church music, the greatest contribution this period made to modern music was the evolution of singing. By 850 A.D., Gregorian chant had given way to polyphonic singing — which is when you have two unrelated voices singing at once (melody and harmony), and by the beginning of the 11th century, it was the music of choice, even after polyphonic music was declared "illegal" by the papacy.

Around 1000 A.D., a Benedictine monk named Guido D'Arezzo completely reworked the crude *neumatic* music notation used for Gregorian chant and designed his own music staff. His staff still used the four lines of the neumatic staff, but he added a time signature at the beginning of the staff to make it easier for performers to keep up with one another. He also devised *solfege*, a vocal scale system that replaced the four tones used by the Greeks with six tones: *ut* (later changed to *do*), *re, mi, fa, so,* and *la,* to be placed in specific spots on the staff. Later, when the diatonic scale was combined with the "Guido Scale," as it's sometimes called, the *ti* sound finished out the octave. *The Sound of Music* just wouldn't be the same without it.

Although most composers from this time wrote anonymously, a few dared to attach their names to their incredible vocal compositions. One such composer — a woman, no less — wrote such incredible choral music that her work is still performed and recorded today. Hildegard von Bingen was the Abbess of Rupertsburg in Germany in the 12th century A.D. She began to record her religious visions in the form of poetry beginning about 1150, providing written melodic outlines using the Church's archaic neumatic notation. She is one of the first identifiable composers in the history of Western music. Her compositions are also some of the only music known from that time that suggest female voices for the high notes, and not boys or men castrated as boys.

## Pre-classical period (1700–1770)

This particular period of music is sometimes divided into two separate periods of music, depending on who's doing the lecturing: the Third Polyphonic Phase of the Late Baroque Period (roughly 1700–1750) and the Pre-classical Period (roughly 1720–1770). However, it works better to lump the two "periods" together because there is so much intermingling of composers and time frames that it's hard to decide which composer belongs to which particular style.

The main thing that sets this period apart, and what makes it really fascinating to study, is that this is the period where composers began to truly break away from the simple and predictable rhythm structures that earmarked nearly 1,000 years of popular music. Musicians such as Antonio Vivaldi (1678–1741) created concertos that were so controlled and tense and such a true study of the mathematics of rhythm that critics accused his work of sounding like finger exercises for the violin. Johann Sebastian Bach (1685–1750) is best known for the prominence of point-counterpoint in his music, where two basic lines of music were played simultaneously on top of one another.

Bach's technique must have seemed liked massive grandstanding back in his day, when most composers relied on having a lead line of music specifically defined, with a lesser line of music designed solely for accompaniment. Two of Bach's 18 children, Carl Philipp Emanuel (his fifth, 1714–1788) and Johann Christian (his last, 1735–1782), also grew up to be major composers during this time frame. The former, known as "the Hamburg Bach," was the principle founder of the sonata style of the classical period; the latter, known as "the London Bach," wrote many symphonies, operas, and harpsichord works that are still played today.

## Nick Currie, a.k.a. Momus

I love baroque music. Bach, of course, is my favorite classical composer. I love that basso continuo thing, that simple, strong counterpoint that happens in baroque music. I love how it defines chords in a fleeting, subtle way rather than the sledgehammer way rock and folk tend to do, with their strummed or fuzzed chord sequences filling out the whole dynamic spectrum of the sound, leaving no space, no ambiguity. I call rock's tendency to hog the whole audible sound area — from deep bass to the hiss of the high-hats — "full-spectrum dominance," and I really think of it as somewhat fascist. Baroque music is more like a sympathetic relationship between two lines, which create harmony and chords by their courtly dance around each other.

# Early 20th century (1910–1950)

This period of time is the true bridge between what was known as classical music and what became known as the *avant garde*. In Austria, composer Arnold Schoenberg (1874–1951) experimented with using the 12-tone scale in his music (as opposed to the 8-tone system considered "normal"), creating some truly disturbing and dark pieces perfectly fit for future horror films. In Hungary, Béla Bartók drew heavily on the dying folk music of his countrymen to create beautifully dark pieces for both orchestral arrangements and solo piano.

Meanwhile, in the U.S., Charles Ives (1874–1954) mixed complex harmonies, polyrhythms, and polytonalities with early American hymns and folk music, leading to his eventual winning of the Pulitzer Prize for Music. His countryman John Cage (1912–1922) laid some of the groundwork for future minimalists in his compositions, requiring audiences to listen to his recorded works via dozens of radios and record players simultaneously — almost overnight making the United States the birthplace of experimental music.

This period of music especially is earmarked by a desperation of composers to really speak to audiences in a time of world-wide turbulence (the two World Wars). Much of the classical music of this time is drawn directly from native traditional music in an attempt to connect with the "common man," as opposed to previous generations of composers, who admittedly were trying to attract the attention of the well-heeled genteel classes.

# Minimalism (1950-present)

If you ever find yourself in a conversation with composer Steve Reich, don't dare refer to his music as *minimalism*, because he'll threaten to wash your mouth out with soap. However, his work, as well as that of Philip Glass, Terry

Riley, John Adams, and Arvo Pärt, has all been lumped together under this category.

Minimalist music springs from the exploratory work started by John Cage and is a genre concerned with finding the absolute right note or rhythm for a piece of music. Philip Glass's work has been earmarked by his songs built around complex rhythms and early use of the synthesizer. In the 1970s, Arvo Pärt put Estonia on the musical map by introducing a new style of composition he called *tintinnabuli*, based on a two-part homophonic texture that is simply breathtaking in its incredible sparseness. In the 1960s, Steve Reich was one of the first to work tape loops into his rhythm-oriented compositions, possibly making him responsible for inspiring much of the electronic loop-based music to come nearly 20 years later.

# Jazz

One unexpected side effect of the Civil War in the United States was that after it ended, pawn shops all over the South were suddenly stocked with brass and percussive instruments hocked by former members of military bands. Suddenly, instruments that had never been owned by anyone outside of the military or nobility were now readily available to the common man. One thing led to another, and, well, jazz *has* been called the one truly American art form.

## Early jazz (roughly 1890–1930)

New Orleans was a fitting home for the birthplace of jazz. The city was a thriving international center of commerce at the turn of the century — unlike the rest of the economically devastated South. Because of its seaport location at the delta of the Mississippi River, it became a melting pot for seemingly a whole world of cultures. Musical influences from Africa, Spain, Italy, South America, and France combined with blues, folk music, and ragtime to create New Orleans jazz, which was invented and further developed by African Americans. Later, in the 1920s, jazz migrated to Chicago, New York, and Kansas City when the black population of the segregated South moved up North to find better job opportunities.

Some of the amazing characters from this time were pianist/composer Jelly Roll Morton, whose massive hands could bang out four octaves' worth of chords at a time. On the brass, Joe "King" Oliver, Freddie Keppard, Louis Armstrong, Sidney Bechet, Jimmy Noone, and Kid Ory blazed a new trail through the tame and timid (and mostly white) music scene of the day with their wild improvisation, unorthodox instrumentation, and obvious sheer delight in just playing music. Anyone who thinks that jazz is something confined to snooty and sophisticated cocktail bars has obviously not checked out any of the guys mentioned above.

## Avant garde (1960s)

With the civil unrest of the 1960s came a slew of brand new types of musical expression, including a brand new form of jazz. The avant garde/free jazz movement encouraged composers to find their own path in music and find their own true individual voice, instead of following the styles and rules of jazz that had come before. In a lot of ways, the only reason that these musicians were considered jazz performers at all was because they used jazz instruments (specifically the whole family of horns), and many critics at the time declared that these pioneers really weren't jazz musicians — and even that the atonal, arrhythmic soundscapes they created wasn't even music.

Building on what composers Charles Mingus, Miles Davis, and John Coltrane had started the previous decade with their own forays into improvisational and modal jazz, Ornette Coleman, Cecil Taylor, Albert Ayler, Eric Dolphy, and Sun Ra stretched the definition of jazz with raw energy and seeming on-the-spot spontaneous performances that challenged everything that had previously been expected of music. Present-day free jazz artists worth checking out include the amazing John Zorn, Mark Feldman, Dave Douglas, and Tim Berne.

# Rock

Rock and roll is now more than 60 years old and still going strong. Its influence on popular music has been so pervasive that some of the more interesting corners of it have been forgotten. Here we mention just a few of these.

## Krautrock

In case you didn't guess it already, Krautrock was German rock. Specifically, it was a style of experimental German rock from the 1960s and 1970s, dubbed *Krautrock* derogatorily by the English press, who were still not open to anything coming out of Germany.

Just as free jazz was called *jazz* mostly because of the instrumentation involved, Krautrock was considered *rock* because it used the guitar/bass/ percussion dynamic of a rock band. The music, though, drew heavily on minimalism and other experimental classical music forms. It sometimes used electronic instruments to give the music a powerfully stark and machine-driven feel and sound.

Krautrock encompassed way too many styles and ideas to truly be considered a single movement. 1970s group Faust incorporated pop sensibilities with rhythmic experiments and tape loops, while other groups like Neu! and Kraftwerk strove to sound as cold and mechanical and devoid of humanity as possible. Can drew heavily on American minimalism and German classical music to create incredibly beautiful and concise rock music, while Popol Vuh took rock instruments and created ambient music that sounded both futuristic and incredibly ancient.

## Math rock (1990s)

Math rock developed in the 1990s as a direct rebellion against rock and roll's traditional 4/4 beat. Math rock is based on complex time signatures such as 7/8, 11/8, or 13/8, giving the music a definite irregular feel.

Perhaps because of the complexity of the music, lyrics aren't a big part of most of these songs. Albums from bands like Slint, Don Cabellero, June of 44, and Bastro were often instrumental-only, whereas other bands such as Shellac, early Modest Mouse, and U.S. Maple included such truly discordant and free-form lyrics in their songs they felt as though they were put there simply to throw off the traditional rock music fan even further.

## Post-rock (1980s–present)

Post-rock can almost be considered the direct descendant of the ambient rock of Krautrock. All the traditional rock instruments are there — guitar, percussion, bass, keyboards — but they are used in completely different ways than in old-fashioned rock and roll. Guitar feedback and static are used to create gorgeous backdrops of ambient sound. Layers of keyboard washes are used to fill in the spaces between notes. Vocals — if there are any — are recorded at the same levels as the instruments, instead of on top of the music, so that the listener's attention isn't immediately drawn to them.

As with the Krautrock genre, the bands that are considered post-rock vary incredibly in construction and sound. The Kentucky band Rachel's is put together like a chamber ensemble, using stringed instruments and piano along with guitars and keyboards, turning out instrumentals that are too dark and tense for most classical audiences, yet not "rock" enough to be considered truly rock and roll. England's Stereolab puts out pleasant pop songs that are so densely layered it's hard to tell where one instrument ends and another one (including the vocals) begins. Canada's Godspeed You Black Emperor! builds incredibly intense arrangements out of traditional rock instruments, drawing both on the traditions of minimalism and ambient music.

## *Right Now*

Every minute of every day, round the clock, something new is being tried out by an artist or an ensemble out there. As of this writing, there's an explosion of new noise, electronic, ambient, rock — you name it — artists out there releasing records, posting MP3s on free download sites, and just playing live at the bar down the street from you. If you're not looking for it, you're not going to find it.

# Appendix A
# Modes and Chords Reference

We talked a little bit about how the seven Greek musical modes are put together in Chapter 6. Well, here are all the possible configurations of the Ionian, Dorian, Phrygian, Lydian, Mixolydian, Aeolian, and Locrian for you to double-check against your own work, or to simply use as a quick reference.

A-Flat Ionian (A♭ Major)

A Ionian (A Major)

B-Flat Ionian (B♭ Major)

B Ionian (B Major)

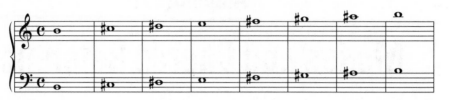

C Ionian (C Major)

D♭ Ionian (D♭ Major)

D Ionian (D Major)

Eb Ionian (Eb Major)

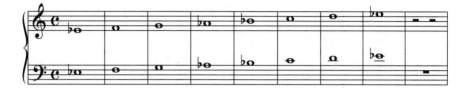

E Ionian (E Major)

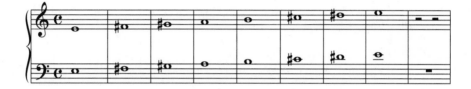

F Ionian (F Major)

F# Ionian (F# Major)

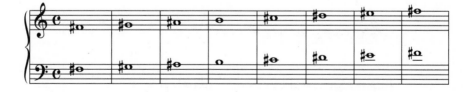

G Ionian (G Major)

A♭ Dorian

A Dorian

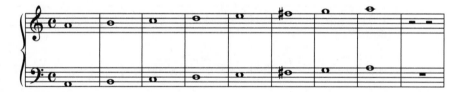

B♭ Dorian

B Dorian

C Dorian

C# Dorian

D Dorian

E♭ Dorian

E Dorian

F Dorian

F# Dorian

G Dorian

A Phrygian

B♭ Phrygian

B Phrygian

C Phrygian

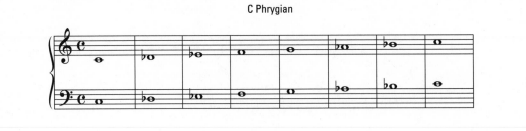

C # Phrygian

D Phrygian

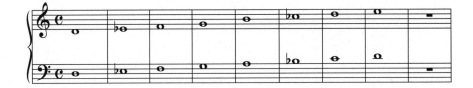

D # Phrygian

E Phrygian

F Phrygian

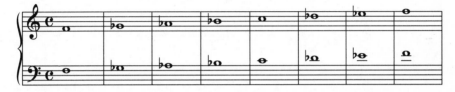

F♯ Phrygian

G Phrygian

G# Phrygian

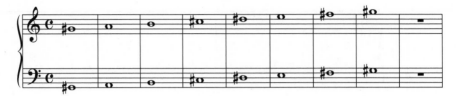

Ab Lydian

A Lydian

A# Lydian

B Lydian

C Lydian

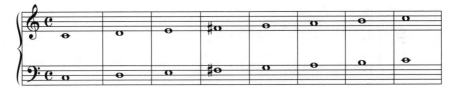

D♭ Lydian

D Lydian

Eb Lydian

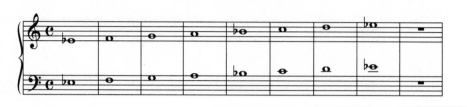

E Lydian

F Lydian

Gb Lydian

G Lydian

A♭ Mixolydian

A Mixolydian

B♭ Mixolydian

C Mixolydian

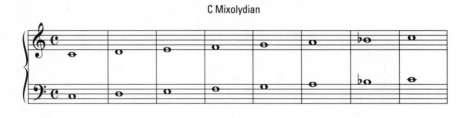

D♭ Mixolydian

D Mixolydian

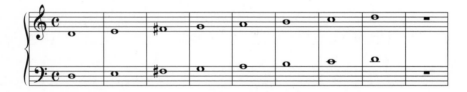

E♭ Mixolydian

E Mixolydian

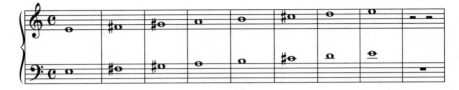

F Mixolydian

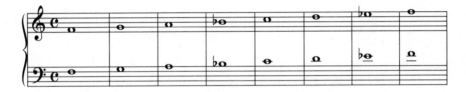

F# Mixolydian

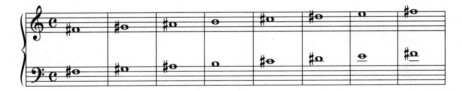

G Mixolydian

Ab Aeolian (Ab Minor)

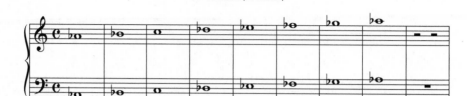

D Aeolian (D Minor)

Bb Aeolian (Bb Minor)

B Aeolian (B Minor)

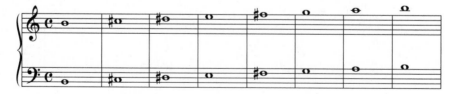

C Aeolian (C Minor)

C♯ Aeolian (C♯ Minor)

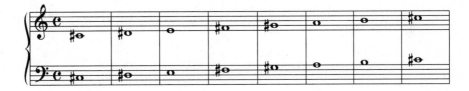

D Aeolian (D Minor)

E♭ Aeolian (E♭ Minor)

E Aeolian (E Minor)

F Aeolian (F Minor)

F# Aeolian (F# Minor)

G Aeolian (G Minor)

A Locrian

A♯ Locrian

B Locrian

C Locrian

C♯ Locrian

D Locrian

D♯ Locrian

E Locrian

F Locrian

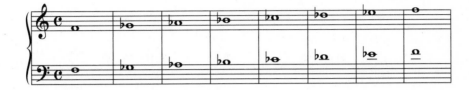

F# Locrian

G Locrian

G# Locrian

The following is a listing of all the chord triads and sevenths for every note on the scale.

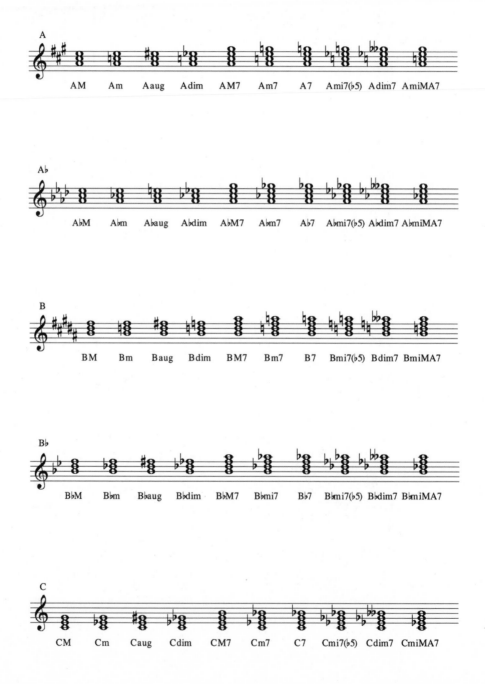

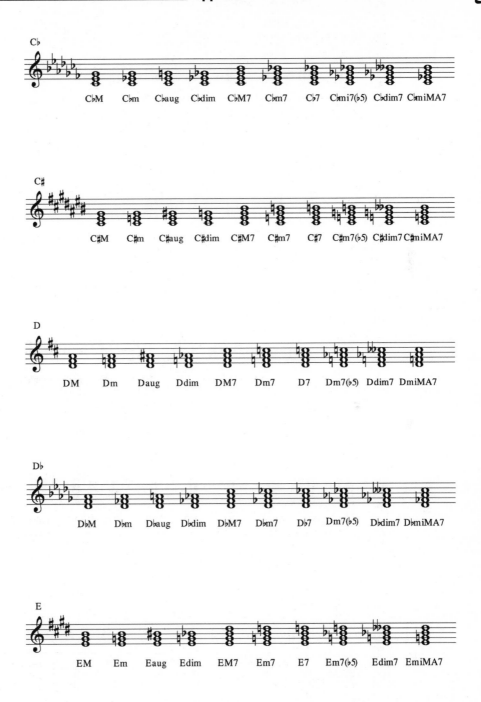

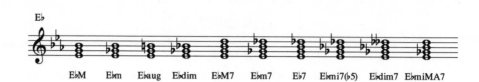

Eb

EbM   Ebm   Ebaug   Ebdim   EbM7   Ebm7   Eb7   Ebmi7(b5)   Ebdim7   EbmiMA7

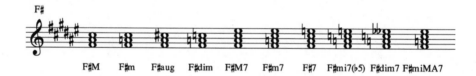

F

FM   Fm   Faug   Fdim   FM7   Fm7   F7   Fmi7(b5)   Fdim7   FmiMA7

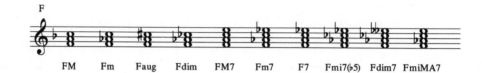

F#

F#M   F#m   F#aug   F#dim   F#M7   F#m7   F#7   F#mi7(b5)   F#dim7   F#miMA7

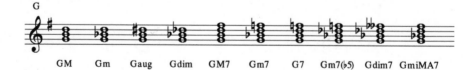

G

GM   Gm   Gaug   Gdim   GM7   Gm7   G7   Gm7(b5)   Gdim7   GmiMA7

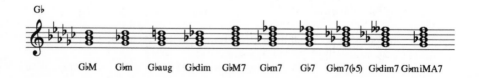

Gb

GbM   Gbm   Gbaug   Gbdim   GbM7   Gbm7   Gb7   Gbm7(b5)   Gbdim7   GbmiMA7

# Appendix B

# Glossary

**accompaniment:** The use of additional music to support a lead melodic line.

**anacrusis:** Note(s) preceding the first full measure in a piece of music, sometimes called a *pick-up*.

**atonal:** Music that is not in a key and not organized diatonically.

**augmentation dot:** A dot placed after a note or rest that extends its value by one half of the original value. (See **dotted note** and **dotted rest**.)

**back phrasing:** Moving a melody to begin later than it is expected.

**bar form:** A typical musical form in three sections: *AAB*.

**bar lines:** Vertical lines in written music that separate notes into different groups of notes and rests, depending on the time signature used.

**bass clef:** The lower staff in the grand staff. The bass clef establishes the pitch of the notes on the lines and spaces of the staff below middle C.

**beam:** A bar used instead of a flag to connect the stems of eighth notes and smaller notes.

**beat:** A series of repeating, consistent pulsations of time in music. Each pulsation is called a beat.

**binary form:** A two-art musical form: *AB*.

**bpm:** Beats per minute.

**bridge:** The contrasting musical section between two similar sections of music. Also sometimes called the B section.

**cadence:** The ending of a musical phrase, containing points of repose or release of tension.

**cadenza:** A solo section near or at the end of a piece of music in which the soloist improvises or plays in a virtuoso style.

**call and response:** When a soloist is answered by another musician or group of musicians.

**chord:** The simultaneous sounding of at least two pitches or notes.

**chord progression:** Moving from one chord to another, usually in established patterns.

**compound time:** A meter whose beat count can be equally divided up into thirds (6/8, 9/4, and so on) with the exception of any time signature that has a 3 as the top number of its time signature (as in 3/4 or 3/8 time).

**counterpoint:** The art of combining multiple complementary melodies.

**cut time:** Another name for 2/2 time.

**da capo:** To repeat from the beginning. Often abbreviated D.C.

**devil's interval:** The augmented fourth (or flatted fifth), a dissonant interval that was once banned by the Catholic Church. Also called the tri-tone.

**diatonic:** Conforming to the notes found in a given key. In a piece written in C major, for example, the C, D, E, F, G, A, and B are all diatonic pitches, and any other notes used in the piece are non-diatonic.

**diminution:** Re-writing of a melody in rhythmic values smaller than what was originally used.

**dotted note:** A note followed by an augmentation dot means the note is worth one and a half times its normal value.

**dotted rest:** A rest followed by an augmentation dot means the rest is worth one and a half times its normal value.

**double bar:** Two closely spaced vertical lines to indicate the end of a composition.

**downbeat:** The accented beats in a measure.

**duet:** A composition for two soloists. May have accompaniment.

**duplet:** Used in compound time to divide a beat that should contain three equal parts into two equal parts.

**etude:** A piece of music composed to help a performer develop technical abilities.

**finale:** The final movement in a multi-movement composition.

**flag:** A curved line added to the stem of a note to indicate a reduced rhythmic value. Flags are equivalent to beams.

**form:** The overall shape, organization, or structure of a musical composition. Forms may arise from very persistent genres.

**front phrasing:** Moving a melody to begin earlier than it is expected.

**genre:** A style or manner of music.

**grand staff:** The combination of the bass clef staff and the treble clef staff.

**half step:** The smallest interval in Western music, represented on the piano by moving one key (black or white) to the left or right from a starting point, or on the guitar as one fret up or down from a starting point. Also called a *semitone.*

**harmonic overtone:** Sympathetic frequencies produced by a tone that are integer multiples of the fundamental tone (as opposed to inharmonic over-tones, which are non-integer multiples).

**harmony:** Pitches heard simultaneously in ways that produce chords and chord progressions.

**heterophony:** Simultaneous use of varied forms of one basic melody. Notes may be omitted and/or changed.

**homophony:** Layers of musical activity that move at the same rhythm, such as melody and accompaniment.

**improvisation:** Spontaneous musical creation.

**incidental music:** Music composed to enhance a film or play.

**interval:** The pitch distance between two notes.

**key:** Normally defined by the beginning and ending chord of a musical com-position and by the order of whole steps and half steps between tonic scale degrees (in the key of C, for example, this would be represented by the first C of the scale and the C an octave above the first).

**key signature:** A series of sharps or flats (or lack of both) at the beginning of each staff following the clef.

**lead sheet:** A scaled-down, notated melody with chord symbols, usually for rock or jazz music, on which a musical performance is based.

**leitmotiv:** A melody, chord, or rhythm used in musicals, opera, cinema, and other visual arts that reoccurs throughout the production to identify a place, object, idea, or character. This compositional technique builds familiarity for the audience.

**libretto:** The text of an opera or other dramatic works.

**measure:** Also called a bar. A segment of written music, contained within two vertical bars, that contains as many beats as the top number of the key signature indicates.

**medley:** A composition that strings a group of well-known tunes together to form a new composition.

**melody:** A succession of musical tones, usually of varying pitch and rhythm, that together have an identifiable shape and meaning.

**meter:** The organization of rhythmic patterns in a composition in such a way that a regular, repeating pulse of beats continues throughout the composition.

**metronome:** A device that maintains a steady beat at varying speeds. It is common for composers to use metronome markings at the beginning of a piece to indicate how fast the piece should be played.

**middle C:** The C note located right between the two musical staffs in the grand staff (numbered as C4).

**modulation:** Transition from one key to another.

**notation:** The use of written or printed symbols to represent musical sounds.

**note:** A symbol used to represent the duration of a sound and, when placed on a music staff, the pitch of the sound.

**octave:** Two tones that span eight different diatonic pitches that have the same pitch quality and the same pitch names in Western music.

**orchestration:** The art of composing or arranging for orchestra.

**pick-up notes:** Introductory notes placed before the first measure in a piece of music.

**pitch**: The highness or lowness of a tone produced by a single frequency.

**polyphony:** Layers of different melodic and rhythmic activity within a single piece of music.

**polytonality:** The simultaneous use of material from different keys.

**quaver:** Also called an eighth note or eighth rest.

**refrain:** A periodically recurring section of music and/or text.

**rest:** Symbol used to notate a period of silence.

**retrograde:** A restatement of notes in the reverse order in which they originally appeared.

**rhythm:** The notation of time in music through the use of symbols and patterns.

**rondo:** A musical form that is divided into five or seven parts with reoccurring refrains: *ABACA, ABACABA.*

**scale:** A series of notes in ascending or descending order that presents the pitches of a key, beginning and ending on the tonic of that key.

**score:** A printed version of a piece of music.

**simple time:** A time signature in which the accented beats of each measure are divisible by two, as in 4/4 time.

**solo:** An entire composition or section within a composition for a single performer.

**song:** A musical composition in which vocals are used.

**staff:** Five horizontal, parallel lines, containing four spaces between them, on which notes and rests are written.

**syncopation:** A deliberate disruption of the two- or three-beat stress pattern, most often by stressing an off-beat, or a note that is not on the beat.

**tablature:** A system of notation that indicates pitches by numbers or letters rather than notes. Generally used for guitar and bass guitar.

**tempo:** The rate or speed of the beat in a piece of music.

**ternary form:** A typical three-part song form. *ABA.*

**timbre:** The unique quality of sound.

**time signature:** A notation made at the beginning of a piece of music, in the form of two numbers such as 3/4, that indicates the number of beats in each measure or bar and which note value constitutes one beat. The top (or first) number tells how many beats are in a measure, and the bottom (or second) number tells which kind of note receives the count of one beat.

**tonal:** A song or section of music which is organized by key or scale.

**transposition:** The transferring of a piece of music from its original key to another.

**treble clef:** Symbol written at the beginning of the upper musical staff in the grand staff. The treble clef establishes the pitch of the notes on the lines and spaces of the staff existing above middle C.

**triad:** A chord of three tones.

**trill:** When a player rapidly alternates between two notes next to one another.

**triplet:** Used in simple time to divide a beat that should contain two equal parts into three equal parts.

**turnaround:** A chord progression leading back to the beginning of a musical composition.

**whole step:** An interval consisting of two half steps, represented on the piano by moving two adjacent keys, black or white, to the left or right from a starting point, or on the guitar as two frets up or down the neck from a starting point.

# Index

books for composers
*American Mavericks*, 277
*Analysis of Tonal Music: A Schenkerian Approach*, 275–276
*How to Grow as a Musician*, 275
*The Norton Scores, Vols. 1 and 2, 10th Edition*, 274–275
*RE/Search #14 & #15*, 277–278
*The Rough Guide to Classical Music, 4th Edition*, 276–277
*The Shaping of Musical Elements, Vol. II*, 274
*Songwriter's Market*, 273–274
*The Virgin Directory of World Music*, 276
bound and free-flowing flow, translation into musical terms, 129
bowed instruments, notation for, 182
bpm (beats per minute), relationship to metronomes, 32
brass instruments, playing scales on, 164
bridge, building, 86–87
business conventions, attending, 270

• *C* •

C
chord triads and sevenths for, 308
playing on piano, 163
playing on transposing instrument, 164
C Aeolian (C minor) mode, notation for, 303
C Dorian mode, notation for, 291
C flat, chord triads and sevenths for, 309
C Ionian (C Major) mode, notation for, 288
C Locrian mode, notation for, 305
C Lydian mode, notation for, 297
C major chord, inversions for, 111
C major scale, notes in, 101
C major with 1-7 chords, example of, 98
C Mixolydian mode, notation for, 300
C Phrygian mode, notation for, 294
C sharp Aeolian (C sharp minor) mode, notation for, 303
C sharp, chord triads and sevenths for, 309
C sharp Locrian mode, notation for, 306
C sharp Phrygian mode, notation for, 294
C4 (middle C), locating on keyboard, 165

cadence
authentic, 115
deceptive or interrupted, 116
ending songs in, 141
explanation of, 114, 142
half-cadences, 116–117
plagal, 115
Cage, John, 282
*cambiata*, definition of, 86
career opportunities
concert composition and performances, 268–269
musical theater, 267–268
producer/arranger, 269
school bands and choirs, 265–266
television music, 266–267
catches (Purcell), popularity in 17th century, 202
cello, pitch range of, 180
Celtic music, use of Dorian mode in, 61
change, introducing to music, 79–80
characterizations, instrumental choices as, 197
cheng free reed instrument, origin of, 193
choirs and school bands, career opportunities in, 265–266
chord changes, using, 119–122
chord charts
writing, 100
writing for atonal compositions, 158
chord moods
augmented, 108–109
diminished, 108
dominant seventh, 105
major, 103
major seventh, 104
major sixth, 105–106
minor, 103–104
minor 7, flat 5/half-diminished, 109–110
minor ninth, 107–108
minor seventh, 104–105
minor sixth, 106
ninth, 107
suspended fourth, 106–107
chord progressions
beginning songs with, 225–226
experimenting with, 140

# Notes

# Notes

## BUSINESS, CAREERS & PERSONAL FINANCE

0-7645-9847-3        0-7645-2431-3

**Also available:**
- Business Plans Kit For Dummies
  0-7645-9794-9
- Economics For Dummies
  0-7645-5726-2
- Grant Writing For Dummies
  0-7645-8416-2
- Home Buying For Dummies
  0-7645-5331-3
- Managing For Dummies
  0-7645-1771-6
- Marketing For Dummies
  0-7645-5600-2
- Personal Finance For Dummies
  0-7645-2590-5*
- Resumes For Dummies
  0-7645-5471-9
- Selling For Dummies
  0-7645-5363-1
- Six Sigma For Dummies
  0-7645-6798-5
- Small Business Kit For Dummies
  0-7645-5984-2
- Starting an eBay Business For Dummies
  0-7645-6924-4
- Your Dream Career For Dummies
  0-7645-9795-7

## HOME & BUSINESS COMPUTER BASICS

0-470-05432-8        0-471-75421-8

**Also available:**
- Cleaning Windows Vista For Dummies
  0-471-78293-9
- Excel 2007 For Dummies
  0-470-03737-7
- Mac OS X Tiger For Dummies
  0-7645-7675-5
- MacBook For Dummies
  0-470-04859-X
- Macs For Dummies
  0-470-04849-2
- Office 2007 For Dummies
  0-470-00923-3
- Outlook 2007 For Dummies
  0-470-03830-6
- PCs For Dummies
  0-7645-8958-X
- Salesforce.com For Dummies
  0-470-04893-X
- Upgrading & Fixing Laptops For Dummies
  0-7645-8959-8
- Word 2007 For Dummies
  0-470-03658-3
- Quicken 2007 For Dummies
  0-470-04600-7

## FOOD, HOME, GARDEN, HOBBIES, MUSIC & PETS

0-7645-8404-9        0-7645-9904-6

**Also available:**
- Candy Making For Dummies
  0-7645-9734-5
- Card Games For Dummies
  0-7645-9910-0
- Crocheting For Dummies
  0-7645-4151-X
- Dog Training For Dummies
  0-7645-8418-9
- Healthy Carb Cookbook For Dummies
  0-7645-8476-6
- Home Maintenance For Dummies
  0-7645-5215-5
- Horses For Dummies
  0-7645-9797-3
- Jewelry Making & Beading For Dummies
  0-7645-2571-9
- Orchids For Dummies
  0-7645-6759-4
- Puppies For Dummies
  0-7645-5255-4
- Rock Guitar For Dummies
  0-7645-5356-9
- Sewing For Dummies
  0-7645-6847-7
- Singing For Dummies
  0-7645-2475-5

## INTERNET & DIGITAL MEDIA

0-470-04529-9        0-470-04894-8

**Also available:**
- Blogging For Dummies
  0-471-77084-1
- Digital Photography For Dummies
  0-7645-9802-3
- Digital Photography All-in-One Desk Reference For Dummies
  0-470-03743-1
- Digital SLR Cameras and Photography For Dummies
  0-7645-9803-1
- eBay Business All-in-One Desk Reference For Dummies
  0-7645-8438-3
- HDTV For Dummies
  0-470-09673-X
- Home Entertainment PCs For Dummies
  0-470-05523-5
- MySpace For Dummies
  0-470-09529-6
- Search Engine Optimization For Dummies
  0-471-97998-8
- Skype For Dummies
  0-470-04891-3
- The Internet For Dummies
  0-7645-8996-2
- Wiring Your Digital Home For Dummies
  0-471-91830-X

**\* Separate Canadian edition also available**
**† Separate U.K. edition also available**

Available wherever books are sold. For more information or to order direct: U.S. customers visit www.dummies.com or call 1-877-762-2974.
U.K. customers visit www.wileyeurope.com or call 0800 243407. Canadian customers visit www.wiley.ca or call 1-800-567-4797.

## SPORTS, FITNESS, PARENTING, RELIGION & SPIRITUALITY

0-471-76871-5

0-7645-7841-3

**Also available:**
- Catholicism For Dummies
  0-7645-5391-7
- Exercise Balls For Dummies
  0-7645-5623-1
- Fitness For Dummies
  0-7645-7851-0
- Football For Dummies
  0-7645-3936-1
- Judaism For Dummies
  0-7645-5299-6
- Potty Training For Dummies
  0-7645-5417-4
- Buddhism For Dummies
  0-7645-5359-3

- Pregnancy For Dummies
  0-7645-4483-7 †
- Ten Minute Tone-Ups For Dummies
  0-7645-7207-5
- NASCAR For Dummies
  0-7645-7681-X
- Religion For Dummies
  0-7645-5264-3
- Soccer For Dummies
  0-7645-5229-5
- Women in the Bible For Dummies
  0-7645-8475-8

## TRAVEL

0-7645-7749-2

0-7645-6945-7

**Also available:**
- Alaska For Dummies
  0-7645-7746-8
- Cruise Vacations For Dummies
  0-7645-6941-4
- England For Dummies
  0-7645-4276-1
- Europe For Dummies
  0-7645-7529-5
- Germany For Dummies
  0-7645-7823-5
- Hawaii For Dummies
  0-7645-7402-7

- Italy For Dummies
  0-7645-7386-1
- Las Vegas For Dummies
  0-7645-7382-9
- London For Dummies
  0-7645-4277-X
- Paris For Dummies
  0-7645-7630-5
- RV Vacations For Dummies
  0-7645-4442-X
- Walt Disney World & Orlando
  For Dummies
  0-7645-9660-8

## GRAPHICS, DESIGN & WEB DEVELOPMENT

0-7645-8815-X

0-7645-9571-7

**Also available:**
- 3D Game Animation For Dummies
  0-7645-8789-7
- AutoCAD 2006 For Dummies
  0-7645-8925-3
- Building a Web Site For Dummies
  0-7645-7144-3
- Creating Web Pages For Dummies
  0-470-08030-2
- Creating Web Pages All-in-One Desk
  Reference For Dummies
  0-7645-4345-8
- Dreamweaver 8 For Dummies
  0-7645-9649-7

- InDesign CS2 For Dummies
  0-7645-9572-5
- Macromedia Flash 8 For Dummies
  0-7645-9691-8
- Photoshop CS2 and Digital
  Photography For Dummies
  0-7645-9580-6
- Photoshop Elements 4 For Dummies
  0-471-77483-9
- Syndicating Web Sites with RSS Feeds
  For Dummies
  0-7645-8848-6
- Yahoo! SiteBuilder For Dummies
  0-7645-9800-7

## NETWORKING, SECURITY, PROGRAMMING & DATABASES

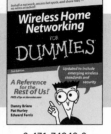

0-7645-7728-X

0-471-74940-0

**Also available:**
- Access 2007 For Dummies
  0-470-04612-0
- ASP.NET 2 For Dummies
  0-7645-7907-X
- C# 2005 For Dummies
  0-7645-9704-3
- Hacking For Dummies
  0-470-05235-X
- Hacking Wireless Networks
  For Dummies
  0-7645-9730-2
- Java For Dummies
  0-470-08716-1

- Microsoft SQL Server 2005 For Dummies
  0-7645-7755-7
- Networking All-in-One Desk Reference
  For Dummies
  0-7645-9939-9
- Preventing Identity Theft For Dummies
  0-7645-7336-5
- Telecom For Dummies
  0-471-77085-X
- Visual Studio 2005 All-in-One Desk
  Reference For Dummies
  0-7645-9775-2
- XML For Dummies
  0-7645-8845-1

## HEALTH & SELF-HELP

0-7645-8450-2

0-7645-4149-8

**Also available:**
- Bipolar Disorder For Dummies
  0-7645-8451-0
- Chemotherapy and Radiation For Dummies
  0-7645-7832-4
- Controlling Cholesterol For Dummies
  0-7645-5440-9
- Diabetes For Dummies
  0-7645-6820-5* †
- Divorce For Dummies
  0-7645-8417-0 †

- Fibromyalgia For Dummies
  0-7645-5441-7
- Low-Calorie Dieting For Dummies
  0-7645-9905-4
- Meditation For Dummies
  0-471-77774-9
- Osteoporosis For Dummies
  0-7645-7621-6
- Overcoming Anxiety For Dummies
  0-7645-5447-6
- Reiki For Dummies
  0-7645-9907-0
- Stress Management For Dummies
  0-7645-5144-2

## EDUCATION, HISTORY, REFERENCE & TEST PREPARATION

0-7645-8381-6

0-7645-9554-7

**Also available:**
- The ACT For Dummies
  0-7645-9652-7
- Algebra For Dummies
  0-7645-5325-9
- Algebra Workbook For Dummies
  0-7645-8467-7
- Astronomy For Dummies
  0-7645-8465-0
- Calculus For Dummies
  0-7645-2498-4
- Chemistry For Dummies
  0-7645-5430-1
- Forensics For Dummies
  0-7645-5580-4

- Freemasons For Dummies
  0-7645-9796-5
- French For Dummies
  0-7645-5193-0
- Geometry For Dummies
  0-7645-5324-0
- Organic Chemistry I For Dummies
  0-7645-6902-3
- The SAT I For Dummies
  0-7645-7193-1
- Spanish For Dummies
  0-7645-5194-9
- Statistics For Dummies
  0-7645-5423-9

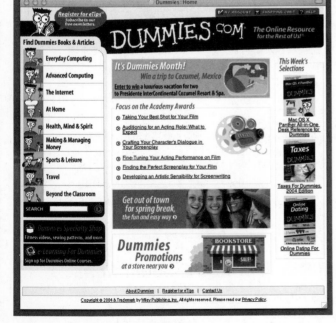

# Get smart @ dummies.com®

- **Find a full list of Dummies titles**
- **Look into loads of FREE on-site articles**
- **Sign up for FREE eTips e-mailed to you weekly**
- **See what other products carry the Dummies name**
- **Shop directly from the Dummies bookstore**
- **Enter to win new prizes every month!**

\* Separate Canadian edition also available
† Separate U.K. edition also available

Available wherever books are sold. For more information or to order direct: U.S. customers visit www.dummies.com or call 1-877-762-2974.
U.K. customers visit www.wileyeurope.com or call 0800 243407. Canadian customers visit www.wiley.ca or call 1-800-567-4797.